AF270083

Praise for *Nothing Gained Is Eternal*

"Throughout the history of Christian theology, the question of tradition repeatedly surfaces in times of crisis, and the greatest theologies of tradition arise from the response to these crises. Here one can recall the work of such leading lights as Irenaeus of Lyons, the Council Fathers at Trent, John Henry Newman, Johann Adam Möhler in the nineteenth century, and Yves Congar in the past century. The discourse around race and colonialism has pressed Christian theologians once again to take up the question of tradition. *Nothing Gained Is Eternal* grapples with this question, and what one finds is remarkable. Carpenter accessibly brings to the fore the problem of tradition and *traditioning* in the course of engaging several key thinkers—Maurice Blondel, Charles Péguy, Hans Urs von Balthasar, Bernard Lonergan, Shawn Copeland, and James Baldwin. What results is not a history or a chronology, but instead nothing less than a 'constructive argument about the *being* of tradition,' an argument surely poised to usher in a new wave of theological reflection on tradition. This book marks Anne Carpenter as a distinctive theological voice worth listening to. I recommend it highly."

—Grant Kaplan, Steber Chair of Historical and
Systematic Theology, Saint Louis University

"Tradition is the *act* of passing on God's self-revelation. But theology, Carpenter argues, has not sufficiently engaged its *action*. Carpenter's metaphysic of tradition turns to its undersides, both its structure—the columns and beams inside its walls—and those on the undersides of history. Carpenter picks up where the twentieth-century authors of *ressourcement* left off, reading tradition through James Baldwin, M. Shawn Copeland, and Willie Jennings. *Nothing Gained Is Eternal* is methodologically inventive and ambitious, fully engaged with the theological tradition but refusing to follow the usual paths."

—Joseph S. Flipper, Mary Ann Spearin Chair of
Catholic Theology, University of Dayton

"Anne Carpenter's *Nothing Gained Is Eternal* builds bridges. It puts important schools of thought into conversation about the nature of history, race, sin, and God's redemptive love. Early twentieth-century Catholic theologians meet contemporary theological critics of church and society, and the result is a provocative work of conceptual synthesis and prophetic insight."

—Andrew Prevot, associate professor of theology, Boston College, and author of *Thinking Prayer: Theology and Spirituality amid the Crises of Modernity*

"At once a celebration, a chastening, and an expansion of conventional formulations of religious tradition, Carpenter's book takes on the ambitious task of integrating a chorus of voices which might not otherwise have had occasion to enrich (and correct!) one another. The book unites detailed theological and philosophical analyses of history and temporality with an exhortative call to action against dark forces of racism and colonialism which shadow Christianity's past and present, making a compelling case that future systematic reflection on Christian tradition ought to be reconfigured to account for a direct confrontation against those powers and principalities."

—Jennifer Newsome Martin, associate professor in the department of theology and the Program of Liberal Studies at the University of Notre Dame, and author of *Hans Urs von Balthasar and the Critical Appropriation of Russian Religious Thought*

"*Nothing Gained Is Eternal* cuts across imagined borders between 'left' and 'right' or 'progressive' and 'conservative.' If 'tradition' and 'liberation' are often considered the possessions of opposing theological camps, in Carpenter's hands they cannot be separated. In the spirit of Charles Péguy and Maurice Blondel, her guiding lights, Carpenter has offered an incisive book that will provoke strong reactions. Here Charles Péguy meets James Baldwin. Blondel meets Willie James Jennings. *Nothing Gained Is Eternal* is a book we have been waiting for, opening up another—doubtless very different—*ressourcement*."

—Kevin L. Hughes, professor of historical theology, Villanova University

NOTHING GAINED IS ETERNAL

NOTHING GAINED *IS* ETERNAL

A THEOLOGY OF TRADITION

ANNE M. CARPENTER

Fortress Press
Minneapolis

NOTHING GAINED IS ETERNAL
A Theology of Tradition

Cover design: Lindsey Owens
Cover image: iStock/DeepGreen

Print ISBN: 978-1-5064-7173-0
eBook ISBN: 978-1-5064-7174-7

Rien d'acquis n'est acquis pour éternellement.

—Charles Péguy

Contents

Acknowledgments

My students. I want to mention them first. I promised them I would. Of all the people to hear the various versions of this book as I worked it out over the long span of years, they were the ones to hear about it most. I collaborated with them constantly, mediated by the fits and starts of my students and I working together to understand one another: in the readings I assigned, in the questions they asked me, in the question that they *are* to me, which is, How will the Catholic tradition that I live, that I know, know them? They are not like me. They are not like one another. How will I know them—know them each? And how does my tradition live in my asking myself, in their asking of me? I am grateful, therefore, immensely grateful, for my students, for the questions that they are by being themselves.

I wrote this book on a sabbatical during some of the worst of the Covid-19 pandemic in 2020–21. Rather than visiting Paris as I had dreamed, I went to my parents' home, back in the Midwest of the United States, where I grew up. My parents' hospitality made a lonely endeavor much less so. Thanks, Mom and Dad. I love you. And I'm grateful for the rest of our family: my brother, Patrick, and my sister, Elizabeth, *à la fois dans mon cœur temporel et éternel,* and everyone they love, whom I also love.

In that same town is my best friend, my childhood friend, my turn-sister, Danielle Cairoli; her husband, Paolo; and their children, Francesca and Sabrina. They broke their pandemic rules for me—no small thing. They gave me a different place to be, people to speak with. Their joy and love helped me immensely in a world crisis that, even still, has us all radically isolated.

It is thanks to Saint Mary's College and my colleagues in the Department of Theology and Religious Studies that I was able to gain tenure and receive pay for a sabbatical, which made this book possible. I'm grateful for their support and collaboration over the years as I worked and wrote toward it. Thank you to Michael Barram, Zach Flanagin, Tom Poundstone, Marie Pagliarini, Paul Giurlanda, Richard Carp, Br. Mark McVann (†), Br. Michael Meister, Br. Michael Avila, Fr. David Gentry-Akin.

As a scholar, I am made of all the people I read and speak to. So I want to especially thank Anna Corwin, Br. Charles Hilken, Erin Kidd, Brian Bajzek, Kirsten Guidero, Joseph Gordon, Jeremy Blackwood, Eric Mabry, Joseph Flipper, Jennifer Newsome Martin, Fr. Christopher Hadley, SJ, Anthony Sciglitano, Kevin Hughes, Matthew Levering, D. Stephen Long, Danielle Nussberger. I hope my work serves them well, as theirs have served mine.

When it comes to actively wrestling with colonialism and responsible theology done in its wake, I must thank Joseph Drexler-Dreis, Jessica Coblentz, and Sergio Bermudez. Joe and Jess were my colleagues for a time, and they are forever my peers. Their passion, thoughtfulness, and knowledge embodied for me a priceless enrichment of Catholic theology, one that I wanted to support and serve and learn from, different as we are from one another. Sergio, meanwhile, is my most unexpected but dearest grace. He changed the way I read, what I read, how I consume media, how I think about the monsters that populate the underside of the colonial world. I am forever thankful.

Then there are *les amis de mon coeur*, to whom I chattered about this book for years and years. The friends I showed paragraphs and pages, whom I asked to help me think that careful richness that is theological orthodoxy; the friends I complained to, wondered with, prayed with. The friends in whom my trust is so sure that I take their corrections as if they have come from my own mind—only better, since from theirs: Jakob Rinderknecht, Jonathan Heaps, Ryan Hemmer, Lyle Enright.

Thank you to Fr. Robert Doran, SJ, dear mentor, blessed of memory.

Lastly, I thank the saints of this book, living and dead: Bernard Lonergan, M. Shawn Copeland, Maurice Blondel, Willie James Jennings, Charles Péguy, Hans Urs von Balthasar, James Baldwin. By their intercession, this book enters the world. By the intercession of the entire mystical body of Christ, may this world rise to its destiny in the triune God, who will be all in all.

Introduction

Christian tradition is a problem. A problem of history, of truth, and of both together. It is a problem made all the more problematic by Christian sin and infidelity. If Christians hand on divine truth in their living of history, it is also the case that they hand on their wrongs in history. This book is preoccupied with the concrete coexistence of truth and sin in Christian historical action, with how the Christian memory of Christ can be in some way a *real* memory, and with how sin might unbind that memory's reality.

To ask how sin affects memory, how it is enacted and carried along in tradition, is to raise the problem of Christian involvement in the creation and continuation of colonialism and race. I am concerned with colonialism and race because together, they help make of Christian tradition a concrete concern. But I am also concerned because the scale of their impact is staggering and because it persists today. My preoccupation is twofold: one addresses the technical problem of the truth of Christian being in history, and the other the concrete problem of the shape that Christian being in history takes with the advent of modern colonialism. I want to know the truth of Christian truth; I want to know the facticity of Christian sin; I want to know what they mean for Christian tradition.

The problem of Christian tradition is a stage play in the middle of its execution. It is not that the play ceases to go on. It does go on. Christians continue to be Christian; Christians continue to have and live a tradition; Christians continue to reflect on, hold, and develop doctrines. But what is the nature of this *continuing*? The play goes on, but what keeps the lights on, what runs under the floorboards, what enables the actions of the players? How are there *today* communities that call themselves Christian, that negotiate the proportions of this identity, that are, in a word, alive?

Christians can say in faith that we are possessed of a divine fidelity to God and, in God, to ourselves. We are bearers of a history that is, we believe, a history that God redeems. But what does it *mean* that we are alive in this history? What does this mean at all, or in the first place? We have not answered this question, and so it causes us pain.

I mean this "pain" in a complex way. Christian theology wrestles with itself over theological questions that are variously backed by tradition, or in contradistinction to tradition, that are variously supported by history (for this is not quite the same as tradition), or in contradiction to history. But this theological wrestling is pained by the questions that it has not asked about the ground, the stage, of the struggle itself, which is our historical being as a tradition. We thus raise banners against one another without a critical, theoretical account of our being in history, or of its specific shape, which is tradition. The ground of our disagreement is our confusion.

But there is a shadow side to the problem of tradition and history that also causes pain. It is the shadow of sin and failure. Though this is not a problem unfamiliar to theologies of many places and times, here I mean a shadow often more familiarly articulated by so-called contextual theologies. It is the trouble of a Christian history and a Christian tradition that has wounded groups of people, that has divided them up *for* wounding, and that repeats its sins with a damning helplessness. Our collective distress about tradition, even if only articulated in fragments, is complex because our confusion about its reality leaves our own shadow only partially recognized.

I slide between images and terms to lay hold of a problem that is perpetually on the move, whose very nature is to be on the move: being alive, being in history, being in time, having or being a tradition, action upon a stage, being responsible for our past and present. Tradition's opacity contributes to the trouble of this slippery terminology, and tradition obfuscates despite its concreteness. Often enough, Christians treat tradition *in* its concreteness, in terms of practices, liturgies, councils, doctrines, texts. The trouble that I am after, in this sense, does not at first appear to be a trouble at all: look at tradition, we say, and see what it is. But what *is* it? What am I seeing, and how do I see it? Can we give it a definition or treat its boundaries with precision? *Has* tradition boundaries so that Jerusalem can turn its back on Athens?

Tradition's urgency and opacity have reared their heads perpetually in Christian history. So Christian theology has approached the question of tradition from the various angles of the various contexts that have provoked its crises: the problem of Jewish practice and Christian practice as recorded in the book of Acts, Irenaeus working to define a public, apostolic Christian tradition over against gnostic Christianity, fractures of communion in the eleventh and sixteenth centuries. Like all such moments in theological history, these reveal some questions and fallow others.

When, in 1965, the Second Vatican Council promulgated *Dei Verbum*, its document on divine revelation, a notion of tradition emerged that itself has a longer history.[1] What is fundamental to the document is an understanding of tradition that is, in one way or another, primarily active: it is a "living" tradition (§8), an "apostolic" tradition (§9) with living apostolic successors, a tradition that is "handed on" (§7). Together with Scripture, tradition forms a single "deposit of faith" to which the church holds fast (§9).[2] Tradition in the council's understanding is primarily a verb, understood in motion *as* a motion—as *tradere*, "to hand over" or "to hand on."

What does this mean? This question is not about what it meant in the minds of the council fathers, or even how it came to be so through the work of theologians.[3] It is not about the organons of judgment by which tradition is understood (which, in a Catholic context, orbit around the magisterium and the *sensus fidelium*). I want to break out of this Catholic contextualizing of the question so that new questions can be asked. My method will be to turn around to others in our recent past (many of them Catholics) and to ask them new questions. But in asking what tradition means, I want to break into the realm of theory, toward a theoretical account of what tradition is.

Theology has grasped that tradition is a verb without providing a full-throated theory for this action. Nor is such a partiality unfamiliar to theology, which wrestled for centuries over notions of grace and freedom without articulating a theorem of the supernatural, or which defined *person* iteratively over time.[4] Still, it becomes necessary for theology to intervene in its own thinking by transgressing the line of reflection into something else, a something-else that is a theoretical account or explanation of the relevant terms, their operations, and

1. See a recent summary in John E. Thiel, "*Dei Verbum*: Scripture, Tradition, and Historical Criticism," *Horizons* 47, no. 2 (2020): 207–31. A magisterial summary is in John W. O'Malley, *What Happened at Vatican II* (Cambridge, MA: Harvard University Press, 2010).

2. Second Vatican Council, *Dei Verbum*, November 18, 1965, https://www.vatican.va/archive/hist_councils/ii_vatican_council/documents/vat-ii_const_19651118_dei-verbum_en.html.

3. Yves Congar, *Tradition and Traditions: An Historical and a Theological Essay* (New York: Macmillan, 1967).

4. Bernard Lonergan, "Philosophy and Theology," in *Collected Works of Bernard Lonergan*, vol. 13, *A Second Collection* (Toronto: University of Toronto Press, 1996), 199–202.

their relations to one another. It is a kind of framework for the work of theology that theologians are forever pursuing as they do their work. As a "framework," it is not itself this work. But it enables the work and breaks open new and graver questions for theology to ask. Bernard Lonergan calls this something-else, or work of a framework, theological speculation.[5]

In this book, I aim to speculate about Christian tradition. I aim to pause, as it were, the rush of theological questions about tradition in all their concreteness, to ask how the world *is* such that Christian tradition itself *is*. I ask for its conditions of possibility. I provide a theory for this action and its possibility.

This kind of theorizing renders my method somewhat unusual. In one way, what I do is what I have mentioned: I turn back to the (for the most part Catholic) past to reason with its thinkers. My context, historically speaking, is the late nineteenth and early twentieth centuries of France, the fin de siècle, and my conversation partners are the Catholic thinkers who inherited Catholic anxieties about the development of scientific history in the nineteenth century: Maurice Blondel and Charles Péguy. Their work, set later than both John Henry Newman and the Tübingen Catholics, approaches the problem of tradition distinctively while relying on the achievements of earlier thinkers. Blondel and Péguy both influenced what came to be known in theological circles as the Ressourcement movement and its associated figures called the *nouvelle théologie*. Through the echo of Blondel and Péguy and others, there emerged a theological stance that influenced the Second Vatican Council.[6] In a sense, this book follows Jennifer Newsome Martin's recommendation that there be a *ressourcement* of the Ressourcement, a searching-beyond the Ressourcement "movement" to the past that made it possible.[7]

I also converse with two twentieth-century Catholic thinkers who were heirs to these nineteenth-century concerns and who developed responses that extend beyond Blondel and Péguy. These Catholic thinkers are Bernard Lonergan and Hans Urs von Balthasar. Though quite different from each other,

---

5. For a summary of Lonergan on speculation, see Ryan Hemmer, "Cathedrals of the Mind: Theological Method and Speculative Renewal in Trinitarian Theology" (PhD diss., Marquette University, 2020).

6. A collection of essays on the movement is in Gabriel Flynn and Paul Murray, eds., *Ressourcement: A Movement for Renewal in Twentieth-Century Catholic Theology* (New York: Oxford University Press, 2015).

7. Jennifer Newsome Martin, "'Only What Is Rooted Is Living': A Roman Catholic Theology of Ressourcement," in *Theologies of Retrieval: An Exploration and Appraisal*, ed. Darren Sarisky (New York: Bloomsbury, 2017), 81–102.

both are burdened with the puzzle that history poses for theology, and in this, they are burdened with the puzzle of tradition. In Lonergan and Balthasar is a searching-beyond that tilts forward rather than backward, enabled as they are by the accident and the grace of being born later, of having different theological concerns, of developing what were for them prior achievements. In Blondel, Péguy, Lonergan, and Balthasar, I explore the history of the Catholic response to the problem of tradition by tracing the details of their individual responses. I gather these responses into a unity, a synthesis, an overall position.

My *ressourcement* of the Ressourcement is also a transfiguration and an argument. It is not chronological. It is not historical, though history founds my theorizing. Each chapter, save the last, is an encounter with a someone—really, *someones*—from recent Christian history. I introduce my reader to these someones. But my purpose is to make a constructive argument about the being of tradition, about its existence in history as a mediator of divine truth. My encounters with these thinkers are thus specified by the argument that I make and that these many minds help me in making. If my theology bears some of the "eclecticism" and "style of life" of the *nouvelle théologie*, or the sharpness of a Lonerganian (and Balthasarian) Thomism, so much the better, but I do so with a single purpose: to provide a theoretical account of Christian tradition.[8]

My theory has a moving viewpoint, one that transitions to new questions with new horizons that integrate previous ones but go beyond them. First, I ask, with Lonergan, what history is. Then I ask, with Blondel, what tradition is. With Péguy, I ask after the impact of temporality on Christian tradition. With Balthasar, I provide a fully theological account of the "action" of tradition in a temporal, historical universe. Because tradition is historical, it demands an account of what history is. But this *what* does not define what tradition is or how it is true. It does not fully relate the "temporal, eternal" Christian to their own tradition, and so I move to that question next. And even this horizon is not an account of what *God* is doing in Christian tradition, or how God accomplishes his doing, which I describe last. So each question relies on the previous questions and their answers, but it also transposes their terms.

I call my theory of tradition a "metaphysic" of tradition. This is because rather than centering inquiries into the content of tradition or its interpretation, my inquiry is into the *being* of tradition, the existence of tradition as it is brought

---

8. The "eclecticism" comment is a reference to various phraseologies of "style" in Jon Kirwan, *An Avante-Garde Theological Generation: The "Nouvelle Théologie" and the French Crisis of Modernity* (London: Oxford University Press, 2019), esp. 89, 105, 137, 149.

into act. A study of the being of tradition first asks what it means for tradition to be historical. This I answer by saying with Lonergan that history is human action. Then I explore the "determinism" of human action with Blondel, who emerges with a definition of tradition as a mediation of truth and history. From there, I emphasize with Péguy the urgency of the present moment, which gives the strength of the past back to itself through an original, revolutionary gesture or *ressourcement*. Balthasar brings together these previous themes to describe the action of tradition in terms of Christ's obedience, itself an action in history that is a handing-over, a tradition-ing, and that animates a theological understanding of God's work in history by emphasizing how human action is the divine instrument of divine grace.

My approach reveals my own training as a scholar, my particular or peculiar context. And in this, I inherit the weaknesses of unasked, incomplete, and erroneous questions. For there was and is a further historical reality putting its pressure on Christian tradition from within, one not treated merely by grappling with the "discovery" of history in the nineteenth century, or by exploring Catholic anxieties that spanned the nineteenth and twentieth centuries. The shadow side of Christian being in history is also at the heart of this book: the question of Christian tradition and Christian sin.

Christians sin. Embedded in our divine fidelity is a constant and quite human infidelity. What, then, must Christian tradition also be if we know this about it? Contemporary theologies of various kinds have been asking this question for decades, and they have more ancient precedents. In this, I follow them, and in following them, I widen my corner of the universe.

Mine is not a *direct* reconciliation of *ressourcement* and liberation, in part because they are not in any case at odds. But furthermore, as a theory, a theology of tradition cannot turn to sin in any fully systematic way, for sin is irrational and unintelligible. It will not yield to systematic treatment.[9] To specify the problem of sin, therefore, I turn to a massive, concrete historical dynamic of sin that Christian tradition has funded and that it remains caught up in: the history of colonialism and of its central product, which is race—race, not as thing, but as en-action.[10] As I turn to *this* history, I admit that all of my conversation partners

---

9. Bernard Lonergan, "Dialectic of Authority," in *Collected Works of Bernard Lonergan*, vol. 16, *A Third Collection* (New York: Paulist Press, 1985), 9–10.

10. I have not yet defined colonialism's "making" of race or what "race" means. This will be a complex arc in the book. What proceeds will be, for example, a study of Alexander Weheliye's gnomic statement here: "Blackness . . . cannot be defined as primarily empirical nor understood as the

in this book, even in their rejections of colonialism, do not fully grasp its disastrous reach in Christian tradition, or the havoc that the lie of race enacts in Christian tradition.

So I bring other partners into the conversation in every chapter, emphasizing especially twentieth- and twenty-first-century Black theological and political thought. I encounter Lonergan's student M. Shawn Copeland; I confront the reflections of Willie Jennings; I engage with James Baldwin. Each of these Black thinkers press my moving viewpoint with their own moving viewpoints, describing in successive horizons what colonialism "did" to the world, how race operates in that world, how Christians and Christian tradition endowed and endow the world with these doings. These Black thinkers speak from out of the secret heart of modern historical being—"secret" if only because one of the functions of race is to conceal what human persons do to these persons in particular; or rather, race's function is to conceal *them* in particular and to conceal the acts of concealing. Race thus eviscerates human being (*ens humanitatis*), cleaving apart the solidarity by which human beings are, the solidarity by which God in Christ brings us to participate in the divine nature. It is not, therefore, an addendum concern for Christian tradition, or for a theological theory of Christian tradition. Race threatens the being-alive of Christianity itself, and so its living tradition.

Race is a historical fiction. It is not *true*: humanity is not in fact divided by ontologized colors that impute value and disvalue to persons. But race is lived as if true. Its life is only in its being lived. It is supported by economic and legal and even spatial structures, whole geographies, complex human actions, and the orders they enact, bringing into the world an irrational way of being, but one that appears as if it were intelligible. And race is supported fundamentally by Christian tradition and its theology. Modern race is a Christian invention, and Christians are, if they are to be historical and to have a tradition, responsible for their history and their tradition. At the same time, Copeland, Jennings, and Baldwin not only respond with a diagnosis of our present situation; they mine theological resources to suggest the sundering of race in a preferential option for the historically oppressed, in the mystical body of Christ, in the "play" of a fragmented existence, in a love that unmasks ugly historical realities to make way for new realities. And so Black thought presents a theory of Christian

---

nonproperty of particular subjects, but should be understood as an integral structuring assemblage of the modern human." Weheliye, *Habeas Viscus: Racializing Assemblages, Biopolitics, and Black Feminist Theories of the Human* (Durham, NC: Duke University Press, 2014), 31–32.

tradition with the revelation of what this tradition is and has been, in all its ambiguity, and Black thought offers in this revelation a fragile potency, one discoverable in what is also true, which is that this Christian sin of race and colonialism was never inevitable; it was freely and irrationally chosen and enacted, and if this really is so, it need not always be.

My encounter with Black thought throws me back upon my resources to ask of them new questions about Christian historical being. In a refracted light, these resources are renewed by the demand for an original gesture to be made with them. So Lonergan is illumined in new ways by his student, Copeland. Blondel's critique of the authoritarian Catholicism of *Action française* receives a new urgency and application under Jennings's guidance. Péguy undergoes a transformation where his temporal musings serve a new and purified purpose. Balthasar's critique of Christian power through christological kenosis receives new moorings in Baldwin.

Each chapter makes a deliberate transition into problems of race and colonialism, and this transition itself bears the weight of a theological world set against asking these questions. My goal is to think these questions *together*, and so to theorize from out of a whole. The problem of tradition and the problem of race, though notionally distinguishable, do not exist separately in the concrete. But this whole can only be viewed from its place in history.[11] My turning to *begin* to reconcile myself with Black thought may appear as a second question. It is not. But that appearance is itself evidence of our simultaneous helplessness and responsibility for standing before our total history of sin. This stance receives my full attention in the final chapter, which considers, or braves, a Christian hope for Christian tradition.

Theological hope is a confident hope, for its object is God. Christians are able to hope that their tradition is redeeming while also, and perpetually, *being* redeemed. But we must be serious in this hope, and serious about its nature. If we peel away the naive realism that would perplex the plenitude of divine revelation with its mediation in Christian history, we seem to lose much, and for a moment perhaps everything. Threatened now before our eyes is the surety of this revelation, which we thought to defend with a Christian tradition that bears neither ambiguity nor sin. (And this ambiguity and sin, once perceived, cannot be unseen except through a refusal that incurs guilt.) But revelation's

11. Cf. Second Vatican Council, *Lumen Gentium*, November 21, 1964, §25, 39, https://www.vatican.va/archive/hist_councils/ii_vatican_council/documents/vat-ii_const_19641121_lumen-gentium_en.html.

trustworthiness and its fullness are divine. They are effects of the triune God. Even tradition's own effectiveness is effectuated by the triune God. So we do not lose *God* when we lose a naive understanding of our tradition. And in a Catholic context, it is possible to say that we do not lose either indefectibility or infallibility. We lose instead the notion that the only thing Christians ever carry with confidence through history is Christ. For we also carry the bewildering, staggering vastness of our sin through history. Like a cracked cup, split by a tragic irony and guilt, we spill poison and grace into the world. Here theological hope is asked to say something of what its hope must mean for Christian tradition.

So the final chapter dares its gesture of hope in the midst of a divine struggle against iniquity that reels its way through the very heart of the Christian and the church, before the world and before God. It is not a gesture toward a lost innocence, one perhaps never had at all. It is, rather, the arduous task of a second innocence, which must struggle under a divine night to cease merely *continuing* yesterday in order to begin again instead today, each day and every day, and so to give yesterday back to itself enriched. This is our living upon the divine manna of time itself, of the order of the universe that rushes forward into being, treated for once as it in fact is. And so this divine hope enables in Christians a struggle to make good on the divine promise in history, not for the sake of our own effectiveness, but in order to entrust ourselves in a living way to the living God, who alone brings good from out of evil.

1

ACTIONS

> She's the end of the world.
> She's dipped in flames
> the color of the sun.
> She's wreathed in the hot sparks
> of an ecstasy, of dying wood.

What is that Christian historicity that we call Christian tradition? What, as John Henry Newman might ask, does it mean for Christ's church to be subject to history?[1] Answering such questions means understanding the relationship between Christian truth and Christian history. But it also means understanding the ways that Christians are agents in history, in their *grandeur et misère*. And because Christians exercise agency in time, answering these questions means wrestling with the lethal racialization of human beings by Christians and by history, by Christians in their history. It is not only the moral urgency of the problem that pulls us to attention; it is also the conviction, available to faith, that the history that is ours is also the history that is God's. To remain blind to history's *grandeur et misère* is to fail in the fullness of a sight that understands God to be at work in the struggle against human iniquity.[2] That failure is nescience, and

---

1. This a reference to John Henry Newman's *An Essay on the Development of Christian Doctrine* (South Bend, IN: University of Notre Dame Press, 1989), see esp. the introduction and chap. 1.
2. This is a reference to a fragment of Blaise Pascal's. See Blaise Pascal, "Fragment *Grandeur* n. 10/14," Les Pensées de Blaise Pascal, http://www.penseesdepascal.fr/Grandeur/Grandeur10 -moderne.php.

nescience is a sin. But underneath all these questions and convictions, holding them together while distinguishing them, is the question of the present chapter: What is human history?

What Bernard Lonergan writes of history is not, perhaps, what we might expect. What Lonergan writes and rewrites is a *theory of history*. The decision is unusual. Lonergan's theorizing might even strike us as far too abstract for the urgent problems of his day, let alone for our own. Why not rise to meet the age on its own level?[3] Why not, if the body bleeds, bandage the wound where it is?

This rising is what Lonergan is struggling to do. He is working to understand what human history is, and therefore what history can become. He writes not just to grasp bandages for the wound but also to grasp anatomical knowledge of the body. He writes to take measure of what is happening in his world. And Lonergan's theory of history is what the present chapter strives to understand, explain, and expand. It is important to my argument because it provides a way to discuss history, and therefore a way to discuss the historicity of Christian tradition. Lonergan also provides the tools by which to understand what it means to build a "metaphysic" of tradition—that is, what it means to operate in the realm of theory, which is one of the fundamental efforts of this book. But to understand this operation, to learn with Lonergan how to take measure of history and what it means to discuss metaphysics within it, we must first understand what theory is.

A Definition of Theory

Lonergan distinguishes between common sense and theory. While both have to do with human intelligence, their standpoints differ.[4] Common sense is that shared practical intelligence that guides people in their daily lives, the communal knowledge that deals with "the concrete and the immediately practical."[5] Lonergan says, "The practical common sense of a group, like all common sense, is an incomplete set of insights that is ever to be completed differently in

---

3. Cf. Bernard Lonergan, *Collected Works of Bernard Lonergan*, vol. 14, *Method in Theology* (Toronto: University of Toronto Press, 2017), 3–4.

4. Lonergan, 79.

5. Bernard Lonergan, *Collected Works of Bernard Lonergan*, vol. 3, *Insight* (Toronto: University of Toronto Press, 1992), 251.

each concrete situation."[6] So common sense is a specific kind of shared understanding. It is the kind that deals with the practical, the concrete. But common sense often cannot understand this about itself, and it mistakes itself for all the understanding that there is.[7]

Theory, by contrast, is at once more general and more specific than common sense. Its specialized language applies human intelligence to systematic inquiry about the world, whether in philosophy or in science.[8] This systematic inquiry is demanded by the questions that common sense cannot answer and by the dynamic structure of human consciousness, which desires such answers and asks such questions. Such a demand is what Lonergan calls "systematic exigence." So theory emerges in its own right as its own realm of meaning, apart from common sense: "The systematic exigence not merely raises questions that common sense cannot answer but also demands a context for its answers, a context that common sense cannot supply or comprehend. This context is theory, and the objects to which it refers are in the realm of theory. To these objects one can ascend from commonsense starting points, but they are properly known, not by this ascent, but by their internal relations, their congruences and differences, the functions they fulfill in their interactions."[9] Theory, then, differs from common sense by seeking the meaning of terms and their relations to one another rather than their relation to the questioner. Per Lonergan's preferred example, the questions that Socrates asks—such as, "What is justice?"—cannot be answered by common sense, because common sense focuses on concrete applications and not on what a thing is in itself.[10] Each of Socrates's dialogue partners can say whether or not a set of circumstances is or isn't just, but none of them can define justice in a way that applies to each just or unjust situation. Socrates wants a universal definition, but common sense cannot provide one. His questions seek answers only to be found in the world of theory, a world in which "things are conceived and known not in their relations to our sensory apparatus or to our needs and desires, but in their relations constituted by their uniform interactions with one another."[11]

6. Lonergan, 236.

7. Lonergan, 251.

8. Lonergan, *Method in Theology*, 80.

9. Lonergan, 79.

10. Lonergan, *Insight*, 251.

11. Lonergan, *Method in Theology*, 242.

Lonergan distinguishes between history and a philosophy of history—that is, between the *events* of history and the kind of theorizing of history that would ask not "What happened?" but "What is history?" This latter question demands not a historian but a philosopher. "A philosopher cannot be content to ask of history, Who holds the power?" argues Lonergan. "He must ask whether this incidence of power is for human progress or for human extinction."[12] Theory, in other words, leads not just to different kinds of understanding but also to its own kinds of judgments about what is the case.

It is worth pausing at this point to consider what, exactly, Lonergan is trying to achieve with theory, and therefore what this book is trying to achieve as a theory of Christian tradition. "While practical people wait for concrete situations to arise before attempting to work out their consequences," he says, "theoretical minds are given to anticipating ideal or typical cases and to determining how a deduction could be carried out in each case."[13] Practical intelligence infers from the given situation; theory tends to be "anticipatory," to be "creative and constructive."[14] Because theory deals in the ideal and typical, it is not useful in every case for every question, just as common sense is not. Indeed, for Lonergan, there is a danger inherent in approaching history through the lens of ideal types.[15]

So this book has a danger latent in its effort, which is the danger of mistaking its theoretical, creative, heuristic understanding of history and tradition *for* history and tradition. The mistake would be a kind of overextension of one form of knowledge beyond the boundaries of its competence. Instead, it is important not only to maintain a "humility" about the argument of this book but also, and more concretely, to maintain that it is a *theory* and so can only bear the weight of what any other theory can bear: it is heuristic, anticipatory, creative.

But the move to theory is fundamental because the goal of the book is to understand Christian tradition, which requires understanding history and revelation in history, a task to which common sense is not equal. To view history in a commonsense way—of which historians perform a sophisticated version—constrains history to the perspective of one's own context.[16] Though

12. Bernard Lonergan, "Essay in Fundamental Sociology—Philosophy of History," in *Collected Works of Bernard Lonergan*, vol. 25, *Archival Material: Early Papers on History* (Toronto: University of Toronto Press, 2019), 5.
13. Lonergan, *Insight*, 70.
14. Lonergan, 70.
15. Lonergan, *Method in Theology*, 214–15.
16. Lonergan, 216.

that kind of history is important, it is not the history that the present work is interested in, because it is distorted and narrowed by group interest, and there is a basic moral imperative to be invested in history beyond our own groups.[17]

A further imperative orients human beings toward the world and beyond groups—that is, toward theory, and beyond common sense. Since the present work is a work of theology, its theory of history must also include an understanding of God not only generally but also specifically as revealed in Christ. The kinds of judgments that such a theory must make will include the "too intelligible," as Lonergan puts it in reference to the supernatural meanings that are above human reason yet known in the light of faith.[18] Theology would be, on this analysis, a theory: it will (and does) have terms and relations, generalizations, principles, and thus a viewpoint that one can properly call theoretical.

Theory's anticipatory measure is what allows for new questions to be asked of history, questions that reach beyond the causal chains of what happened, beyond one's own group, and even beyond what was moving forward in a time or place.[19] Theory can ask what history is. More than that, a theory of history allows for an approach to the whole of history, which otherwise remains beyond our grasp. Lonergan calls such a theory of history "knowing why history is what it is" through a conceptual network that operates at "maximum generality."[20] Such a "why" and "generality" is the ultimate goal of this chapter, and understanding fully *why* will require the patient building of an actual theory of history. But before moving into that theory of history, it is important first to consider what, exactly, I mean by the term *metaphysics*. It, too, is a theoretical discourse, and an important one, since one of the things I want to do is to build a "metaphysic" of tradition.

A Definition of Metaphysics

The term *metaphysics* denotes an exploration of *being*, of what is. "Being," from the Latin *esse* ("to be"; *ens*, "being"), refers to all that in some way "is." So metaphysics has to do with inquiry, since it is a *study* of being, and it has

---

17. Lonergan, *Insight*, 247–50, 253.

18. Bernard Lonergan, "Outline of an Analytic Concept of History," in *Early Papers on History*, 105.

19. Lonergan, *Method in Theology*, 174.

20. Bernard Lonergan, "Analytic Concept of History," in *Early Papers on History*, 157.

something to do with the object of that inquiry, since it is a study of *being*. It asks questions about what is, but in a specific way. As a method of inquiry with an object, metaphysics both is an expression of being asking about itself (you and me, who are, asking about what is) and refers to the object of its own questioning (being, what is). Erich Przywara calls these two qualities of metaphysics "meta-noetics" and "meta-ontics."[21]

But what is this object, this being, this *to be*? "Being," Lonergan explains, "is (1) all that is known, (2) all that remains to be known."[22] Being is thus what intelligence understands when it understands correctly. Lonergan argues that everyone has a spontaneous *notion* of being. Our very desire to know is a kind of supposing that there is something to know. This supposing is conscious and intelligent, and so it is notional.[23] As a notion, it is more than a mere "orientation toward" being. It is a structured anticipation of being that motivates *all* of our intelligent inquiry. It is "the supreme heuristic notion. Prior to every content, it is the notion of the to-be-known through that content."[24] This characteristic is essential for the argument of the present book because it derives its notion of reality from Lonergan's description of being here.

Beyond the notion of being, there is our experiencing of being. Beyond our experiencing, there is our "thinking out being." And beyond this thinking, there is our knowing of being. Lonergan explains that in our acts of judgment—our acts of affirming answers to our own questions—we *know* being. So in every correct answer to every question for understanding, from the simplest to the most complex, being is known.[25]

Knowing being as such is not quite the same as knowing all the answers to all possible questions. It is a knowing of the *that there are* of all questions and

---

21. See Erich Przywara, *Analogia Entis: Metaphysics: Original Structure and Universal Rhythm*, trans. John Betz and David Bentley Hart (Grand Rapids, MI: Eerdmans, 2014), 119–24.

22. Lonergan, *Insight*, 374.

23. Lonergan, 377–79.

24. Lonergan, 380.

25. Hans Urs von Balthasar explains the same problematic through the act of human consciousness itself. "Consciousness," he says, "implies not only the abstract property of being *conscious*, but also, with equal immediacy, the reality of *being* conscious, the being of consciousness." In other words, I am conscious. This is consciousness that I am. And in my "consciousness-that," I also know being; I know what-is in a generalized way through this, my consciousness, a specific what-is. Says Balthasar, "Here is the proof, then, that being, precisely *as* being, can be unveiled and apprehended." Hans Urs von Balthasar, *Theo-Logic: Theological Logical Theory*, vol. 1, *Truth of the World* (San Francisco: Ignatius, 2000), 37 (hereafter *TL*).

their answers. I do not know this "that" except from out of the specificity of my own asking. So metaphysics, as a human discipline that makes a study of what-is, is heuristic in nature, since my knowing of being is at once concrete and, instead of total, anticipatory. "Metaphysics," Lonergan explains, "is the whole in knowledge but not the whole of knowledge."[26] It is important, then, not to confuse metaphysics and its discussion of being with all the knowledge available to human intelligence. It is fundamentally heuristic. Nevertheless, it is a way in which to heuristically approach all that there is. "Hence," says Lonergan, "being has at least one characteristic: it is all-inclusive. Apart from being there is nothing."[27]

What Lonergan means by "heuristic" here is important. Already I have used the concept at several points, and it bears clarifying. Lonergan notes, for example, that questions anticipate answers: "Before man actually understands, he anticipates and seeks to understand."[28] That is, we can in some way name what it is that we do not yet understand by asking questions about it. Such anticipatory naming is what Lonergan means by heuristic.[29] "Of themselves," says Lonergan, "heuristic structures are empty. They anticipate a form that is to be filled."[30] Metaphysics is theoretical. Its work is in the realm of theory. And while theory is abstract, the being that it explains is concrete. And this is another essential idea in the theory of tradition that follows: it must explain the concrete.

Lonergan contrasts concreteness with abstraction. "Are you talking about an abstraction when you talk of the concrete?" he asks. "That is precisely what you are not talking about."[31] We tend to think of abstraction as an impoverished imitation or representation of the concrete.[32] But for Lonergan, abstraction enriches the concrete. Abstraction anticipates an intelligibility to be had about the concrete and sets up heuristic structures by which to grasp that intelligibility by prescinding from what Lonergan calls the "empirical residue" of

26. Lonergan, *Insight*, 416.
27. Lonergan, 374.
28. Lonergan, 565.
29. Jonathan Heaps and Neil Ormerod, "Statistically Ordered: Gender, Sexual Identity, and the Metaphysics of 'Normal,'" *Theological Studies* 80, no. 2 (2019): 353.
30. Lonergan, *Insight*, 127.
31. Bernard Lonergan, *Collected Works of Bernard Lonergan*, vol. 10: *Topics in Education* (Toronto: University of Toronto Press, 1988), 28.
32. Lonergan, *Insight*, 111–12.

concreteness.[33] This empirical residue is the nonintelligible elements of the concrete: time and place, which are intelligible not in themselves but only as the duration or extension of something else.[34] In a sense, the concrete is what abstraction abstracts from. It is that totality of an instance of being, in its intelligibility and in its instantiation. In another sense, the concrete always pertains to that remainder, the empirical residue, which cannot be systematized, since the concrete is, *as* an instance, precisely *not* a system. The concrete has both an intelligibility that yields to inquiry (and thus to the enrichments of abstraction) and an empirical residue that has no intelligibility.

But is not this definition of the concrete all rather abstract? By explaining concreteness in a way that applies equally to all instances of concreteness and to nothing else, concreteness is not itself concrete.[35] In other words, human inquiry about the concrete yields intelligibility, but as inquiry, it is abstraction and not concrete. Thus, metaphysics is abstract, while its object of study (being) is not.

The present study, which proposes a "metaphysic" of Christian tradition, shares its major qualities with the description of metaphysics earlier in this section. It intends the concrete: it is about the concrete tradition that is ours, which persists in the history that is ours. But as a form of inquiry that abstracts from the concrete, it is not itself this concrete tradition. It is heuristic: it concerns the "whole" of tradition without itself being the whole of tradition.

It is "narrower" than a pure metaphysic, since it is not about *all* of being. It is different, too, than a pure history, since it operates from a theory of history in order to include all of human history in its basic perspective. This book is in many ways about a particular quality of historical—which is to say human—being. That quality is tradition. As a quality of historical being, tradition is universal to all human beings, and in that sense, this book is about the heuristic structure of all traditions. But though all human beings are historical, and all tradition is historical, traditions do not have their being apart from their concreteness, and there are many traditions that exist and have existed concretely. Thus, this book is specifically about the Christian tradition, especially as expressed in Catholic thought and history.

As a metaphysic of tradition, the present work will not touch on many of the major objects and contents of Christian tradition. Nor will it, except in a

---

33. Lonergan, 112.
34. Lonergan, 51.
35. Thanks to Jonathan Heaps for pointing this out to me.

heuristic way, lay out laws of interpretation for that tradition, since interpretation is a different horizon than the metaphysical one. Nor will it, finally, be a florilegium of Christian tradition—as in the medieval tradition, or in the vein of Henri de Lubac—though it does martial the resources of Christian tradition in its task.[36] That task is to order and describe the heuristic structure of Christian tradition, of its *being* in the world, such that this tradition *is*. This chapter's effort is to understand what it means to call anything at all historical, which in turn anticipates some qualities of what it might mean to call tradition "historical." And so it turns now, properly, to the theory of history.

A Theory of History: General Principles

There is, Lonergan says, the history that is written and the history that is written about.[37] There is, in other words, the history that historians write, reconstructed from a multitude of sources and angles, and then there is this other history— but what would I call it? The what-really-happened, the whole of the happening, all the human beings who made and make it? In other words, how should I name this event-quality, this permanent feature of every single human existence, such that I have in some way spoken both the unique *event* and the *universal* (the *every* human) of this particular thing called history?

Moreover, studying *this* history will not be the same as the studying that historians do. This totality, history, is not caught sight of in painstaking reconstruction, since every moment of every human life cannot be reconstructed. Nor is it the history contained in archives, since archives only contain the past and human historicity includes the present and the future.[38] Indeed, this total human history—as Charles Péguy argues—is not in fact viewable in its totality.[39] Because of this, others have said that the study of history itself is impossible,

---

36. Florilegia were collections of quotations bound together, often arranged by a master. Henri de Lubac (d. 1991) frequently assembles collections like this in his writings, two of his most well-known versions being *Medieval Exegesis*, 3 vols. (Grand Rapids, MI: Eerdmans, 1998–2009); and *The Discovery of God* (Grand Rapids, MI: Eerdmans, 1996).

37. Bernard Lonergan, "Method in Catholic Theology," in *Collected Works of Bernard Lonergan*, vol. 6, *Philosophical and Theological Papers 1958–1964* (Toronto: University of Toronto Press, 1996), 38; Lonergan, *Method in Theology*, 164; Lonergan, "Outline of an Analytic Concept," 97.

38. Lonergan, "Essay in Fundamental Sociology," 35.

39. For a summary, see Glenn Roe, *The Passion of Charles Péguy: Literature, Modernity, and the Crisis of Historicism* (Oxford: Oxford University Press, 2014), 16–50.

since it is impossible to really reconstruct.[40] And though such an impossibility is not my focus, I will note how this conclusion conflates the "history that is written" with the "history that is written about." History may escape writing, but does it escape theory? For Lonergan, history is at least *heuristically* available to human intelligence in a manner analogous to how being, and human being, is available to it.[41]

A theory of history moves away from common sense into generalized systematic operations and their terms.[42] It is dynamic, since history—as with all the sciences—studies change. "Theory of history," Lonergan explains, "is an a priori construction; it deduces the forms of historical movement from the inherent laws of human nature; and it is an explanatory account of these laws in their origin, their combinations, their effects."[43]

There are, therefore, overlapping theoretical questions at stake in my argument, one of which is, What is history? and the other of which is, What is a theory of history? They overlap because the answer to one implicates the other. They are not the same because a theory is not identical to what it studies. What this means is that, on the one hand, the more the problem of history unfolds, the more complex it becomes. Lonergan's answer to the first question—What is history?—is that history is "external human action."[44] Or, as he says elsewhere, history is *the making and unmaking of man by man.*[45] In other words, human history is what human beings *do*, and not only does history shape our doing; our doing also constitutes history. This might not strike the reader as sufficient. What about the "big events" of history? Or what about the lost or erased past? What about the "great men" who have contributed to history? What of the methodologies used by historians? Without waving away such questions, it is important to understand that historians and their methods are not answering the question of what history *is*; they are interpreting what

40. For example, Terrence Tilley, *Inventing Catholic Tradition* (Eugene, OR: Wipf & Stock, 2011). A separate monograph on the problem of tradition and history that notes their difficulty but resolves it differently is Paul Ricoeur, *Memory, History, Forgetting*, trans. Kathleen Blamey and David Pellauer (Chicago: University of Chicago Press, 2004).

41. Cf. Lonergan, *Method in Theology*, 176, 211–19.

42. Bernard Lonergan, "Philosophy of History," in *Philosophical and Theological Papers*, 69.

43. Bernard Lonergan, "A Theory of History," in *Early Papers on History*, 81.

44. Lonergan, "Essay in Fundamental Sociology," 6; cf. Bernard Lonergan, "Analytic Concept of History, in Blurred Outline," in *Early Papers on History*, 131: "History essentially is the course of human action in its causes."

45. Lonergan, "Outline of an Analytic Concept," 99; emphasis original.

has happened in it. Human action, however, heuristically attains this desired universality and specificity intended by asking *what* history is. All of human history is all human deeds. In Lonergan's words, "The material object of history is the aggregate of human actions, past, present, and future: every thought, word, and deed of every man."[46]

Humanity is one.[47] This statement is not aspirational. It is, for Lonergan and the Aristotelian-Thomist tradition out of which much of his language comes, a statement about how human beings are. We are not like the angels, spiritual beings who are distinguished from one another by their own unique species; we are instead one species individuated by matter. Or, to put it another way: I am a human being, but I am not humanity; *we*—through all time—are humanity.[48] Lonergan refers to this oneness as human solidarity, and by it, he means that fundamentally we are, together, humanity: "The radical solidarity of man is that he is a species, one nature, one intelligible, in many material individuations."[49] This means that when Lonergan refers to "human action," he does not primarily mean the action of one human being, a few "great men"; he means *human* action: the actions of all of us.[50]

It is worth pausing at this point to consider what humanity's radical solidarity means for a theory of history. It does *not* mean aggregation, a combination of many pieces together.[51] No, human solidarity is more radical than that. Our action is *one*, which involves a profound interdependence of willing that grows in importance over time.[52] Human solidarity also means that for a theory of history to be serious, it must include every single human being over all of time. *That*, and nothing less, is what history is, and therefore what a theory of history is about.

46. Lonergan, 97.

47. Since I must select those notions that I argue for, I will not argue for the use of "humanity" or "human nature." Suffice it to say, I align myself with Lonergan's argument in "Natural Right and Historical Mindedness," in *Third Collection*, 169–83; and with Achille Mbembe's desire to retain the category of the human, as expressed in *Out of the Dark Night: "Essays on Declonization."* (New York: Columbia University Press, 2021).

48. Lonergan, "Theory of History," 80.

49. Lonergan, "Outline of an Analytic Concept," 100.

50. Lonergan, *Early Papers on History*, 50, 52, 90, 98.

51. Lonergan, "Essay in Fundamental Sociology," 26.

52. We begin with Lonergan, "Analytic Concept of History, in Blurred Outline," 135. It will grow in importance in the next two sections.

For Lonergan, humanity is not the cause of its own motion. This might seem contradictory at first, since I have been talking about history as human *action*. But from a Thomist point of view, human beings are but instruments of the original agent of our motion, the original agent both in the order of the universe and with respect to our individual willing, which is God.[53] Lonergan refers to this original agential moving of human being as "premotion."[54] I will not review the conflict over divine premotion as it has occurred in Thomist circles.[55] Instead, it is important to understand how, in our transmission of this single premotion, a new world opens up for a theory of history: either we can follow the dictates of reason, in which case we "add" nothing to the premotion while continuing it, or we can reject reason, in which case we subtract by sinning. "Every individual," says Lonergan, "is an instrument in the transmission of the premotion: but he may be an instrument for more sin or less. He may be an instrument of sin or of Christ."[56] A kind of chasm, a dialectic, opens up in our willing and in the world. Premotion emphasizes that we receive the situation that we are presently in *and* that we mold the situation of the future through our present action. This is one way that human action is dialectical: action occurs through our continual response to and creation of situations in an ever-evolving feedback loop.

Lonergan, because he understands human action to also be intelligent, considers this dialectic to be essentially progressive: it builds "upward," as it were, in rising complexity. Here Lonergan imagines things like the invention of alphabets or the discovery of philosophy.[57] But really, this progress is any elaboration that human action makes upon itself over time.[58] Human action either conforms to reality or does not. This fact makes the dialectic of human action

53. Lonergan, "Essay in Fundamental Sociology," 34.

54. See Lonergan, *Early Papers on History*, 35–36, 71.

55. For a review of the discussion, see David S. Oderberg, "Divine Premotion," *International Journal for Philosophy of Religion* 79, no. 3 (2016): 207–22; Thomas Osborne, "Thomist Premotion and Contemporary Philosophy of Religion," *Nova et Vetera* 4, no. 3 (2006): 607–32.

56. Lonergan, "Essay in Fundamental Sociology," 35.

57. For example, Lonergan, *Method in Theology*, 30.

58. Though it has yet to be explored by students of Lonergan's thought, in principle, "primitive" societies take up a place in the "line" of progress not merely as origins for what is greater but as themselves elaborations of human action. Really, we ought to say, "All non-Western societies are elaborations of human action." Their authenticity is not determined by their "degree" of progress, or by their semblance to the West, but in their attention, intelligence, reasonableness, and responsibility.

complex in another way because it introduces absurdity into human action, or what Lonergan calls decline. Decline is also a progressive or building response to situations, an elaboration of human action, but in the inverse direction: toward lesser complexity, toward fragmentation.[59] Human action has a kind of directionality, a motility embedded in it that is not only or simply temporal. This is not the same as saying that history has a "side" (a "right" side) or a will of its own. No, *history is all of our willing for all time*.[60] But to say this is also to say that human willing is an "incidence of power" that "is for human progress or for human extinction."[61] Human action is more than temporal; it endures and effectuates qualitative change.

Christians recognize that history also has as its principle of motion the supernatural action of God, the world of grace in Christ. Lonergan describes this quality of history too, and in his early work, he refers to it as "supernatural action" or even "renaissance."[62] History is not only progress and decline; history is also recovery in the wake of decline. But for Lonergan, such recovery is not available to the human will on its own, not even to all of us together. The situation of decline is essentially intractable because it contains absurdity, the unintelligible.[63] Only an intervention beyond human power, and so a properly supernatural intervention, can address the complex tangle of sense and nonsense that human beings find themselves in. By integrating supernatural action, Lonergan provides a theory of history with a fully theological point of view, which complements the motility of human action in general, with its qualities of progress and decline, by adding (supernaturally accomplished) redemption.[64]

59. Cf. Lonergan, *Early Papers on History*, 58, 143–44.

60. Lonergan, "Essay in Fundamental Sociology," 8.

61. Lonergan, 5.

62. Cf. Lonergan, "Outline of an Analytic Concept," 99.

63. Cf. Lonergan, *Method in Theology*, 222.

64. The reference to "redemption" as the third heuristic comes from Lonergan, *Philosophical and Theological Papers*, 7.

The Turn to Interiority

We live in a world mediated by meaning.[65] Knowledge of that world is not writing or reading or speaking. It is not "taking a good look."[66] Knowledge is a much more profound and intimate achievement than this. It requires a mind; it requires a mind that makes a judgment.[67] In other words, thinking is something that we *do*; it does not arrive to us ready-made (as Péguy would say: *tout-fait*).

Lonergan's insight into insight is twofold: it expands both the Thomist idea that truth is known by a mind that makes a judgment and the idea that human beings arrive at knowledge through mediation. We experience the world as meaningful. We have intellects that not only ask about meaning but also creatively assemble entire complexes of meaning, making meaning into a world that we (together) make. Meaning is, at one angle, the difference between human knowledge—the way that humans know—and what Lonergan calls the "world of immediacy."[68] This latter world is not unimportant. It is the world of sense and sense-response. But the difference between an infant and a child, or between the insensate person and the awake one, is this world of meaning that we constitute and that constitutes us. Meaning is also, at another angle, a way of describing how much of the world that we consider "the world," or real, or real to us, is the world not of bare fact but of meaning. Meaning that makes us and that we make. It is, too, a way of describing human potential: the world that we make in many ways determines the world that we might make.[69]

For Lonergan, meaning is as complex as human consciousness. With the same mind, a person experiences, knows, judges, decides, loves. Lonergan calls this complexity-in-unity the "differentiation" of human consciousness.[70] And since consciousness is or can be differentiated, so is human meaning. We make a world intelligently in the *way* that we are intelligent, in the very manner of our intelligence, and we fail to make a coherent world inasmuch as we abandon our intelligence and its basic shape.[71] In this fashion, Lonergan is able to

---

65. Cf. Bernard Lonergan, "Dimensions of Meaning," in *Collected Works of Bernard Lonergan*, vol. 4, *Collection* (Toronto: University of Toronto Press, 1993), 233.

66. Cf. Lonergan, *Insight*, 27–37.

67. See Lonergan, 296–303.

68. Lonergan, *Method in Theology*, 30, 75.

69. Cf. Lonergan, 55–95.

70. Cf. Lonergan, 81–82.

71. See Lonergan, *Insight*, 241–42, 252.

describe our mediated world as both structured and dynamic: it is structured as an image of our immanent intellectual structure; it is dynamic inasmuch as we continue asking questions, and inasmuch as human being is perpetually self-transcending.[72]

It is important to understand that Lonergan's model of human consciousness, and therefore of the world of meaning, is fundamentally ecstatic: our "pure," "unrestricted" desire to know pulls us out of ourselves and into the world, most especially into the world of meaning.[73] We ask questions, make judgments, make decisions. Each successive quality of our intelligence enfolds the others in an ecstatic movement upward or outward. This ecstasy is radically decentering, since what animates the ecstasy fundamentally is a movement beyond the self. "For Lonergan," explains Frederick Lawrence, "self-transcendence means exactly what it says."[74]

This self-transcending movement or, *ek-stasis*, explains what Lonergan means by the word "transcendental" and by the "transcendental precepts": be attentive, be intelligent, be reasonable, be responsible. By "transcendental," he means the movement of consciousness beyond itself, and he means the structure of that dynamism; he means that this movement is intentional, or has a "direction"; he means that this movement is not out-there but is in the intentionality of human consciousness itself. Being attentive, intelligent, reasonable, and responsible is the being of self-transcendence, of ecstasy beyond the self. This underlines what Lonergan means when he calls human consciousness "intentional" at all: humans reach toward in their desire to know. "The point," explains Jeremy Blackwood, "[is] to be able to talk about the operations of human subjects that seek to know (cognitional) and reach toward (intentional) objects."[75]

The transcendental precepts—be attentive, be intelligent, be reasonable, be responsible—do more than describe the operations of intentional human consciousness. They also provide the standard for what Lonergan calls "authenticity." At one level, authenticity and its opposite, unauthenticity, are descriptions of whether the conscious subject or community is "doing" what it is that they

72. See Lonergan, 78–93.

73. Lonergan, 28; Lonergan, *Method in Theology*, 55–60.

74. Frederick Lawrence, "The Fragility of Consciousness: Lonergan and the Postmodern Concern for the Other," in *The Fragility of Consciousness: Faith, Reason, and the Human Good*, ed. Randall Rosenberg and Kevin Vander Schel (Toronto: University of Toronto Press, 2017), 249.

75. Jeremy Blackwood, "The Heart of the Mystical Body of Christ: Subjectivity and Solidarity with Poor Women of Color," *Theological Studies* 77, no. 3 (2016): 661.

"do," or whether they "are" what they "are." Is the creature that is capable of attention, intelligence, reason, and responsibility *being* attentive, intelligent, reasonable, and responsible? That is to say, the standard or norm for authenticity is immanent to human consciousness. And as standards, they are heuristic: they are measures that are "empty," as Lonergan says, and so able to be sufficed in any number of ways in accord with specific circumstances and situations. But the transcendental precepts are also a description of self-transcendence. They are measures of a decentering ecstatic movement, found beyond the self and ultimately in God.[76] "He made us in his image," explains Lonergan, "for our authenticity consists in being like him, in self-transcending, in being origins of value, in true love."[77]

The pure, unrestricted desire to know is fundamental to Lonergan's philosophy and theology. It is not only ecstatic. It also shapes his understanding of what understanding is: we are driven by the "tension" of "the pure question," and we do not cease asking questions.[78] This pure desire that moves us beyond ourselves is more than wanting to know all that there is to know, though it involves that. Because we are structured this way, we are also responsible for it. To reject the "pure desire" is to stand against oneself; it is to reject the world of responsibility, which demands that we ask further questions.[79] So embedded in the desire to know is the latent world of decision and its responsibilities. Therefore, besides the unrestricted desire to know, besides the world mediated by meaning, there is also our encounter with the world of value.

With these concepts in place, it is possible to say something about what it means for human beings to be in a (concrete, historical) "situation." At least on Lonergan's account, a *situation* is a particular instance of a world mediated by meanings and motivated by values, and indeed by meaninglessness and disvalue. A change of situation must, therefore, be not only a change of the practical circumstances that shape our creation of meanings and values but also a change of the meanings and values themselves. "Situations," argues Robert Doran, "are constituted by meaning, and a change in constitutive meaning is in the long run the most effective form of praxis."[80]

76. The "decentering" language is drawn from Lawrence, "Fragility of Consciousness," esp. 248–49.

77. Lonergan, *Method in Theology*, 113.

78. Lonergan, *Insight*, 34.

79. See Lonergan, 750.

80. Robert Doran, *Theology and the Dialectics of History* (Toronto: University of Toronto Press, 1990), 4.

Finally, it is important to understand the ultimate change of the concrete situation that is the "law of the cross." For human subjectivity is not only involved with itself but also involved in, involved by, the economy of salvation.[81] By the gift of God, the human being becomes part of a new society, which is the church. The human being radically falls in love with God, and so also with the order of the universe. We are taken up into the action of God, which is fundamentally cruciform: exchanging good for evil, loving our enemies, acting in terms of that ultimate dialectical attitude toward the problem of evil that is God's to give and God's to make effective.[82]

Lonergan's great effort as a theologian is to understand how, for the Christian, for the world, God intervenes in a way that perfects and elevates what he has already made. *Gratia perfecit naturam non destruit.* Or, in Lonergan's words, "The solution [to the problem of evil] will be a harmonious continuation of the actual order of this universe."[83] And in this universe is a creature that is historical as well as corporeal, a creature that is intelligent and free: the human being. This means that the great hinge of salvation is not only flesh but also history. God's intervention in the world is a redemption not just of human beings but also of human meaning and human action.

In the Wake of Interiority

Human action has a "directionality." It can occur according to reason and to the benefit of human beings, or it can be unreasonable and inhumane. Because human action is *human*—involving all humans for all times—and not purely individual, and because human intelligence shares this quality of togetherness, it is collaborative and open to change. For the same reasons, human action is also progressive and regressive: actions taken together over time build on one another toward achievements, or toward their undermining.

Progress is not at all automatic. Progress only happens when we apply ourselves together, and *humanly*—which is to say, including everyone. As Lonergan argues in the 1930s, "Only the conspiracy of all human intelligences can discover the 'better' of progress, which is concrete and particular."[84] Indeed, for

81. Lonergan, *Insight*, 718–19.
82. Lonergan, 721.
83. Lonergan, 718.
84. Lonergan, "Analytic Concept of History, in Blurred Outline," 140.

Lonergan, progress is not really progress unless its achievements, discerned by everyone, are applied to everyone.[85] It is complex because society is complex: its activity involves us all, but differently, and that difference depends heavily on the concrete circumstances and the types of multifaceted states, cities, or communities that we find ourselves in.[86]

Like human intelligence, progress is dialectical. We are constantly involved in a kind of feedback loop between subjectivity and situation, between "thought/deed" and "circumstance," each affecting the other through a series of ever-working refinements and responses. Lonergan sees the basic task of human intelligence as that of reality conforming the mind to itself.[87] He envisions this process as, precisely, a process: as taking time, as enduring improvement, as requiring evermore sophisticated intellectual tasks and responsibilities, in evermore diversified societies.[88]

Progress is also complexly dialectical: it involves more than one dialectical engagement with reality. This is not only so because human societies have many parts. It is also so because besides individual intelligence, there is also human intersubjectivity, and besides intersubjectivity, there are higher and lower "integrations" that treat different parts of society differently.[89] Even politics, for example, is not monofunctional. And besides politics, there is economics. And besides economics, there is the whole practical working out of the scale of values: vital, social, religious, and so on. These values are "lower" and "higher" in the same manner that various integrations can be: some rely on others to be the case before including them in what is "higher." We can hardly have a religion if none of us can eat, and yet religion involves itself in much more than food. Or again, philosophy can draw together the various complex insights required to view the "whole" of a society—and yet it does more than this. Socrates does not ask only about just laws; he asks what justice itself is.[90]

These higher viewpoints, which include the realm of theory, are necessary for the functioning of progress, for its application, for its discernment. The more complex a society becomes, the more necessary these higher viewpoints and their integrations are. For Lonergan, we cannot remain only in the theater

85. See, for example, Lonergan, *Insight*, 249.
86. Lonergan, *Early Papers on History*, 24, 35, 86–88, 103, 135; Doran, *Theology and the Dialectics*, esp. 205–6.
87. Lonergan, "Analytic Concept of History, in Blurred Outline," 132.
88. Lonergan, *Method in Theology*, 190; Lonergan, "Analytic Concept of History," 164–65.
89. Cf. Lonergan, *Insight*, 255–57.
90. Lonergan, *Early Papers on History*, 13–14, 86, 108; Lonergan, *Method in Theology*, 79.

of common sense. Practical intelligence deals with practical problems, but not all problems and their solutions are practical. Every new situation requires not just a grasp of the situation but also a grasp of the meanings that make the situation. This higher grasp is what Lonergan often calls a "higher control."[91]

It is important to understand that "control" here is not meant in a common-sense way, where control is essentially identical with mere power over outcomes. Lonergan means *control* more in the sense that a scientist might use the word. Control is what allows for the discernment of relevant and irrelevant factors in an experiment or, here, in the ideal line of progress. But at the same time, "control" is also meant as *integrative*, as what allows for a higher viewpoint that can take the disparate elements of progress and consider them together.

Not only is progress not automatic; its inverse frequently occurs. In fact, for Lonergan, (purely) human progress is *always* accompanied by decline.[92] Decline is, basically, sin. It is not to do what reason asks; it is, in other words, a failure to follow the transcendental precepts, and this "not-doing" introduces to the world not *something* but no-thing, a nonintelligible surd.[93] Human intelligence cannot address a surd, which has no meaning, and yet the social surd becomes part of the facts of the situation.[94] The temptation, therefore, is to partially solve the problem: to take a fragment and resolve only it, and for only some. "This disorder is like the complex number," Lonergan argues, "it contains the irrational."[95] This irrationality further fragments the situation, which further fragments the human beings in the situation. Decline becomes a "cycle" that feeds upon itself, resulting in ever-greater fragmentation and absurdity.[96] For Lonergan, decline is marked at once by the "atomization of man"—which is to say, by the increasing destruction of solidarity—and by the rejection of reason and any "higher control" or "higher viewpoint." Decline is a kind of double movement against human unity and against human intelligence, since the two are ultimately linked to each other.

Lonergan distinguishes between "minor" and "major" decline, or between the "shorter" and "longer" cycles of decline. Both have to do with how we treat common sense. The shorter cycle includes problems like individual and group

---

91. It is all over his early work: Lonergan, *Early Papers on History*, 10, 15, 28.
92. Lonergan, *Insight*, 720.
93. Lonergan, "Theory of History," 85.
94. Lonergan, *Insight*, 249–50.
95. Lonergan, "Outline of an Analytic Concept," 112.
96. Lonergan, *Insight*, 257–59.

bias: both are failures to develop intelligence beyond the narrow world of one's own interests.[97] Both apply the practical intelligence of common sense, but only within the narrow ranges of their own biases. And bias, as M. Shawn Copeland reminds us, is about more than personal preference or temperament. "Bias," she explains, "is the more or less conscious and deliberate choice, in light of what we perceive as a potential threat to our well-being, to exclude further information or data from consideration in our understanding, judgment, discernment, decision, and action."[98] Biases are failures of intelligence and therefore also are failures of responsibility.

With the longer cycle of decline, Lonergan highlights the general bias of common sense against anything other than itself: all else is "impractical."[99] It might not strike us as obvious that the foundation of major decline is an overreliance on common sense, an overreliance that forsakes theory. But here is where Lonergan's move to interiority is helpful: the human being as such is more than their practical intelligence. We all want to make of life a dramatic work of art.[100] So though theory is indeed in "danger" (from common sense) in the case of major decline, Lonergan is more concerned with the stakes not of our ideas but of our subjectivities. "Practical intelligence," Doran explains, "is not a sufficient intellectual development to meet the requirements of social artistry."[101]

Refusing theory leads to long-term decline. So even if practical intelligence can carry itself quite far, especially in our day-to-day labors, its solipsism is the seed of a fatal flaw, one whose fruit is widespread, long-term structural collapse. "One way to understand at least one dimension of the major principle of decline," says Doran, "is to view it as a neglect of the questions that are pertinent to true order."[102] For there has been a failure to acquire a higher viewpoint that can successfully, artfully integrate all lower viewpoints; a failure, that is, to attend to anything but the practical. Common sense goes on unable to critique itself or its methods until its failure and limitation fund not just day-to-day lapses of intelligence and action (minor decline) but also civilizational disintegration (major decline).[103]

97. Lonergan, 247–50.

98. M. Shawn Copeland, *Enfleshing Freedom: Body, Race, and Being* (Minneapolis: Fortress, 2010), 13.

99. Esp. in Lonergan, "General Bias," in *Insight*, 250–51.

100. Esp. in the "dramatic pattern of experience." Lonergan, 210–12.

101. Doran, *Theology and the Dialectics*, 373.

102. Doran, 392.

103. Cf. Lonergan, *Insight*, 257–59.

With decline, we are in fact *responsible* for the things we leave out or fail to do, for the standpoints that we do not take up. But in this phenomenon, culture is also important. Because culture stands "above" practical human endeavor, it serves as the essential lifeblood for a viewpoint that can independently judge the efforts of practical intelligence. In decline, however, culture is made subservient to common sense's concerns and ceases to be able to judge the situation as it ought.[104]

Progress, for Lonergan, follows the basic lineaments of conscious intentionality: we desire to know, a desire that drives our self-transcendence. Our responsibility is to follow this desire, which is pure and unrestricted. To deny either quality of this desire is to step into decline; it is to submit to bias, to refuse to ask further questions, to forsake rationality itself. In this way, while Lonergan describes structures and dynamics much larger than any single human being, he never ceases to remember that everything that humans make resembles their own humanity.[105]

It is not possible to respond to decline with more progress. Progress cannot treat the surd of sin, which remains unintelligible. Decline basically funds its own continuation, a spiraling dialectic of widening blends of sense and nonsense, and we are helpless before it. According to Lonergan, a higher integration is needed, one that can address both progress and decline. But this viewpoint is not available to human intelligence.[106] For Lonergan, the only proper solution to the problem of decline is beyond human every power: it requires a supernatural response, which is to say, God's response.

Progress and decline are qualities of human action. God's redemption must (therefore) address human action. It must treat situations, which are situations of meaning. It must also be new, because what is old has broken down. "The troubled times of crisis," Lonergan explains, "demand the discovery and communication of new insights and a consequent adaptation of spontaneous attitudes."[107] In other words, whatever God does in history has to both address the problem and address human beings as they in fact are, all while introducing to them what is new. Redemption is concrete, and it is also supernatural.

If sin is, fundamentally, the unwillingness to do the good, then the gift that God gives us in Christ is willingness. But this willingness is more than a mere

---

104. Lonergan, 262; Doran, *Theology and the Dialectics*, 208–9.
105. Cf. Doran, *Theology and the Dialectics*, 402.
106. Lonergan, *Insight*, 719.
107. Lonergan, 241.

restoration of willingness to do the good; it is the gift of a radical being-in-love that commands our absolute willingness. It is a pure gift that brings about total conversion. "In its most mature form," explains Doran, "the grace of willingness is love for God that is motivated by God's own goodness."[108] This includes a commitment to, a love for, the whole world.[109] God grants the human being that radical and loving disposition that is God's own. This is not available to us naturally, which is to say, by our own power; but God's gift of himself to us in Christ enables in us a whole series of new responses to the world.

Here is where Lonergan's law of the cross plays a fundamental role in the life of the Christian: like Christ, we are to exchange good for evil, charity for hatred, penance for sin.[110] As Doran argues, these new actions, which are also new meanings, are what is able to treat the surd of sin and the ideal line of progress while surpassing both. At the same time, it means that the community of the suffering servant will continue to be cruciform in the world. In Doran's words, "The community of the suffering servant, neither wavering nor being crushed until true justice is established on earth, can be an agent of an alternative to the distorted dialectic of community only by permanently remaining a countersign to it. But then it will also permanently be shot through with the law of its participation in the cross of God's suffering servant."[111] Lonergan's law of the cross, in other words, is the "how" of God's perfecting grace in the world.

The intervention of God in Christ and through the church means opening up a new world by being responsive to the old one. This includes a kind of inversion of the sins of decline: where there is hatred, there is charity; where there is the flight from understanding, there is penance; where there is a rejection of reason, there is faith.[112] These are not just corrections but also higher integrations, beyond where natural reason would lead us. As Doran argues, "Meeting the problem on the level of the disease, then, and so truly ministering in the world, involves in part what Lonergan calls a new and higher collaboration of intellects through faith in God."[113]

Theology and the theologian in the church, like the church itself, are self-transcending. The church "goes out" into the world.[114] So too, both theology

108. Doran, *Theology and the Dialectics*, 201.

109. Lonergan, *Insight*, 721.

110. See esp. Lonergan, *Early Papers on History*, 27–29, 74, 87–88, 174.

111. Doran, *Theology and the Dialectics*, 205.

112. Lonergan, *Insight*, 718–25.

113. Doran, *Theology and the Dialectics*, 384.

114. Doran, 420.

and the church are witnesses to that "newer and higher collaboration of intellects." Such collaboration is a way of life, one that follows the scale of values in all their vitality and rigor rather than their distortion through sin, bias, and decline. And for Doran, it is a collaboration that must be world-cultural rather than monocultural. "It is the community of the church as a whole," explains Doran, "that is to evoke a world cultural community, by its fidelity to the integral scale of values and its incarnate witness to the mission of the suffering and risen servant of God under the just and mysterious law of the cross."[115]

It would be too easy to miss the Christocentrism of Lonergan's description of redemption, involving as it does the complex mechanisms of human action through Christian virtues like charity, poverty, obedience, and penance.[116] But the major force behind or underneath redemption, including the dynamism of our own actions, is God in Christ: all of history, all the wonder of progress and the devastation of decline, is summed up and transfigured through Jesus's historical life, death, and resurrection. The Christian participates not on their own or under the animus of their own power but in what is God's initiative. Says Lonergan, "The Christian . . . participates [in] the supreme act of Christ and partakes in the supreme act of history."[117] So Christ is not just God's response to history, a response to decline with redemption, but also history's ultimate meaning.

For Lonergan, decline requires more than a mere reversal. It requires the intervention of the supraintelligible through revelation in Christ, and it requires our participation in this revelation in the life of the church. Moreover—and as Doran makes clear—theology is obligated to participate in the praxis of the church through its own mediation between faith and culture. This brings the chapter to its final theme, which presses Lonergan beyond himself into new areas of inquiry.

In the Wake of Colonial History

A theory of history is more heuristic than it is descriptive. It anticipates through its categories a whole that is not simply the sum of history's parts. It emphasizes

115. Doran, 418.
116. This list of virtues echoes his 1930s work rather than *Insight*. See, for example, Lonergan, "Analytic Concept of History, in Blurred Outline," 148.
117. Lonergan, "Outline of an Analytic Concept," 123.

that human history is human action and that such action has "direction" in the forms of progress, decline, and redemption. Such direction describes human action and so expresses not phases or epochs of history but possibilities for all of human action. But so also is human history meaningful, composed of situations that are constituted by meaning. This meaning, too, endures change, as human action endures change. And at this point, one could, in theory, describe almost any quality of history: our fundamental solidarity with one another, the developmental nature of our building of a world of meaning, the breakdown of solidarity and meaning, God's redeeming action in and through history. But to stop here would in fact leave the theory incomplete.

Besides the systematic exigence that leads to theory, there is the critical exigence that leads to interiority. We are led, in Lonergan's way of speaking, to our own self-appropriation. We are led not just to the world of mediated meaning but also to our own mediation, to our consciousness as adverted to.[118] For Lonergan, we do not stop there. We return again to the realms of common sense and theory, and we return changed, able to deploy a method suited to the structure of our own consciousness, the method that emerges in the wake of the turn to interiority.

And we do not stop even there. In addition to systematic and critical exigences, there is that ultimate exigence that Lonergan calls "transcendent." This exigence leads us beyond ourselves, "beyond the realms of common sense, theory, and interiority, and into the realm in which God is known and loved."[119] The *ekstasis* of our being, the pure drive of our desire to know, draws us beyond ourselves and into that supraintelligibility that is God. So Lonergan describes a kind of double movement, one where we are able to reflect upon our own knowledge *and* move beyond ourselves into the love of God, in absolute self-transcendence. These are not opposed efforts. We must think of them as a single ecstasy in a double direction.

For Shawn Copeland, operationalizing this ultimate exigence in contemporary US theology requires a "turn" in that theology that renders it more authentic, a *turn to persons*.[120] Such a turn reforms theology by also seeking its roots, which reach down deep into a creative, culturally and intellectually polyphonic way

---

118. Cf. Lawrence, "Fragility of Consciousness," 246–48.

119. Lonergan, *Method in Theology*, 81.

120. M. Shawn Copeland, "Turning Theology: A Proposal," *Theological Studies* 80, no. 4 (2019): 767.

of being.[121] Turning to persons is a way of approaching human beings not only in their abstract and shared qualities but also in those many and various things that distinguish them. "Persons," says Copeland, "are plural, many, diverse, different, at one and the same time so very alike and unlike one another."[122] It is a heuristic turn, for there are many kinds of persons; it is a heuristic turn toward concreteness, for persons are always concrete.

A theory of history, in other words, to be fully and responsibly historical, and so also in order to be fully and responsibly theoretical, ought to be able to make a mirroring turn to persons, since it is not simply a blank-faced humanity that makes history to be in human action and in human meaning but a humanity that is one and many through human persons. To be historical in this, the fullest sense, requires attention to persons. There is a danger here in this turn from the outset, inasmuch as it resembles a different turn, the Enlightenment's famous "turn to the subject." This turn, Copeland says, "coincided with the dynamics of domination."[123] Descartes and Kant and others—far from transforming philosophy into an exploration of a pure, idealized human nature and a pure, idealized human rationality—in fact idealized white, male, European being-in-the-world.[124]

Concepts have histories.[125] And those histories include both word and deed. The Enlightenment was a time of rapid cultural change in Europe, and also a time of Europe's domination of large swaths of the world.[126] So Copeland not only describes a deformed set of *ideas* in their deformation—the turn to the subject—but also describes the historical *action* by which they persisted, the creation and domination of cultural and racial others. These are some of the principle moments of this history: the Enlightenment oversaw the vociferous expansion of colonial and racial logic; Enlightenment philosophical categories were used to describe who was human or civilized *and who was not*; in these categories, Europe was said to "have" history, while all other peoples and

121. Copeland, 755–59.

122. Copeland, 768.

123. Copeland, *Enfleshing Freedom*, 88.

124. Copeland, 89.

125. Cf. Jeremy Wilkins, *Before Truth: Lonergan, Aquinas, and the Problem of Wisdom* (Washington, DC: Catholic University of America Press, 2018), 235–37.

126. See, for example, Daniel Carey and Lynn Festa, eds., *The Postcolonial Enlightenment: Eighteenth-Century Colonialism and Postcolonial Theory* (Oxford: Oxford University Press, 2009); Andrew Curran, *The Anatomy of Blackness: Science and Slavery in an Age of Enlightenment* (Baltimore, MD: Johns Hopkins University Press, 2013).

places, as "primitive," did not.[127] Charles Long emphasizes the way religion itself changed under the weight of these new categories: "Both religion and cultures and peoples throughout the world were created anew through academic disciplinary orientations—*they were signified*."[128]

All of these ideas and their dynamics are part of a much larger historical arc that witnessed the emergence of the modern idea of race during the emergence of modern ideas of commerce. This modern racial notion operates to "assign" power, grace, glory, intelligence—the adjectives and their ontologies move around—to some and not to others. But race itself assigns nothing at all; it is human beings who do the assigning, and race operates in this operation with a certain mediatory power. Since it divides human being, which is one, we can call this operation irrational and sinful. Since it mediates a denial of the humanity of certain human beings and titanically aggrandizes the humanity of others, we can say that race scotomizes human being in its being. We stare and do not see; we move through the world, and certain urgent questions do not arise in our minds, for we refuse their very emergence; we ourselves are the question that is refused; our world results from this refusal and institutes it as our situation. So this world that we call "world" is a world of mediating meaning, a world of concrete nonintelligibilities, a world of persons, and it is our being whose being we vitiate. It is in a resonant sense that Copeland calls the racialization of persons "metaphysical violence."[129]

Race, then, is a historical product, a meaning that mediates our world, one that endures a number of transmutations over time, and today it is a continuing, transmutative reality. This historical product, race and its transmutations, is locatable in various times and places, always differently, but it is not—especially *as* sin—locatable in a single monument or moment of birth.[130] And since race

127. Walter Mignolo is extremely influential in regard to uncovering this dynamic, and he tracks it beyond the Enlightenment. See Mignolo, *Local Histories/Global Designs: Coloniality, Subaltern Knowledges, and Border Thinking* (Princeton, NJ: Princeton University Press, 2012); Mignolo, *The Darker Side of the Renaissance: Literacy, Territoriality, and Colonization* (Ann Arbor: University of Michigan Press, 2003); and Mignolo, *On Decoloniality: Concepts, Analytics, Praxis* (Durham, NC: Duke University Press, 2018).

128. Charles H. Long, *Significations: Signs, Symbols, and Images in the Interpretation of Religion* (Aurora, CO: Davies Group, 2004), 4.

129. M. Shawn Copeland, "Anti-Blackness and White Supremacy in the Making of American Catholicism," *American Catholic Studies* 127, no. 3 (2016): 7.

130. It is difficult to pin down a historical "whence" for modern racial ideas, and attempts are various, from the Marxist emphasis on the rise of capitalism to studies of medieval racial ideas

in the sense I mean it here fundamentally divides human beings, fragmenting them, and plies the wealth of development only to a few, it is at its heart an instrument of decline.

There is a tension in the chapters that follow this one, and at this moment it appears for the first time. That tension is contorted across three modes of reflection about modern dynamics of race, which are, broadly, race as meaning or ideology, race as imbricated of and "made" by human action, race as unintelligible "fact" of concrete situations. The distinctions I just made between reflective modalities do not mirror specific schools of thought, though there are many such. As distinctions, they will emerge as Blondelian in origin by the end of the next chapter, particularly with respect to the meaning of "human action," though they are influenced by Barbara Fields and Karen Fields's *Racecraft*.[131]

I contribute my odd demarcation of thought about race to indicate an oddness in its being-thought. And the trouble I name is immense: even if we say that race is a not-real, even if it has no biological basis, it is a process of meanings and pseudomeanings applied to bodies by way of human action, an operation that simultaneously conceals human action and the human relationships this action makes and is made by. Even if race, as an operation, is sin and so is surd, it is embedded in the world we confront today. The "craft" of race is, in other words, concrete. To call it not-real is not to make it stop being concrete. And it is not possible to think "beyond" a surd, to think the being of a world beyond the impossible-to-understand, just as it is impossible to see-no-color, to remove from the facticity of the present situation the surds in its facts. What is more, surds fragment our attention into small, understandable pieces of situations rather than allowing us to attend to situations themselves.

Such fragmentation is explanatory of more than one disagreement about how to confront problems of racism, about whether race is a product of colonialism specifically, about the ways that race and racism are systematic rather than individual, and about what sense there is in calling theologies "Black," or in accusing theologies of being "white"—indeed about whether such terms

---

and so on. Here I gesture, in a way, at them all, without choosing any particular one. For further reference, see Mignolo, *Local Histories*; as well as Geraldine Heng, *The Invention of Race in the Middle Ages* (Cambridge: Cambridge University Press, 2018); and M. Lindsay Kaplan, *Figuring Racism in Medieval Christianity* (Oxford: Oxford University Press, 2018). Finally, I will only mention that there is disagreement among scholars on how and whether the late Hellenic system of slavery lasted into the Middle Ages, a literature that I will not review.

131. Karen E. Fields and Barbara J. Fields, *Racecraft: The Soul of Inequality in American Life* (New York: Verso Books, 2012).

can be applied across distinct historical circumstances at all.[132] With Charles
W. Mills, the Fieldses, and others, I suspect that American discourse about
race conceals problems of class, impoverishing our discussions of both.[133] With
Achille Mbembe and others, I see "Blackness" as ambiguous, as a negation of
persons reappropriated against itself by those negated persons, as the "remainder" of modernity, and so, for all this, Blackness is important to think through
and think about and think with, however challenging it is to do so, with its
quality as complex number.[134] Race is only ever inexplicable of problems, and
yet as embedded fact, it is necessary to descriptions of historical situations,
including situations that are problems of class. In other words, we must discuss race and racism, the processes of colonialism, the sins of our recent history. But we must not allow this necessity of ours to make race *necessary* in the
Scholastic sense of "necessity," which means (among other things) *real*. Race is
real-not-real, out-there-now, "body" but not *body*, historical but not explanatory
of history—for what explains human history is human action, and by way of
race, we forever threaten to defer discussing these decisions and their reasons (or
un-reasons) in favor of discussing a person's flesh, all while we forever threaten
to refuse our own responsibility for history by refusing to discuss flesh at all.[135]

132. It would be difficult, for example, to consider any one version of "whiteness" to be "just
as white" any other, inasmuch as such a statement would be forced to attribute the patterns of
intelligibility by which the surd "is" to the surd (whiteness), as if it were real. At best, we can draw
analogies—but how could analogies of surds possibly be? The problem of anachronism is only
part of the problem; the other part of the problem is the nonintelligibility struggling under the
mask of intelligibility. And what is intelligible is human action. The Fieldses give a concrete example by describing the conditions and actions under which indentured servitude in the English
colonies shifted into use of slaves and then shifted into associating "slavery" and "Blackness." The
acting, as it were, came first; its explanation came a posteriori. The explanation, "race," describes
neither that meaning nor that irrationality by which the action was enacted but the situation now
that this action made a world to be. And yet now, such a world, with its a posteriori delirium, exists.
See Fields and Fields, 120–40.
133. See Charles W. Mills, *The Racial Contract* (Ithaca, NY: Cornell University Press, 2014), esp.
1–39. Or, from Fields and Fields, "From very early on, Americans wove racist concepts into a public language about inequality that made 'black' the virtual equivalent of 'poor' and 'lower class,'
thus creating a distinctive idiom that has no parallel in other Western democracies" (*Racecraft*, 10).
The language of "impoverishment" comes from Joseph Drexler-Dreis, for whom I am grateful.
134. Achille Mbembe, *Critique of Black Reason*, trans. Laurent Dubois (Durham, NC: Duke University Press, 2013), esp. 7, 11, 77–94.
135. With this language, I blend Lonergan, *Insight*, 275–80, and what will emerge in the next
chapter in Maurice Blondel's *Action (1893): Essay on a Critique of Life and a Science of Practice*, trans.
Oliva Blanchette (Notre Dame, IN: University of Notre Dame Press, 2003).

"Skin," Copeland explains, "morphs into a horizon funded by bias."[136] *Horizon* is, for Lonergan, our "maximum field of vision." Horizon is that quality of human consciousness that always-already selects what is relevant for us and what is not. "As our field of vision," explains Lonergan, "so too the scope of our knowledge and the range of our interests are bounded."[137] While horizons can change, we never begin without one. This simple fact, added to bias, results in the basic field of vision and field of action that is race. Race is real to us because we act like it is real. Moreover, race preselects our range of possible interests, leaving out entire ranges of alternatives. That is, race *mediates knowledge* and *mediates action*, and *we made it* and *it makes us*. But race does not perform its functions with the radical indifference of the desire to know. It burdens human being with profound asymmetries, appearing as their explanation and covering-over their in-explication. W. E. B. Du Bois lays hold of this disproportion and its effect on human consciousness when his imaginary white colleague asks him, "How does it feel to be a problem?"[138]

For Copeland in particular, race intersects with our concrete world at the site of bodies. It visits these bodies with violence, but it also conceals them in their valence as bodies of persons, persons evinced of rational agency and a divine calling.[139] But by "it," we must think of race not as a thing but as the crossways of horizon and bias in human consciousnesses, and we must think about it in terms of that world of meaning that such human consciousnesses make, and remake, in the dialectic of history. As ever, race points beyond itself as an impossible juncture of human persons in action. In this sense, I quote *Racecraft*: "Unreasonable divisions of humankind seem to be born from reason itself, not from its opposite."[140] This unreasonableness born from reason will be important to remember, even as this book's discussion of such an "impossible juncture" in its concreteness will always threaten to shatter language.

Copeland's response to the conundrum of our history is instructive for a Christian theory of history. She turns her eyes to poor Black women as a location of reflection for theology, which fills out what it means to "turn to persons,"

---

136. Copeland, *Enfleshing Freedom*, 13.

137. Lonergan, *Method in Theology*, 221.

138. Cited in Fields and Fields, *Racecraft*, 242. The result is double consciousness: "For Du Bois, double-consciousness meant an irreducibly complex awareness of himself as his own self, an unsettled and always evolving subject, and at the same time as a despised object, fixed in caricatures, braced for the daily ritual insults of outsider-hood" (242).

139. Copeland, *Enfleshing Freedom*, 29–38.

140. Fields and Fields, *Racecraft*, 228.

and she renews the Christian understanding of the radical solidarity of human beings in Christ, doing so through doctrine of the mystical body of Christ. The first move, Jeremy Blackwood stresses, is not the replacement of one standard with another: "Rather than replacing the anthropological supremacy of white male bourgeois Europeans with an anthropological supremacy of poor women of color, Copeland places the emphasis on victims of oppression, those without power, who throughout history have been the victims of utter objectification, dehumanization, and oppression. That is, the criterion is not *poor women of color* as such, but is instead those *who are oppressed and powerless*, which keeps her position from becoming a tool of the powerful."[141] Copeland's move unhinges the identification of "human" with "those in power" (in our recent history: the white male bourgeois) and instead emphasizes the oppressed and powerless not only as human but also as at the heart of a fully realized authenticity. It is important because it follows the Catholic preferential option for the poor; it is also important because it helps remedy a historical reality, that of oppression, by proposing an alternative heuristic.

This chapter's theory requires a similar addition, a further heuristic, one where we are allowed to encounter "the other."[142] And it is not just any "other" that we must encounter but the one who is systematically left out of major narrational and political centers, which in our concrete history has been people of color. There are many others whom we could and whom we need to encounter. The point is that in order to talk about history as human action, which is *human* and so *all of us*, it is necessary to take a corrective step and to ensure that the "all" really is "all." That corrective step is to make that *all* first mean (in its heuristic form) *the oppressed*. This corrective step exists because our past and our present exist. Our past and our present inform us unavoidably. In other words, it is more than possible, it is likely, that one will inadequately understand the term *human* in the heuristic term *human action*. Therefore, one must see Lonergan's theory in its own historicity by adding Copeland's corrective.

Copeland is after more than a corrective, more than a countermovement in the wake of the concrete movement of history. Our first hint is the double way that Copeland articulates the turn to persons, which elevates their solidarity with one another in the concreteness of their differences, and which flowers fully in a turn to the oppressed. One of the things that this version of solidarity

---

141. Blackwood, "Heart of the Mystical," 655.

142. Brian Bajzek, "Cruciform Encounter in a Time of Crisis: Enfleshing an Ethics of Alterity," *Theological Studies* 80, no. 1 (2019): 79–101.

achieves is its reorganization around the human species understood as historical, with its concrete character of varied and varying attributes: a single species differentiated materially in history. But the burgeoning heart of Copeland's turn to persons is the heart that God has for the oppressed. This is the heart that God has revealed in the economy of salvation and the heart that centers Copeland's efforts. And through it, we enter upon another doubling, one that is inextricably both moral and metaphysical.

The moral valence is expressive of a theorizing funded by the preferential option for the poor, which places the vulnerable at its center. We care for the vulnerable because the self-revealing God cares for the vulnerable. But this God is also the Creator of the universe, of its order and its being. And if we are tempted to articulate the morality of the preferential option as an exterior addition, as an unforeseen (because supernatural) addition "from above," we must recollect that the unanticipated heart revealed on the cross is the heart of the universe that is, of its order and its being. Christian morality, in other words, is indeed an elevation of human nature; but it is also an exaltation of that nature, in a participated likeness of God's own divinity.[143] What, then, has Christian morality to do with the universe that is? By way of answer, Lonergan often speaks of the *passionateness of being*; this a characteristic of all of being, which glorifies God in the expressiveness of its be-ing and drives the major arc of conscious being in its self-transcendence. "Human consciousness," explains Frederick Lawrence, "is conditioned overwhelmingly from below and from above by the gift of the passionateness of being that underpins, accompanies, and reaches beyond the conscious subject."[144] So "disinterested" morality, which loves the good in itself and so also loves being, is the passion of being in its passionateness. And so also Christian morality, in its passion for the poor and the vulnerable, is the passion of being in its passionateness. What I am saying, in other words, is that a theory—any theory, but most of all this present theory of history—in order to rise to the fullness of being in its passionateness, must bear up that disinterested morality that flowers fully in love for the poor. This is because a theory's full rigor not only is to be found in its heuristic exactitude but is also found in its passion for being, which it is an expression of, since it is an expression of conscious being with its attention, intelligence, reasonableness, and responsibility.

---

143. Cf. Thomas Aquinas, *Summa Theologiae* I–II.112.1 (hereafter *ST*).
144. Lawrence, "Fragility of Consciousness," 249.

Lonergan's theorizing endured transformation toward more authenticity in his own life. In the 1930s through to *Insight* (1957), there is a particular narrative that shapes Lonergan's ideas of progress, decline, and redemption. He associates decline especially with the decline of Christendom—that is, the decline of the medieval unity of culture, state, and church, which splinters first with the Reformation and then further over time, arriving in Lonergan's own era with liberalism (on one side) and the Bolsheviks (on the other).[145] Such a narrative sets up the Western European Middle Ages as something of an ideal. Such an ideal is not rare among Catholics, especially Catholics of this era. In this kind of perspective, there is an ideal time period and an ideal culture, which is the Western European one (of a certain time period). All other cultures that fail do so because they fall outside of this basic horizon.

Lonergan rethinks this horizon. During the 1960s, he moves from what he calls a "classical" theory of culture to an "empirical" one. This move mimics the transfiguration that the sciences had already endured in the transition from classical science into modern science, with its approaches to statistical probabilities. Here Lonergan moves from the idea that there is but one "stable," ideal culture (almost invariably associated with the West) to the idea that there are many cultures. For Lonergan, then, what theology at present endures in the modern era is not a crisis of faith but a crisis of culture: theology is enduring a transformation in its thinking-through of empirical culture.[146]

No longer is it the case that Christendom is a kind of ideal "height" for Christianity, one that then disintegrated. No longer is there a particular era in the past that Christians might long for. No longer is classical Western literature a kind of litmus test for the civilized and the uncivilized. Rather, every era and every culture makes its demands even as the gospel remains the same. Fundamentally, what Lonergan does here is fully relativize historical epochs *as historical*. This is not to say that progress no longer occurs, or that we can no longer judge what is authentic and inauthentic about the culture that we are in, the history we have made, and so on. It is to say, instead, that the measure of such authenticity is fully organized by self-transcendence: it is not a comparison to one era or one culture. It is a judgment of what is attentive, intelligent, reasonable, responsible.

Copeland furthers Lonergan's development by pressing him not just to relativize culture but also to turn to the oppressed as a further essential measure for

---

145. For an example, see Lonergan, *Insight*, 260.
146. Lonergan, *Method in Theology*, 3, 30, 120.

understanding the transcendental precepts. Copeland's final move, her opening up of Lonerganian and Western thought, is at the same time a turn toward radical Christian solidarity, which is more than the essential solidarity of being-human. Her turn to this solidarity complements her turn to the oppressed. It is radical because it is also Christic and therefore both concrete and supernatural.[147] As such, this move does more than ensure that the oppressed are not sectioned off as a mere "part" of humanity: "Solidarity," explains Copeland, "preserves the universality of love, without renouncing the preference for these women of color."[148] In other words, our memory of the other becomes an ethical and moral task: we must live and move toward solidarity with one another, especially with the oppressed. Here is a solidarity that, while rooted in the original solidarity of being-human, is a moral and a Christian task; one that is ecclesial and so concrete; and one that is supernatural because it is made effective by God.

The invocation of this kind of solidarity transforms, as a final measure, a heuristic understanding of redemption. In the first place, such redemption *begins* with the oppressed as its center. In the second place, redemption does not "merely" restore that solidarity of human nature that the chapter began by considering. Redemption returns good for evil and does so through human persons who participate in Christ's action. This participation occurs through radical, decisive solidarity with one another in Christ, which is more than essential human solidarity because it is also supernatural. Therefore, redemption is not God's impersonal action in the world: it takes place in and through the action of Christ and, then, in Christ, in and through you and me.

But to say all this is not to *resolve* the problem of a theory's embedment in its own time. It is to describe that problem, and in Copeland, it is to suggest two necessary corollaries that a (Christian) theory of history must include: a turn to persons that is in particular a turn to the oppressed and a turn to the solidarity of the mystical body of Christ. As I have argued, a turn to the oppressed not only mimics the gospel but also is a corrective to concrete historical circumstances, where the oppressed are precisely those who receive no attention in their fully human action and meaning in history. So too, a turn to the mystical body of Christ not only has scriptural warrant but also is a response to the fundamental fragmentation that is decline, and it is a response to the decline that racializing meanings and racializing actions in particular provoke. Both of these

147. Blackwood, "Heart of the Mystical," 659.
148. Copeland, *Enfleshing Freedom*, 100.

"turns" are concrete responses to concrete history, to the concrete history that this chapter's present theory is embedded in.

Copeland provides a keener, more specified sense of what redemption in history involves. She also offers a generalized response to the problem of race, in its aspects as constitutive (pseudo)meaning and constitutive action, by dealing with its effects according to the law of the cross. So too, Lonergan's turn toward an empirical view of culture transfigures a theory of history from a reflexively Eurocentric endeavor to one fundamentally open to the "other." But here a theory of history at last exhausts itself. There can be no heuristic "measure" of race in history, since it does not occupy *all* of human history, since it is not real to human nature qua nature, and since it is essentially a surd that is part of the facts of our situation. Race is, we might say, a distortion of human development, an iteration of human decline, but it is not a thing in itself. Even so, race remains a historical "reality" because it structures the present history that is ours.

Since the present work strives to describe a theory of Christian tradition, what remains unasked and unanswered in this chapter is the problem of Christian tradition's responsibility with respect to race; in other words, the problem of a tradition that partakes of a concrete human history where race is a "reality," one that Christians have been involved in. To understand such a problem *as* a problem requires understanding what tradition is, and how it is historical. That consideration takes up the next chapter.

A Final Dialectic

This chapter has made the case for a theory of history such that Christian historicity in Christian tradition might be understood, and the thought of Bernard Lonergan has provided just such a theory. According to this theory, human history is human action. History is the action of all human beings for all time. Lonergan nuances this theory by adding to human action the qualities of progress, decline, and (in Christ) redemption. So history not only is what human beings do; history also makes human beings who they are. History is, as Lonergan says, "man making man," for progress or extinction or—in God—redemption.

But theories do not occur apart from history, and so the last portion of this chapter was devoted to developing an understanding of what recent human history has in fact involved, which is a particular rise of racial ideas and their structures. This reality, in turn, means that the present theory has to be responsible for and with that history. M. Shawn Copeland develops Lonergan's thought in this direction; emphasizes a turn toward persons, especially the oppressed other; and emphasizes the solidarity of the mystical body of Christ.

This is, even for Copeland, but a beginning. What remains, still, is the trouble of responding to concrete history and its systems of domination. What remains, indeed, is the problem of what it means for Christian tradition to be part of a concrete history, to be involved in systems of domination. This raises the question of what Christian tradition is, and of what its relationship to history is. So too, a theory of history as human action raises the question of what human action is, and therefore the question of human freedom. These are the questions that will occupy the next chapter.

2

MEDIATIONS

Memory of millions under
the shadows of her archways,
those watchers at her fiery gate,
the dyed at her glass, long
their light gathered at sunset.

History is human action. But action and the history it effectuates are mediated by tradition. Under the guidance of the early twentieth-century French Catholic philosopher Maurice Blondel, this chapter explores human action, its "determinism," its freedom, and its radical reliance on the supernatural action of God in order to be. These explorations put a magnifying glass to the previous chapter's theory of human history. But more essentially, they result in an argument about the whole "body" of human action, which breaks forth first in the breathless intimacy of human consciousness and extends outward in a perpetual law of self-transcendence. Human action reveals not its own self-mastery but its total dependence on the structure of a world and of a self that together and everywhere rely on what absolutely outstrips them: the supernatural, which in its disproportion to us makes our inmost freedom real. Our real world is, then, intimately and integrally a natural and a supernatural one. And it is in that world, a world whose history is constituted by both natural and supernatural meanings, that tradition lives.

The reality of our world and of our action in it leads Blondel into a confrontation with the sundering of these meanings in the form of both historicism and fundamentalism—the latter's monstrous height taking the shape of

French Catholic "integralism," where the face of the church becomes the face of domination. It is by way of this double conflict that Blondel arrives at a heuristic grasp of what Christian tradition is, offering my argument at last a definition of its major object. And it is, too, before this double conflict that Blondel offers a countervision, one that cleaves to the real in its integral wholeness while dethroning understandings of Catholicism and of Catholic tradition—and, most of all, of divine revelation—that justify violently exacting our submission.

Blondel's real-life confrontation with integralism is the hinge of a major turn in the chapter, which is an effort to comprehend what it means for Christian tradition to be involved in truth but also domination. And in this major turn, both I and Blondel encounter the faces of colonialism, race, and Christian responsibility, as expressed by Willie Jennings, who is my final and most important "face" in the chapter. Rather than effecting a resolution, the encounter will lead the chapter and myself beyond ourselves to describe together the situatedness of Christian tradition in its truth and in its history, leaving us at the doorway of theology and a theological description of Christian tradition.

Because of my constructive goals, the theological controversies that Blondel is normally associated with—Modernism, the natural desire to see God—do not receive attention as such. Though they appear, they appear at an angle, discoverable in certain implications of Blondel's thought that are nevertheless not the focus of the chapter. The focus is instead on the fabric of Blondel's thought, on its fundamental threads, and on how those threads might come into contact with the struggle of the present book: to present a metaphysic of tradition and to frame that metaphysic according to an encounter with the problem of race.

Maurice Blondel's Integral Reality

Blondel defended his doctoral thesis in 1893 at the École normale supérieure, one of the premier secular universities in Paris. He had already met with his jury in the days before the examination, doing so at the urging of his director, Émile Boutroux. "These colleagues," explains Blondel's biographer, "were so irritated upon reading such an unusual dissertation, that [Boutroux] advised Blondel to try by all means possible to visit the other members of the jury at their homes, before his defense, so that they could vent their anger in private rather than in public."[1]

---

1. Oliva Blanchette, *Maurice Blondel: A Philosophical Life* (Grand Rapids, MI: Eerdmans, 2010), 6.

Blondel's dissertation, called *Action: Essay on a Critique of Life and a Science of Practice*, is unusual in several senses, much to the vexation of his original jurors. The subject "action," for example, does not appear in the *Dictionnaire des sciences philosophiques*.[2] To make action a topic of a dissertation is, therefore, quite strange. But Blondel's *method* is also unusual, charting "action" as it does at every possible hinge-point, however small, from the beginnings of human consciousness to action's entrance into the world, and even unto action's expansion across the world itself, to absolute human solidarity—and beyond.

None had seen Blondel's like before. Like later phenomenologists, Blondel is interested in the "phenomenon" of human existence as it tangibly appears. Unlike some phenomenologists, however, Blondel is not out to reject metaphysics.[3] Blondel calls his position a "dynamic philosophy" that is rooted in human thought and action.[4] Against his classmates and professors, who at the time emphasized abstraction, Blondel sets out in search of what is concrete, which in turn leads him to that most omnipresent human reality—action. In Henri Bouillard's words, "Blondel was . . . led to the study of action by the search for a concrete philosophy."[5]

Blondel's purpose in assembling this "science of practice" or "science of action" is to argue that philosophy, in order to be true to itself, must acknowledge not *only* the natural world but also the presence of that which outstrips it. "My aim," Blondel explains at his defense, "has been to constitute a philosophy which, though quite distinct from the supernatural order, would be its natural and necessary underpinning."[6] By contrast, the philosophy of Blondel's day was intent on its "separation" from religion; Blondel shows such separation to be at best illusory.[7]

---

2. Blanchette, 4.

3. Blondel added a final chapter to his dissertation in response to the objection that he had rejected metaphysics. He did so in order to indicate that he had not. See Blanchette, 90–92. Much of his later work, which I do not explore in this chapter, explicitly confronts and appropriates metaphysics, esp. *L'Être et les êtres* (Paris: Librairie Félix Alcan, 1935); and *La pensée*, 2 vols. (Paris: Librairie Félix Alcan, 1934). Here I remind my reader that these chapters are arguments and not surveys.

4. Maurice Blondel, *Une alliance contre nature: Catholicisme et intégrisme; La Semaine sociale de Bordeaux 1910* (Brussels: Éditions Lessius, 2000), 30.

5. Henri Bouillard, *Blondel et le christianisme* (Paris: Éditions du seuil, 1961), 24. See also Kirwan, *Avante-Garde*, 52: "By exploring the dramatic, free, and concrete character of human existence, Blondel provided, with Henri Bergson, an anticipation of existentialism."

6. Quoted in Blanchette, *Maurice Blondel*, 7.

7. Maurice Blondel, "The Letter on Apologetics," in *The Letter on Apologetics and History and Dogma*, trans. Alexander Dru and Illtyd Trethowan (Grand Rapids, MI: Eerdmans, 1964), 151–52,

Both "natural" and "supernatural" are technical terms for Blondel, with specific if somewhat idiosyncratic meanings. The *natural* is all that is available to human beings proportionately. It is that which is available to human nature to be and to do. The *supernatural* is that which is disproportionate to human nature, that which is not available to human nature either to be or to do. The supernatural is "above" nature in the sense of being "beyond its power" rather than literally or spatially. And theologians like myself must resist the temptation to associate Blondel's "supernatural" with grace. Blondel's position, because it is philosophical, is broader than this: as Jonathan Heaps argues, for Blondel, the supernatural refers to the entirety of God's *ad extra* agency, which would include grace but also more than this, even the act of creation itself.[8]

Blondel strives to show that the natural does not exist apart from the supernatural.[9] These realities, the natural and the supernatural, are absolutely distinguished, but they are not divided. So the world, the world that we concretely encounter, reality itself, is a *réalité intégrale*:

> If integral reality [*réalité intégrale*] is what our faith affirms to us, if man, not as he might be in an unreal [*irréel*] state of nature, but as he is universally in the present state, where he is constituted by supernatural vocation, by degradation, and by the recollection of redemption, [where] the inevitable effect of these divine dispositions or his own infidelities manifests in his personal and social life, is it not correct to affirm, with [Henri] Lorin, "the real [*réel*] is a continuity in which there is no watertight bulkhead and no element of which can be treated as non-existent with impunity"?[10]

Here Blondel describes a humanity at once involved in redemption and involved in sin. This is the concrete world, and the concrete human nature, that we encounter: the one being redeemed, the one in need of redemption, the same world. But more importantly, this world in its concreteness requires attention

---

175–84; cf. Blanchette, *Maurice Blondel*, 11.

8. Jonathan Heaps, "The Ambiguity of Being: Medieval and Modern Cooperation on the Problem of the Supernatural" (PhD diss., Marquette University, 2019), 151–53; cf. Bouillard, *Blondel et le christianisme*, 88–89.

9. Blanchette, *Maurice Blondel*, 97–104.

10. Blondel, *Une alliance contre nature*, 7 (translation mine).

to *all* of its qualities rather than to some of them. This is part of what Blondel means by "integral."

Reality is also integral because it is heterogeneous. "What reality is" is two horizons, one disproportionate to the other: the natural and the supernatural. The natural and the supernatural are radically distinguished and not to be confused, since they are disproportionate. Nevertheless, they persist—in the real world, in the world as we find it—in "vital solidarity and practical assistance" (solidarité vitale et concours pratique).[11]

It is helpful to look backward to Bernard Lonergan for some sense of what Blondel means here. For Lonergan, human beings are not "agents" of their own action: I did not give myself my own aliveness, or my own willing.[12] I share in "premotion." Indeed, it is God who acts in my own acting in order for me to act.[13] Blondel, using a method organized around phenomenal concreteness, argues for a similar conclusion. "There is in me," Blondel explains in *Action*, "a disproportion between the efficient cause and the final cause; and yet neither the one nor the other can be in me what they already are without the permanent mediation of a perfect thought and a perfect action."[14] In other words, for both thinkers, the natural cannot be without the supernatural (without God's *ad extra* agency). Therefore, Blondel insists, "the divine is to be found not only in what seems to surpass the familiar powers of men and of nature but everywhere, even where we are tempted to think that man and nature are sufficient."[15]

Blondel intimates that the natural in some way *supposes* the supernatural. He then brings this intimation to the surface: to nature, he insists, the supernatural is "both necessary and impracticable."[16] This position is difficult and complex.[17] On the one hand, Blondel thinks that the natural, to be understood, must posit the supernatural—which, however, cannot be known in itself by nature.[18] In other words, we can at least surmise that nature is the effect of some disproportionate power. Similarly, and logically, nature must be able to be not only *effected* by what is supernatural but also *affected* by it. Should we have a supernatural destiny at all, it would be effected supernaturally in our nature,

11. Blondel, 7–8.
12. Heaps, "Ambiguity of Being," 93–97.
13. Heaps, 104–6.
14. Blondel, *Action*, 320.
15. Blondel, "Letter," 135.
16. Blondel, *Action*, 297; cf. Blondel, "Letter," 159–62.
17. See also Bouillard, *Blondel et le christianisme*, 20–22.
18. Cf. Blondel, *Une alliance contre nature*, 32–35; Blondel, "Letter," 134.

affecting it. And if nature can indeed receive supernatural action in this (double) manner, then, Blondel argues, this ability-to-receive must be affirmable on the "side" of nature.[19] In this sense, the supernatural is necessary to the nature that we concretely know: "For if our nature is not at home with the supernatural, the supernatural is at home in our nature . . . to turn away from one's destiny is not to free oneself from its control. That is the meaning of the *necessity* which connects these two heterogeneous orders without infringing their independence."[20]

On the other hand, Blondel insists that nature can neither produce nor influence the supernatural, which remains in radical heterogeneity and disproportion to nature. The supernatural remains *supernaturam*. In Blondel's parlance, the supernatural is *impracticable* to nature—that is, no human action is proportionate to the supernatural; I cannot make-to-be the supernatural, or command it to my level, either through the action that is my consciousness, or through the procession of my action into the world, or otherwise. "For," says Blondel, "what we find in ourselves is precisely *not* what we have to receive."[21]

It is not possible to hold Blondel's position sensibly without recalling both features of the supernatural at once: necessity and impracticability. If the first is lost, if nature exists as a pure and complete edifice, then supernatural religion can make no claims on nature. If the second is lost, if nature can bring the divine down to its level, then there is no need for a supernatural revelation or for a supernatural intervention in history.[22] So for Blondel, one must hold fast to nature's need for the supernatural, which functions as a kind of capacity, *and* to the supernatural's absolute transcendence of nature, by which all divine activity condescends to nature as pure gift. Here Blondel approaches something like Thomist obediential potency: nature has a potency for the supernatural that nature nevertheless cannot bring into act.[23]

19. Cf. Blondel, *Une alliance contre nature*, 8–11; Blondel, "Letter," 140, 152–55.
20. Blondel, "Letter," 163.
21. Blondel, 153.
22. Cf. Blondel, *Une alliance contre nature*, 56–59; Blondel, "Letter," 154–57.
23. Blondel more than once relates his own thought to Thomas Aquinas's, and this familiarity grows in Blondel's later work. See, for example, Blanchette, *Maurice Blondel*, 262–365; and two studies by Michael Conway, "From Neo-Thomism to St Thomas: Maurice Blondel's Early Encounter with Scholastic Thought," *Ephemerides Theologicae Lovanienses* 83, no. 1 (2007): 1–22; and "A Thomistic Turn? Maurice Blondel's Reading of St. Thomas," *Ephemerides Theologicae Lovanienses* 84, no. 1 (2008): 87–122. In terms of Blondelian texts that I use here, see, for example, Blondel, *Une alliance contre nature*, 47, 58, 66, 68.

Blondel emphasizes the real as concretely encountered. Through this emphasis, he argues for a "heterogeneity" (and so a difference) that is "integral" (and so found together).[24] The concrete world that is ours is a reality of difference-found-together. So it is necessary, when reading Blondel, to always have this double vision in mind: the natural and the supernatural are absolutely distinguished, even as they are united without confusion. This position, for Blondel, reflects the gospel and the tradition of the Catholic Church: Christ proclaims the (supernatural) good news to the (natural) world, and the church maintains the integrity of natural reason, even while insisting that nature cannot produce or discern the supernatural.[25]

Key to the Blondelian position is what he calls a "double *afférence*," a double reference or movement.[26] One takes the form of an interior preparation for the supernatural in the natural; the other takes the form of an external gift of supernatural revelation. Each *afférence* moves in different directions: one from "below" and "interiorly," the other from "above" and "exteriorly."[27] Both movements are necessary to each other: the preparation for and reception of supernatural action and the exterior gift of supernatural revelation by way of its instrument, the church. Blondel clarifies his claims in contrast with the neo-Thomism of his day:

[The neo-Thomist position is] true, salutary, necessary, insofar as it condemns and represses any theory that claims that religious life is only a production of nature, or even that the supernatural order reveals itself by the means of reason and individual and collective conscience, even from a germ previously sown, but without an explicit revelation and without a divinely entrusted teaching to an authority, [it is true insofar as it is] the doctrine that affirms the essential and gratuitous *afférence* of the gift of above . . . it becomes false insofar as, under the pretext of affirming that neither reality nor knowledge of Christianity proceed *ex natura and per naturam* [from nature and through nature], it disregards the work of God internal to the soul and the interior work of the

24. Cf. Blondel, *Une alliance contre nature*, 11.
25. Blondel, 13.
26. See Blanchette, *Maurice Blondel*, 242–48.
27. Cf. Blondel, *Une alliance contre nature*, 65.

soul towards God, *in natura* and *ad modum naturae* [in nature and by way of nature].[28]

Double *afférence* sums up and concretizes what Blondel means by an integral reality. When he speaks of reality as "heterogeneous," he is referring not simply to the natural and supernatural as such but rather to a set of relations with certain laws one must maintain: necessity and impracticability, exterior gift and interior preparation, cooperation and pure gratuity. To say that reality is "integral" is to say that these two orders, one disproportionate to the other, persist together in the world; it is to say indeed that in reality exists a double *afférence* by which these two orders greet one another without being confused.[29]

Blondel's "double *afférence*" is essential for understanding the political and ideological implications of Catholic positions in Blondel's day and the puzzle of race, history, and Christian tradition in our own. For now, it is important to understand that the world as Blondel understands it is only made possible by God's *ad extra* agency, and God's action in the world in Christ contains in it a design for our free reception of supernatural revelation.

It is not possible to cordon off the supernatural from human history, even if that history is conceived of in a purely secular manner. For Blondel, *all* human action, whatever its type, requires the supernatural in order to be. But this need on nature's part does not bring nature into proportion with the supernatural. Human history, therefore, as human action, requires the supernatural in order to be—yet without rendering human history "level" with God.

Blondel nuances a theory of history through his phenomenological emphasis, through his focus on concreteness, urging such a theory to consider not an "unreal" (*irréel*) world but the "real" (*réel*) one. This renders the problems of race and colonialism more urgent to such a theory, since the *real* history that is ours involves the development of racial ideas and their economic structures, underlining not only the moral urgency of examining race but also the phenomenal incompleteness of a theory that does not. Though separated by time and language, Copeland and Blondel share a compassion for reality: not just a passion "for" it but a focus on thinking-with reality as it really is (Lonergan can be counted in this company too), a thinking-with that in Blondel surfaces as concern for concreteness and that in Copeland emerges as concern for persons.

---

28. Blondel, 65–66 (translation mine).
29. Cf. Blondel, "Letter," 152.

In Blondel, human action receives a further character as not *only* immanent to itself. This is one of the things that an integral reality means. Human action cannot be only its immanent playing out in the world because the world is more than that which is immanent to human power. And yet this "more than" is not known apart from human experience. Here I gesture forward to Blondel's encounter with historicism in the scientific history that emerged in his day. But to grasp what he does there requires understanding what Blondel understands the sciences to be. It also requires following Blondel in his turn to human action in general. Together, these three thematic explorations—integral reality, the sciences, human action—shape how Blondel arrives at a notion of Christian tradition.

Positive Science and Human Action

Blondel lived in a century during which the positive sciences dominated as never before. The progress of science was then seen as basically unlimited. This perspective impacted the development of scientific history, especially in the mid-nineteenth century, which saw in France a shift from narrative-oriented Romantic history to "evidence-based" textual history.[30] So prevalent was this rationalist point of view that French Catholicism often pressed in the other direction, emphasizing intensity of personal experience and supernatural miracles over against human reason (really: over against rationalism).[31] It is no surprise, then, that Blondel is interested in understanding these sciences and their possible limitations. But the sciences also deal in the concrete world in various ways, and so understanding what they are and what they are not, and what it means for them to deal in a world that is *concrete*, is an important fulcrum for Blondel's philosophy.

Action begins first with a distinction between mathematics and the sciences: the one works from a kind of ideal world that is then deployed to describe the concrete world, by which Blondel means the world of experience; the other

---

30. Samuel Tomei, "Nation, Religion, Future: In the Footsteps of Ernest Renan," *Revue Historique* 691 (2019): 734–37; Robert D. Priest, "Reading, Writing, and Religion in Nineteenth-Century France: The Popular Reception of Renan's Life of Jesus," *Journal of Modern History* 86, no. 2 (2014): 258–94.

31. See Ruth Harris, *Lourdes: Body and Spirit in the Secular Age* (New York: Penguin, 2000), esp. 320–56.

works from empirical observations that it then organizes (mathematically) into terms and relations.[32] Mathematics and science are, as it were, inverses of one another. And they are taken to, together, describe the whole of the (concrete) world that is.

But there is a problem. Secreted away in both mathematics and science is a confession of their insufficiency. "The positive sciences," says Blondel, "are not sufficient for us, because they are not self-sufficient."[33] In other words, the positive sciences *rely on something that they are not* for their own efficacy. Both mathematics and science presume that the world can be brought together into a unity, into a system; this drives their efficacy. But neither human experience nor (mathematical) symbols, Blondel points out, indicate of themselves that the world can be integrated. The pure data of sense, on which the empirical sciences are based, are in fact a cacophony. In other words, there is nothing *in* sensation that says that the empirical world can be theorized. So too, mathematics does not realize that its symbols are, though rationally related to one another, arbitrarily applied to experience itself—for the symbol is not the same experience: "Mathematics can be adapted to experience, but it does not start from it."[34]

Blondel's point is that the *understanding* provided by science and mathematics, though immense, is not *in* either science or math: "In these sciences where everything seems penetrated with light and where the distinction of ideas reaches its perfection, the competence of the science does not belong to the science; *what* they know, they do not *know* as they know *it*."[35] For Blondel, two related facts—together a single action—rest submerged underneath the competency of the sciences. One fact is that every science supposes the unity and relation of things, and so second, in every science, minds do the supposing. Thus, underneath science is action, the action of human beings, who suppose the unity of their science. Science and math exist because human beings do them. "Our power," explains Blondel, "always goes further than our science, because our science, risen from our power, needs that power still to find in it its support and its end. . . . It is therefore impossible for science to limit itself to what it knows, since it is already more than it knows."[36]

<hr>

32. Blondel, *Action*, 63.
33. Blondel, 65.
34. Blondel, 70.
35. Blondel, 71.
36. Blondel, 88; cf. Blondel, "Letter," 177–82.

Here it is helpful to disambiguate what Blondel means by the "concrete." The exact sciences, he notes, are often taken to *be* concrete, the result of observation. And so the scientific positivism especially of Blondel's day tends to serve as a definition of what is most "concrete" to us: the observed. But this is not Blondel's approach. Blondel points out that in order to operate successfully, both the sciences and mathematics rely not on the concrete as such but on the same fiction, or imagined supposition, that the cacophonic heterogeneity of sensory experience is unitary or whole. For Blondel, the very multiplicity of the sciences, including their differentiation from one another, relies time and again on the supposition of their relation to one another, on the possibility of integration into a whole. We imagine that sciences testify to concrete experience, to simple observation, when, for Blondel, all sciences—including the exact sciences—are abstractions.[37] "In short," says Blondel, "the bond between the closest states is never perceived by direct experience, even when we know their conditions, their relation and their connections."[38]

But *we* do suppose their connections.[39] We perform this supposing through an analogous hinge, by relating science to our own experience of ourselves and our world. For we ourselves are an intelligent integration of chaotic sensation; we are so in our very consciousness. Blondel says, "[Sense] is only inasmuch as it is felt; and it is felt only insofar as it is represented at the same time as present, imagined at the same time as experienced . . . : 'I am what I sense, I sense what is.'"[40] We ourselves, as conscious, are a unity of sensation and sensing. Blondel calls this root unitive gesture "action" in order to stress its persistent dynamism, which we often indicate in a heuristic way simply by saying "I." This creative, dynamic unity that we are forms the basis of our integrating anticipations in mathematics and the sciences.[41]

For Blondel, *consciousness* is not what we often think of as self-reflection or inward perception.[42] It is the action by which such self-reflection can be at all. "Consciousness," he argues, "emerges from the organic functions [of the human organism], without being conscious of it and without letting itself be reduced

37. Blondel, *Action*, 69.
38. Blondel, 84.
39. Blondel, 70.
40. Blondel, 57.
41. Cf. Blondel, 60, 73–74.
42. Here I refer to what in French is Blondel's *conscience*, which Blanchette translates for the most part as consciousness. See Blondel, "Note on Translation," in *Action*, xxix.

to them."[43] And in this I think it is helpful to fall backward for a moment on Lonergan: consciousness, Lonergan explains, "is not an object, not part of the spectacle we contemplate, but the presence to himself of the spectator, the contemplator. It is not an object of introspection, but the prior presence that makes introspection possible."[44] We are possessed of a creatively self-constituting consciousness that can attend to the concrete world intelligently, and *this* is what animates and unifies all of our disciplines of inquiry.

Blondel's "concrete philosophy" that treats a concrete universe is, therefore, complexly intended. Concreteness is what is abstracted from, an operation we unfailingly perform even in the exact sciences. It also bears an intelligibility, or else we could not apply intelligence to it. But Blondel is most of all interested in what he calls "the imprint of this mediating action in all knowledge," this hinge by which consciousness confronts concreteness.[45] And that "hinge" is the action that *is* consciousness, an action that—as "action"—extends further in the "determinism" of its own élan. This élan, too, is concrete; it is that concreteness by which we are and by which our knowledge comes to be. So Blondel's own study of action is what he calls a "science," and it is a practical science, since it is about that concrete dynamism by which we are in the world, by which we in the action of our consciousness *are*, even if to speak of it requires, ever and always, the mediating intervention of that self-same élan.[46]

In this fashion, Blondel undermines the scientism of his day while not rejecting the science of his day. He does so by pointing out that the intelligibility of the sciences requires intellects supplying intelligence. For Blondel, the sciences rest upon the "action" that is human knowing. This notion will be important when I discuss the nature of scientific history. But before I do that, this phenomenon, human action, needs to be described and understood.

43. Blondel, 85.

44. Bernard Lonergan, "*Existenz* and *Aggiornamento*," in *Collection*, 229.

45. Blondel, *Action*, 88.

46. Blondel discusses his "science" and the indirect method—indirect because to reflect is to step away from the immediacy of the concrete—that he will deploy to arrive at a conception of action in Blondel, 9–11.

Human Action

Blondel's science of action is something other than a colloquial understanding of "action"—that is, action as *a* deed, *an* act, discrete and meted out in the world. When Blondel speaks of *action*, he means the entire phenomenon, from its roots in the human being as a systematic organism to action's outer reaches in the radical solidarity of all human action, and the solidarity of that action with the action of the universe. Essential to the science of action is a distinction between "the voluntary" (*le volontaire*) and "the willed" (*le voulu*).[47] When human beings will something, a "hidden contradiction" occurs. On the one hand, there is the willingness whence a particular willing emerges, and on the other, there is the particular will for some particular thing. Should I desire to lift a glass to my lips, there is in me both the well of willing—the will itself—and my particularized desire to do *this* thing. These two elements of the act are not the same. It is not that I have two wills but rather that there is a distinction in my own willing. Blondel calls this distinction the difference between the "willing will" (*volonté voulante*) and the "willed will" (*volonté voulue*).[48] Is it possible for the human will to "equal" itself? Is it possible for the willing will and the willed will to be meted out wholly together? Is there an act that exhausts my willing? Blondel asks, "Yes or no, for one who limits himself to the natural order, is there any concordance between the willing will and the willed will?"[49]

Blondel does not immediately answer these questions. Instead, he goes looking for where the human will does seem to reach, so long as one constrains oneself to the natural order. But even here, Blondel notes something unusual about human action: it seems to suppose, when willing a thing, what it is not. "To conceive an act distinctly," Blondel points out, "is to imagine at the same time at least the vague possibility of different acts, which play the role of a foil."[50] Human action is more than it appears; or rather, human action supposes more than itself. In the conceiving of a particular act, there is the supposition of other actions not taken.

Elsewhere, Blondel associates this imagining of other possibilities with a notion of the transcendent: "The very notion of immanence is realized in our

47. Blondel, 32.

48. Cf. Blondel, 53; Henri Bouillard, "The Thought of Maurice Blondel: A Synoptic Vision," *International Philosophical Quarterly* 3 (1963): 393.

49. Blondel, *Action*, 53.

50. Blondel, 116.

consciousness only by the effective presence of the notion of the transcendent."[51] This is not yet a transcendence that can be associated with God.[52] It is transcendence in the barest sense: an order that stands above another order, with the "above" being the power to organize and render effective what is below it. More than once, Blondel indicates the way that human action is self-transcending, moving into ever higher orders. It begins in the act of consciousness itself, which organizes all the various powers of the sensate human being and, in organizing them, stands "above" them before a specific act is even conceived. Right from its roots, there is a dynamism, an élan of human being and of human acting in the world.

The dynamism of human action is stranger still. In supposing other acts in my conception of a single act, I at the same time suppose a wholeness or an infinity by which to understand that single act. I posit a *universal*. Blondel calls this "infinite" a "regulative idea."[53] It is what allows me to judge and compare not just my possible actions but also the various motives for those actions. So I, in following the dynamism of my own action, conceive of an infinite by which to understand my immanent activity. This infinite transcends me, just as I, as conscious, transcend (and yet require) my heartbeat. "There is no effective synthesis, no internal act, no state of consciousness, however obscure it may be," says Blondel, "that is not transcendent regarding its conditions, and where the infinite is not present."[54]

This infinite is not God. But it does, along with transcendence, allow Blondel to characterize human activity as in some way transcendent and infinite. At every point, action moves beyond its determinant conditions; at every point, action has not equaled itself. "Conscious action," explains Blondel, "is conscious of its own initiative only by attributing a character of infinitude and transcendence to itself."[55] It is against this mirror of infinity that action can become an action without yet exhausting itself; because of this infinity, we are able to call action free.

Freedom emerges from out of a "determinism," the determinism of action itself, the irresistible playing out of its élan. I did not *choose* to be conscious, for example, but I am, and this consciousness is at the same time an act that I freely

51. Blondel, "Letter," 158.
52. Cf. Heaps, "Ambiguity of Being," 142.
53. Blondel, *Action*, 122.
54. Blondel, 123.
55. Blondel, 123.

make my own. And we must call this action free because, from out of the infinity that the will supposes, none of that infinity comes to be in the concrete world apart from my acting. In other words, even to lift my hand, I not only must *think* that I want to but also must *do* so, and this doing-so does not come to be unless I make it so.

Human freedom is not merely, not even primarily, our ability to choose *between* options. It is our ability to decide to enact action. Freedom is that leap by which an action comes to be at all. "What was contained in the natural expansion of [the subject's] energy," Blondel explains, "he can dominate and exploit. . . . Hence we find in our acts a kind of creative sovereignty."[56] For Lonergan, "Freedom is a special kind of contingence. . . . It has the twofold basis that its object is merely a possibility and that its agent is contingent."[57] A free action, then, is the contingence by which an action comes to be, depending on the contingent subject for its being. That leap into decision is the beating heart of what Lonergan calls free action, an action that, as free, communes with the order of the universe. Human action also en-acts its order.[58] For both Blondel and Lonergan, freedom is that mystery whereby we bring action into act.

This freedom is, therefore, rational. Even should my action be in error, and in that sense irrational, still I will attribute reason to my action. It is not only the case that human beings need and develop reasons for their actions, and not only that this reasoning informs the character of human freedom; it is also the case that for a human action to be free, it has to be *conscious*, an application of the act of consciousness: Blondel says, "There is free activity only where there is consciousness of acting."[59] And so our action is free only when it is *rational*. Our presumptions about the operations of human rationality, therefore, have an impact on the way we talk about human freedom.

When our action enters into the world, we make efforts to unite our actions with the actions of others: "To succeed in being better and more completely one, we must not, we cannot remain *alone*."[60] So individual action becomes social action. This social action builds in character, including as it does so the family, the community, the nation—but also beyond these. For Blondel, as with

---

56. Blondel, 124.
57. Lonergan, *Insight*, 642.
58. Lonergan, 632, 647.
59. Blondel, *Action*, 124.
60. Blondel, 192.

Lonergan, human action involves the essential solidarity of humanity itself. "Indeed," says Blondel, "whatever we do, humanity has an interest in the action of each individual as in a new element of the general equilibrium: the action whose origin man attributes to himself is one which could take place in the name of the entire species."[61]

Blondel argues for more than a kind of collective solidarity where human actions are "added up," as it were. This "more" takes up a double sense. We *want* to act in light of the universal that we have first perceived. We ourselves desire the expansion of our will into this total solidarity of acting, a solidarity beyond any single grouping of human beings. And here human solidarity reveals itself not simply to be because we are but to be what we make to be in our bringing action into act. At the same time, in my wanting to act in light of the universal, I act as an image of the totality of humanity, bearing "all" in my action "by the impulse of its first *élan*."[62] Human solidarity is made microcosmic, in each of us, in the dynamism and determinism of our human action.

But beyond humanity is the universe, whose action is the foundation for human action and whose action is that into which human action extends. "Indeed," Blondel insists, "voluntary action concerns the whole system, from which it has taken its nourishment," and "to act is in a way to entrust oneself to the universe."[63] The self-transcendence of human action, in other words, is rooted in the "action" of a universe; we might say in metaphysical terms that everything that the being we call "human" is and that it brings into act relies on a universe that also is, and so is in act. That which we bring into act is also a bringing into act of the being of the universe—not absolutely, but precisely in terms of our contingency, which is also free.

My action has still not reached a resting point. It has arrived at no equality between the willing will and the willed will, though it has arrived at the absolute borderland of all that is immanent to it: myself, my whole world—the whole universe. So my action continues to require something equal to itself, though no such thing is available to it by nature. For Blondel, at this point, we have finally arrived at the horizon of the properly supernatural. And here we encounter what is a familiar twofold idea: "There follows only this doubly imperious conclusion: it is impossible not to recognize the insufficiency of the

---

61. Blondel, 261.
62. Blondel, 261.
63. Blondel, 263.

whole natural order and not to feel an ulterior need. . . . *It is necessary* and *it is impracticable*."[64]

Action is where Blondel first surfaces his definition of the supernatural as "necessary" and as "impracticable" (to nature). It bears repeating that Blondel still speaks in a philosophical mode, one that cleaves to the modern interest in purely "immanent" argumentation, though he shows how such *immanentism* is in fact insufficient to describe the concrete (integral) world.[65] The temptation here is to import theology and theological terms, which would only render a disaster upon Blondel's original intent. This intent is, to recall his own words, "to constitute a philosophy which, though quite distinct from the supernatural order, would be its natural and necessary underpinning."[66] He wants to show that modern philosophy cannot ignore the supernatural, that it cannot ignore the way that the supernatural impinges on the natural while remaining beyond it (remaining, that is, *super-natural*). Philosophy, much like the sciences, does not describe the totality of the integral world, though it does describe this world in part (via a method of immanence).[67] And this totality makes itself known, at least conceptually, to a philosophy that is able to arrive at the insufficiency of pure immanence. Thus, the supernatural is necessary to nature, and the supernatural is impracticable to nature. Blondel follows this rule—that the supernatural is, to nature, necessary and impracticable—to its very end. He insists "the entire order of nature is inevitably a guaranty of what surpasses it."[68] And philosophy can say more than this.

For Blondel, the supernatural indicates that human action has an origin beyond itself in God, in the supernatural power that makes its natural and finite effectiveness effective at all. "In a sense," he says, "action has to be entirely from man, but it first must be willed as entirely from God. . . . There is a communion of two wills only on this condition: the one cannot do anything without the other. And action, a common work, proceeds nevertheless in its entirety from each."[69] But there is a further corollary to this argument, and for Blondel, it emerges as an option: either I acknowledge a supernatural will in my willing and allow that will to transform me or I refuse change according to any will

64. Blondel, 297.
65. Blondel, "Letter," 156–59.
66. Quoted in Blanchette, *Maurice Blondel*, 7.
67. Blondel, "Letter," 156–59.
68. Blondel, *Action*, 318.
69. Blondel, 354.

other than my own.[70] With this option, Blondel opens the door to the possibility of supernatural revelation and to the concrete practice of (supernatural) religion but also to their closure in free rejection.

Blondel presses philosophy into what his contemporaries would decry as religion and would therefore name as outside the purview of philosophy. But Blondel's point is that the philosophy of his day has artificially cordoned itself off from religion and that, if modern philosophy follows its own immanent logic, this restriction is revealed as false. Blondel does not fill out the content of supernatural revelation and supernatural religion so much as he lays out what nature, to be transfigured, requires by virtue of its very structure. Here Blondel can go quite far. "God alone," he says, "acting in us, grants us to be and to do what we will."[71] In this way, human action is transformed, or in its refusal, it remains the same.[72] And similarly, modern philosophy, which has refused to speak of God, must be transformed or refuse itself and remain the same.[73] "Man," explains Blondel, "thrown back upon himself and cut off from the higher life, whose source is not in himself, is condemned simply because he has not changed."[74]

It would be a mistake to take Blondel's protoexistentialism as a rejection of metaphysics.[75] Instead, Blondel shows how what action must constantly postulate by the necessity of its movement or élan can be affirmed as real by human knowledge.[76] As with Lonergan, then, being is the intelligently understood and the rationally affirmed because being is intelligible and true. For Blondel, human action "has" being. This means, on the one hand, that it exists. It means, on the other, that this existence is the subject of intelligibility or of its absence.

Blondel calls human action "metaphysics in act."[77] But this being of action is complex. It is concrete, and so it bears material facticity. At the same time, human action bears, *as* concrete, meaningfulness or intelligibility. Blondel's notion of the supernatural means that such intelligibility is not quite "two" intelligibilities (the one an immanent meaningfulness, the other supernatural), since instead Blondel means that the truth of human action is not self-sufficiently so.

70. Blondel, 328.

71. Blondel, 388.

72. Blondel, 328.

73. Cf. Heaps, "Ambiguity of Being," 150.

74. Blondel, "Letter," 201.

75. Blanchette discusses the revisions Blondel made to *Action* (1893) in response to his board on precisely this question. See Blanchette, *Maurice Blondel*, 88–94; cf. 493–546.

76. Blondel, *Action*, 390–91.

77. Maurice Blondel, "History and Dogma," in Dru and Trethowan, *Letter on Apologetics*, 237.

"We can never touch being at any point," he says, "without encountering at least implicitly the source and bond of all being, the universal Realizer."[78] So human action in its concreteness has an eternal significance, disproportionate to itself, as much as it also bears proportionate or immanent significance.[79]

If human history is human action, then a purely "natural" history is impossible; or rather, it is incomplete by virtue of its own logic. Human action requires what is impracticable to it in order for it to be: the supernatural. Human history is therefore not *only* the product of human beings, though it is the work of all human beings; it is also supernaturally conceived, ordered, and constituted. If I require God to act in all of my acting in order for me to freely act, then so also does human history. In other words, human history is not only natural; it is also integrally supernatural.

Tradition as the Mediator of Truth and History

Blondel develops a theory of tradition in response to a crisis over the nature of Scripture. The essential question in this crisis is not only about whether Scripture is historically true but also about what historical truth means and how it relates to the truth that is believed. In other words, is Scripture true? And in what way might it be said to be true? Does it indicate what is historically the case, or does it cover-over history with later religious traditions? In a time when Ernest Renan's *Vie de Jésus* (1863) still reverberated in France, sundering as it did the received tradition about Jesus and the historical existence of Jesus, and in a time, too, where Alfred Loisy's major theories upended the French Catholic world, these questions were painfully urgent.[80]

For Blondel, the problem requires a clarification. In the essay *Histoire et Dogma*, he points out that historical facts and claims of faith cannot be *the same*: "If Christian facts (history) and Christian beliefs (dogma) coincided in the light of immediate experience or complete evidence; if one only had to *believe* what others have *seen* and affirmed, the difficulty [of history and dogma] would

---

78. Blondel, "Letter," 202.

79. See Blondel's development of his idea as it continues in "Letter," 202–3.

80. See Alan Pitt, "The Cultural Impact of Science in France: Ernest Renan and the *Vie de Jésus*," *Historical Journal* 43, no. 1 (2000): 79–101; Perrine Simon-Nahum, "The Scandal Surrounding the *Vie de Jésus* by Ernest Renan: Literary Success, Scientific Failure," *Mil Neuf Cent. Revue d'histoire Intellectuelle, How One Argues* 25, no. 1 (2007): 61–74; and C. J. T. Talar, "Creating Critical Distance: Pierre Batiffol and Alfred Loisy on the Church," *Downside Review* 137, no. 1 (2019): 14–24.

not arise."[81] So the very fact that Christians struggle to reconcile historical claims with the claims of faith indicates some kind of distinction between them. This distinction makes their total identity a nonoption, but it also leaves wholly open the matter of what relationship they do have.

Blondel identifies two common positions that contradict each other. The first is what he calls "extrinsicism." This position considers historical facts to be signs or proofs of divine action.[82] But *how* historical facts function as that proof is purely external: the sensible sign—like a miracle, for example—is a mere veil for its true form, which is its divine meaning. And this is a problem because "although he had performed so many signs in their presence, they did not believe in him" (John 12:37). And this is not extrinsicism's only problem. "The worst of it," Blondel explains, "is that the thesis I have just sketched does not provide any means of accommodating itself to the facts, or any rule of interpretation: it cannot set bounds to itself."[83] Because the relationship between facts and belief is purely external, facts or proofs can be exchanged for other facts or proofs without at all adjusting the interior belief that is supposed to be attested to by the facts. All that is really needed is the belief; the facts do not matter. It does not matter, for example, that after the resurrection, Jesus first spoke to Mary Magdalene; it does not matter that he ate meals with the disciples; what matters is what is believed, and each of these things proves belief, whatever belief, equally as much.

Essentially, Blondel describes a naive realism where there is no interpretive trouble between historical facts and what they "prove." But the problem is that facts are interpretable, and this is so because facts—including miracles—are not identical with what they indicate. The whole reason that modern historical scholars can question the fact of the resurrection is because of the persistence of this "space," we might say, between facts and belief. Naive realism resolves the problem basically by ignoring it. And it is therefore a path that we cannot follow.

The second common position is more forthrightly modern. Blondel calls it "historicism" and relates it directly to the critical historical science of his own time. Historicism identifies *history* with historical *facts*. It limits everything that there is to know about history to its facts, in a kind of reduction of history to critically verifiable events. It is this type of thinking that would say, for example,

81. Blondel, "History and Dogma," 223.
82. Blondel, 227.
83. Blondel, 229.

that an empty tomb is merely a sign of an empty tomb—nothing more, and nothing less. In this kind of a thought system, there is no belief that facts can "point to" as real. Historicism not only limits itself to facts but also subjects itself to a "determinism" where those facts are all that *could have* happened because they are what *did* happen.[84] This is a double reduction of sorts: facts are all that there "is" to history, and the causality of history therefore is simply and wholly "in" the facts.

For Blondel, this way of thinking is also a problem. It is a problem because it forgets that facts are expressions of what they are not. "Historicism," he argues, "tends to mistake the external act, the expressive trait, the concrete image, for the object itself."[85] There is, in other words, more to history than its facts. There are also the human beings who make the facts come to be. "Real history," says Blondel, "is composed of human lives; and human life is metaphysics in act."[86] So, like Lonergan, Blondel argues that history is human action. Because it is human action, he says, history is not reducible to its facts, which is to say to its particular instances of occurrences.[87] A study of history equal to its object would have to be able to make a study of human action as both a particular instance and a *réalité intégrale*. Such meaning is at once immanent to it and supernatural to it. The facticity of history, of human action, in other words, bears in itself a divine intention, even as it bears the immanent truth of its facticity—even we ourselves only come to know any truth at all by way of particulars.[88] So for Blondel, the truth of history has to be complexly conceived, with an intelligibility available to human intelligence and an intelligibility (distinguishable but not divided therefrom) that is not. In Blondel's own words, "For while [Catholicism's] mission is to preserve and propagate the gift of Revelation, which is always something limited, it does not forget the universal gift of the Redemption, which is the divine reality, the absolute term, to which revealed knowledge refers, though this is not identical with it."[89] History,

---

84. See Blondel, 238–41.

85. Blondel, 240.

86. Blondel, 237.

87. A fuller discussion of what "facts" are, either for Blondel or in a more generalized theory, is not possible here. So I am borrowing a conceptuality that Kevin Hughes first indicated to me, one that is a helpful and heuristic term for a larger set of notions.

88. By "particulars," I refer to a handful of aspects of Lonergan's discussion of "things" in *Insight*, esp. 274–75. As for the position on truth here, thanks to Jonathan Heaps again for pointing out to me, forcing a reread esp. of Blondel, "History and Dogma," 273–81.

89. Blondel, "History and Dogma," 281.

while it is competent according to its horizon of inquiry, is not equal to the task of studying the total phenomenon of human action.

In *Histoire et Dogma*, Blondel expands his critique of the positive sciences to include scientific history. Blondel points out that science (here: history) is insufficient because it derives its power from something other than itself. Blondel also indicates that history's subject, which is the action of human beings, in fact surpasses the science that studies it. Historicism falls apart because it fails to describe human history as it in fact is, because it forgets what human beings are (self-transcending action), and because it forgets that human action is more than its historical facticity. We must find, says Blondel, some way to mediate between truth and history. We must find what it is for Christians that bridges the "gap" between the truths of belief and the facts of history. This mediation is tradition.

Take, for example, the vexed question of Christ's relationship to his disciples. Is it true to say, with Loisy, that "what was expected was the Parousia; what came was the Church"?[90] Is the "Jesus of history" necessarily opposed to the "Christ of faith"? These questions lead to (1) a crisis about how to relate the facts of history to faith-claims and, as an extension of the first, (2) a crisis about how to understand the earliest epoch of Christian existence in its relationship to Jesus. What we *know*, the fact that is not under contestation, is that the community around Jesus existed and in some way continued to exist.[91] But what this *means* seems to lead us back into the inoperable pathways of historicism and extrinsicism: at one angle, all we are able to "see" is the fact of early interest in the Parousia and then the fact of the church's perpetuation, facts that cannot interpret themselves (as pure facts); at another angle, all we have in view is Christology, the theology of what Christians believe about Jesus, and the facts do not matter.[92] So for Blondel, it is necessary to interrogate the relationship between history and dogma, between facts and belief.

Knowledge of Christ cannot be reduced to texts. "The only way in which we can penetrate into his mind," Blondel argues, "is through the *consciousness of his consciousness* on the part of simple men deeply involved in the prejudices of their restricted background, and better able . . . to observe and maintain the facts."[93] Blondel insists that Christianity *also* is not reducible to texts or facts.[94] As

90. Cited in Blondel, 249.
91. Cf. Blondel, 244.
92. Blondel, 248–49.
93. Blondel, 246.
94. Blondel, 264.

with history, so with Christianity: because Christianity involves human beings, rising to meet the phenomenon itself will require more than (but not less than) the facts. What we need then, for Blondel, is something other than either critical history or faith, something that bridges their difference. What we need is *tradition*.

Tradition, Blondel admits, tends to be associated with transmission.[95] But this is not primarily what he has in mind when he refers to Catholic tradition. Tradition is, precisely, "consciousness of Jesus's consciousness." For Blondel, "[tradition] relies, no doubt on texts, but at the same time it relies primarily on something else, on an experience always in act which enables it to remain in some respects master of the texts."[96] As a kind of consciousness, as an experience-in-act, then, tradition is both a recovery and a creative work, mediated by the collective life of the church, which does not avoid history but exists in it, and yet transcends the facts of history precisely by being in act.[97]

Against the idea of tradition as a pure deposit, a kind of bankroll that the church must judiciously if not parsimoniously maintain, Blondel suggests that tradition is experience-in-act. Because it involves human beings in act, it involves our rationality, our textuality, our concreteness. At the same time, tradition is not summarized by the lights of any of those qualities, certainly by none of them by themselves, since tradition vitally organizes (and so transcends) each.[98] Blondel suggests, in other words, a reality that is "in" the facts and "beyond" the facts, and it is this double movement or double existence that allows tradition to be the mediator between dogma and history, binding them while also distinguishing them.

So to return to the division between the Jesus of history and the Christ of faith, Blondel suggests that neither framework is comprehensible in its wholeness without Christian tradition. Rather than facing a decision between Parousia or church, there was and is a consciousness in act that yearned for the Parousia *as* (what became) church. Or again: rather than facing a choice between historical facts and belief, between a Jesus of history and one of faith, the historical facts of Jesus's life were and are organized by a living memory of his relationship to the facts, a memory that is the founding shape for all belief. Rather than a crisis of opposites between critical history and ecclesial faith, Blondel suggests a third pathway—tradition: "The Gospel is nothing without the Church, the

---

95. Blondel, 265.
96. Blondel, 267.
97. Blondel, 269.
98. Blondel, 270–71.

teaching of Scripture is nothing without the Christian life, exegesis is nothing without Tradition."[99] Historicity is but one quality of human action. From out of this same logic, more-than-history is possible: truth, and human engagement with it, is possible. This engagement necessitates the mediation between human historicity and the truth that transcends that historicity. Such mediation is tradition. This means that tradition is identical with neither history nor truth but is rather the concrete (and so historical) appropriation of truth (and so of dogma).

Tradition is therefore an action, a "life," the life of all Christians. The problem of history and dogma therefore can only be resolved by turning to human being-alive and, in the case of Christianity, to Christian practice: "Christian practice nourishes man's knowledge of the divine and bears within its action what is progressively discerned by the theologian's initiative. The synthesis of dogma and facts is scientifically effected because there is a synthesis of thought and grace in the life of the believer, a union of man and God, reproducing in the individual consciousness the history of Christianity itself."[100]

For Blondel, hinging Christian thought on Christian life does not make thought any less objective; it rearranges the frame for that objectivity, which is to be sought in the concrete unity of God and human beings in the life of the church. And this "rearrangement" in turn impacts what Christian thinking is for, which is in service of a living practice effected in the believer by God.

Christian tradition is "a union of man and God," a surrender of the will to its supernatural source; a surrender that, by allowing the supernatural to act in and with it in a new way, transforms human willing and so fulfills it. It is the recapitulation of the incarnation in the consciousness of the believer ("synthesis of thought and grace"). This is the very heart of a supernatural religion that is borne in history—in a nature it affects. It is what renders Christian tradition, for Blondel, unique. But more importantly, it offers a sharp and bright description of Christian tradition, of its "what" that is always "in act."

At last, then, we have an operating definition of Christian tradition: it is the mediation between history and dogma. It is concrete because it deals in the facts of history, and because its action is also concrete; it is objective because it deals in the truth of God. But tradition itself is neither history nor truth, since it is the active appropriation, in history, of divine truth in the life of the church. What this "looks like" is complex, since it involves the complexity of the people of God. At the same time, what tradition "looks like" is always the same, since

99. Blondel, 275.
100. Blondel, 287.

the life of the Christian is the unity of God and the human being in Christ. But beyond this operating definition of Christian tradition, Blondel is forced by his historical situation to elaborate further how Christians relate to history and truth through the medium of tradition, how Christians relate concretely to ideas, and how Christians conceive of their relationship to human power.

Tradition and the Politics of Rule

Blondel's era witnessed the great creativity and chaos that was the French Third Republic. In many ways, the French people had not moved on from the revolution of 1789: they still lived in its shadow, either to exult it or to decry it. Most French Catholics in the early twentieth century, working from memories of religious suppression, remained stubbornly antirevolutionary and promonarchy.[101] Supporters of the revolution and the Third Republic, meanwhile, tended to be firmly secular.[102] Blondel fits on this map as one member of a small group of bourgeois Catholics who were more moderate, struggling to find a way to confront the modern world with a Catholic way of being.[103] Indeed, Blondel was an influential member of these French "social Catholics."

Social Catholicism itself is a topic beyond the reach of this book. But it is important to understand that social Catholics were those Catholics who responded to the challenge of economic modernization as a new and particular social problem, beginning in Belgium and France in the 1820s and 1830s.[104] The term *social* refers to the specific sense that the Industrial Revolution had produced a new societal problem requiring a Catholic response. They saw the poverty of the working class produced by economic modernization as a grave reality of special, and new, concern. They strove, too, to articulate a particularly *Catholic* response to this modern condition, a Catholic response that avoided both liberalism and socialism. As Paul Misner explains, "If social Catholics, for their part, remained for the most part hostile to continental or classical liberalism (economic as well as cultural), in the second half of the nineteenth

101. Joseph Byrnes, *Catholic and French Forever: Religious and National Identity in Modern France* (University Park: Pennsylvania State University Press, 2005), 69–75, 85–94.

102. Byrnes, 75–81, 85–94.

103. Adrien Dansette, "Contemporary French Catholicism," in *The Catholic Church in World Affairs* (Notre Dame, IN: University of Notre Dame Press, 1954), 238–41.

104. Paul Misner, *Social Catholicism in Europe: From the Onset of Industrialization to the First World War* (New York: Crossroad, 1991), 3.

century they become increasingly opposed to the now 'godless' or anti-religious socialism."[105]

The *Catholiques sociaux* in *this* chapter refers not primarily to that group of Catholics scattered throughout Europe with their various theories and responses across the nineteenth century but specifically to the French Catholics who gathered during yearly *Semaines sociales* beginning in 1904. Inspired by Leo XIII's *Rerum Novarum* (1891), these Catholics sought to carry out the pope's vision in their own society.[106] Their *Semaines sociales* were seen as an "itinerant university" that convened in different locations each year, where French Catholics of various expertise, including then new fields like sociology, would discuss the modern economic problem and possible approaches to it.[107] Their first president, Henri Lorin, explains, "Social Catholics have repeatedly affirmed, as a rigorous consequence of their faith, the will [*la volonté*] to be living and active members in the society of their time and of their country, through ideas, through feelings, through example; [the will] to be citizens, in the full scope of the rights that this title gives them, in full acceptance of the requirements that this quality imposes on them."[108]

Despite their claims of faithfulness to the Catholic Church and specifically to Rome, the *Catholiques sociaux* came under fire as "Modernists" for their methods. Many of the social Catholics' opponents came from that larger bloc of French Catholics who were antirevolutionary and promonarchy. These opponents tended to be supporters of the royalist movement *Action française*, and they tended to come from the neo-Scholastic school of theology and philosophy.[109] But for Blondel, the argument between the *Catholiques sociaux* and their opponents is more than the rather academic matter of monarchy or republicanism, or of Scholasticism and modern philosophy. It is about how Catholics conceive of the world and their place in it.

Blondel names his opponents "monophorists" because they tend to think of reality in terms of one quality alone: what is exterior and abstract. This then is how they conceive of supernatural revelation: as an abstraction achieved apart

105. Misner, 4.

106. Michel Mercier, prologue to *Les Semaines Sociales de France: 1904–2004* (Paris: Éditions Parole et Silence, 2006), 22.

107. Mercier, 23.

108. Quoted in Mercier, 26 (translation mine).

109. Jon Kirwan describes the debate between neo-Scholasticism and Blondel as primary in Blondel's work. See Kirwan, *Avant-Garde*, 56–60. I have taken a different angle, following Oliva Blanchette, and have framed Blondel primarily in terms of his *philosophical* interlocutors.

from its concreteness and, in revelation's operation from above to what is below, wrought through what is exterior and visible—that is, through the Catholic Church.[110] In other words, they tend to think with respect to only one *afférence* of Blondel's double *afférence*: the external one, which comes from above.[111] Similarly, these royalists imagine the world from the top down: the state's obedience to the church, the people's obedience to the state, and so on, in a hierarchy that moves from the higher to the lower.[112] Finally, this position informs their conception of the relationship between the natural and the supernatural: the supernatural stands "above" nature, which is below it and subservient to it.[113] For them, the world works through a chain of obedience.

The monophorists of movements like *Action française* can justify this position because of the way that they imagine ideas operate in the world. They understand ideas as separated entities, and similarly, they imagine a world in which separate realities are superimposed on one another, connected through the exteriority of obedience. In this conceptuality, ideas become things rather than acts of living minds. One need only come to know the concepts that exist in the world whole and entire, and then submit to them. But this results in disaster. Blondel writes, "The illusion of any exclusive ideology is not only to isolate ideas as intellectual atoms and logical blocks, but also to isolate things, on the pretext that concepts are distinctly thought out and separately defined; [it] is to break up the world into compartments that are simply juxtaposed; it is sometimes even, since things can and must be distinguished, to implicitly conclude that they cannot be united *re et actu* [in being and act]; and finally, it is to make us think and live everything conceptually."[114] For Blondel, this sort of conceptualism not only misconceives the world—that is, wrongly supposing the world to be a set of concepts rather than operating according to the dynamism of action. It also enables the rationalization of domination, because concepts just *are*, and so concepts must be obeyed, according to the implacable logic of reality. If one has the truth—say, the truth of revelation—then one has everything that there is. This, then, is a "theory according to which supernatural being is brought and

<hr>

110. Blondel, *Une alliance contre nature*, 65.
111. Blondel, 74.
112. Cf. Blondel, 74.
113. Blondel, 35.
114. Blondel, 30 (translation mine).

imposed only by way of external *afférence*, making Christianity fall under the law of fear which is summarized in two words, domination and servility."[115]

For the royalist monophorist, the watchword is *obedience*. Obedience of what is lower to what is higher. But Blondel questions the nature of this obedience, not with respect to whether God's commands ought to be obeyed, but with respect to whether monophorist obedience renders nature a pure receptacle, a "footstool," of commands.[116] The monophorist conceives of Christian effectiveness through the execution of exterior power. The monophorist "needs the external prestige of a powerful authority: precisely because nothing in man echoes with response to nor does it appeal to the [supernatural] gift which imposes itself as a right."[117] Acting according to this perceived need for external prestige, the monophorist ends up with a political religion rather than a religious politics.[118] The supernatural is only ever a kind of cloak that rests on top of creation without ever penetrating or animating it; and, as exterior, the supernatural demands naught but absolute submission—a suffocating cloak indeed.

Blondel contrasts this position with that of the social Catholics. For them, "the supernatural order is completely free and absolutely transcendent; but it is not only superimposed, it is supposed [by] and responsible for the natural order, existing such that it can never be *naturalized*; it is intended to penetrate [nature] and to assume it in itself without being confused with it."[119] Therefore, in order to be faithful to religious questions, what emerges in the natural order must be attended to by Catholics as much as supernatural revelation must be, for they are not *separate* even if they are *distinct*. This attention would include economic problems, which are not religiously indifferent problems.[120]

For Blondel, monophorists do not have a sufficient account of that other *afférence*, that movement from "below" to what is "above," where God prepares the human will to freely accept the gift of supernatural revelation. Like scientific positivism, which Blondel critiqued as early as his dissertation, the political positivism of monophorism eliminates "all that would be the work of the soul, spiritual anxiety, need for research, and an inner life: by the simple fact that [the monophorists] communicate in positivism, they exclude, willingly or not, this

115. Blondel, 74 (translation mine). See also Blanchette, *Maurice Blondel*, 242–48.
116. Blondel, *Une alliance contre nature*, 76.
117. Blondel, 108 (translation mine).
118. Blondel, 109.
119. Blondel, 32 (translation mine).
120. Blondel, 32.

spirit."[121] Here Blondel turns his eyes to *Action française*, which was led by the agnostic positivist Charles Maurras, and with whom many royalist Catholics allied themselves. For Blondel this "practical" union of instrumentalized religion (in Maurras) and Catholic religious fervor is itself evidence of the deeper errors that run through the monophorist position like massive fissures.[122]

Blondel's point is not that no one should obey the church or that the church is not necessary in God's saving plan. His point, rather, is that the monophorist conception of the world, matched together with the practical outcome of their politics, renders supernatural religion nothing but force and power. If the supernatural only acts upon nature from above—if the world is split between the rigid concepts of the natural and supernatural, divorced according to two ends, if nature is whole and complete, after all, and in no interior need of the supernatural—then supernatural religion can only ever be an external imposition upon what is already unabridged and, so to say, entirely itself.[123] Supernatural religion confronts pure secularity and crushes it by force.

So Blondel opposes the "integralism" of the monophorists with the *réalité intégrale* of the social Catholics. For the latter, the concrete human nature that we encounter in the world has but one *intégrale* destiny and so is nurtured—from above, below, and within—into the reception of what it needs: the supernatural.[124] "In fact," argues Blondel, "man only treats man as man if everyone sees in each one Christ invisibly present."[125] In other words, it is not only that humanity *needs* supernatural revelation (and thus also the church) but also that nature is secured by and engendered to fullness by the supernatural. Therefore, the social Catholics are both "social" and "Catholic," concerned with social problems and concerned with the church.[126] *This* kind of integralism cannot be violent in the sense of a power that overcomes another, for the bloom of need for the supernatural in the natural is that space where the supernatural grows the germ of a free cooperation with its disproportion. To overpower it would be to remove it, and so to tear out the marrow of concourse. Empty bones can do anything a greater power wishes—except cooperate, except surrender in sweetness, except be alive. To put it another way: there is no "purely"

---

121. Blondel, 136.
122. Blondel, 140.
123. Cf. Blondel, "Letter," 154–55.
124. See Blondel, *Une alliance contre nature*, 7–8, 11.
125. Blondel, 147.
126. Blondel, 178.

secular world out there to grovel in obeisance to a cloud-temple, any more than there is a purely religious world up there in the sky to demand it. There is just the human world. The integral world. So Blondel's riposte to his modern philosophical peers becomes one to his fellow Catholics.

What the monophorists most of all forget is the radical, supernatural equality of all human beings before one another in Christ.[127] Here Blondel directs his opponents to the heart of supernatural revelation, which is also a radically supernatural *action* that elevates all human beings before the God who loves each of them, both lending to them and cherishing their infinite dignity. French Catholic integralism, most especially Charles Maurras's sort, has no plan except to enforce itself through greater power over the weak. No *convincing* is necessary at all. In fact, quite the opposite. But this violent imposition of one schema over another through the effective and practical execution of exterior force, a Catholic realpolitik, forgets absolutely the dignity and freedom *in Christ* that everyone has, including that of the monophorists' opponents.

Blondel opposes authoritarian conceptions of Catholicism, but his reasons for doing so matter. For Blondel, the monophorist imagines that having the right ideas in the right order will result in the right reality—if not by persuasion, then by force. This perspective is the function of a positivism in line with the scientism of Blondel's day: all there is, is what is understood, and what is understood is understood simply or immediately. Thus, error has no rights. It could not have any, because it is wrong. But the monophorist forgets human action, from its nascence to its maximum in radical human solidarity, to its supermaximum in an infinite need for that which acts in all its activity. It is this human action that is made possible by the supernatural and that—through the supernatural—receives the supernatural. It is this action that makes the sciences possible. It is this action, too, that freely carries itself out in the world.

"Freedom," for Blondel, is that mysterious doing of the action that has been conceived; no one can supply this doing for anyone else, and no one's mere conception of the act can supply the deed. There is a kind of "gap" here between (mental) word and deed that is bridged by human action, and by human action alone. So even to arrange one's mental world rightly is not yet to follow the full "determinism" of one's own action, and even to exalt supernatural revelation is not yet to conceive revelation's transfiguration of human action. Thus, the social Catholics are concerned for social problems as well as religious ones, doing so according to the double *afférence* of a *réalité intégrale*. It is not just the

____

127. Blondel, 148–49; Blanchette, *Maurice Blondel*, 252–53.

case that the monophorists are conceptualists who are in error; it is also that their error consumes wholly human action, both in theory and in practice. In other words, they impose a superficial and false schema on the world, and they—through *their* action—freely act it out. Now that we understand Blondel's critique of monophorism, its tragic politics, and its overcoming through the social fullness of integral tradition, Blondel must encounter and be critiqued by an examination of the politics of race, by an exploration of the ways tradition is actively enmeshed in colonial conquest, in its theory and in its practice, in its theology and in its history.

Tradition and the Politics of Race

In *The Christian Imagination*, Willie Jennings describes a triple construction at the heart of modern colonialism: the invention and application of a "racial scale," the dislocation of human bodies and geographies, and the theological distortions that support these economic and aesthetic transfigurations. The "racial scale" envisions humanity with two poles, "white" and "black." These designations are applied to bodies (and the lands they occupy), and they carry with them economic and theological meanings: "Black indicates doubt, uncertainty, and opacity of saving effects. Salvation in black bodies is doubtful, as it was in (Christian) Jews and Moors. White indicates high salvific probability, rooted in the signs of movement toward God (for example, cleanliness, intelligence, obedience, social hierarchy, and advancement in civilization)."[128] The racial scale is not only a mechanism for justifying cross-continental slavery, kidnapping, and land seizure; it is also *theologically* evaluative, placing Europeans and "whiteness" at the center of Christian salvation and placing the other end of the scale ("Blackness") at its edge.[129] God's providential guidance of history operates within the racial scale and its new geography. There develops a theological rationalizing of the events occurring in the "New World" that justifies the actions of God's people, who are Europeans (first: the Spanish). It is a vision that, Jennings says, "discerns the guiding hand of God in the way the Spanish

---

128. Willie James Jennings, *The Christian Imagination: Theology and the Origins of Race* (New Haven, CT: Yale University Press, 2011), 35.

129. Jennings, 37; Willie James Jennings, "Whiteness Isn't Progress: How the Missionary Project Went Horrifically Wrong," *Christian Century* 135, no. 23 (2018): 28.

arrived and remained in the New World, while discerning no such divine involvement in the lives of native peoples."[130]

For Jennings, there is an equally important "transformation of space" that occurs alongside this aesthetic-economic-theological European endeavor, a kind of unmooring of people *from* the land. They are de-connected from one another. From out of this shift, theological meaning becomes constrained around bodies. "The gospel," explains Jennings, "is always embodied in the acts of faithful Christians, and yet the gospel is without constrictors of space. It is quintessentially movable, elastically stable over vastly different locations. The age of discovery entails that the European body will take on these exact characteristics."[131] So the flexibility of the gospel is applied to European ("white") bodies, whose geographic "space" is then universalized: white bodies have dominion and obligation toward the whole world, including the "new" one. So also, the African body (indeed, "Africa") receives its own elaboration, and "Black" is applied to Africans and to new peoples and new lands.

But colonialism is more than this. It involves the forcible (and free) moving of whole peoples into new places with new relationships to the land. Says Jennings, "Four things are happening at the same time: first, people are being seized (stolen); second, land is being seized (stolen); third, people are being stripped from their space, their place; and fourth, Europeans are describing themselves and these Africans at the same time."[132] With these massive changes come new economic patterns that further order into a hierarchy both people and their relationship to the land. The New World is characterized as "raw" land that needs to be "tamed" or brought to a kind of maturation.[133]

For Jennings, theology is intimately involved in every one of these movements, and that theology is transformed, deformed by that support. Theology constricts Christianity to the European body, which, by identifying the gospel and Europe (European culture and bodies), succeeds in supplanting the gospel with European "civilization." For Jennings, such deformation occurs according to the energies of a much older problem, that of supersessionism: the replacement of Israel with the church (theologically, but also concretely in anti-Semitism). "Indeed," argues Jennings, "supersessionist thinking is the womb in which whiteness will mature. Any attempt to address supersessionism

130. Jennings, *Christian Imagination*, 90.

131. Jennings, 31; Jennings, "Whiteness Isn't Progress," 29.

132. Jennings, *Christian Imagination*, 24.

133. Jennings, 43.

must carefully attend to the formation of the racial scale and the advent of a new vision of Christian social space."[134] If the church can replace Israel, then the church can replace any (Indigenous) culture—for the sake of the salvation of those people. It is in this way that colonialism is not merely the operation of Europeans who happened to be Christians but rather an operation of Christian tradition itself: "The inner coherence of traditioned Christian inquiry was grafted onto the inner coherence of colonialism."[135] Thus, Jennings articulates a certain crisis with respect to Christian tradition: How is one to describe that tradition as mediating the mind of Christ when it is enmeshed in colonial structures even today?[136] Thinking that happens within a tradition repeats the gestures of that tradition—including its deformations.[137]

What happens to the meaning of tradition when it is involved in historical movements like colonialism? For Jennings, Christian tradition is altered as it operates, altered in ways that are concretely and profoundly harmful to those who come into contact with it. "Traditioned Christian existence," explains Jennings, "first that of the Iberians and then that of all Europeans, fundamentally changed as they ascended to hegemony in the New Worlds. It is indeed traditioned imperialist modernity."[138] At the same time, Christian tradition contains a long legacy of a prior actions meant to supplant Israel with the church. The "fundamental change" has, as it were, a genetic pedigree. Jennings himself often uses spatial metaphors to describe such a change: the wideness of theology moves "inside" the confines of the racial scale, and it is presaged by an earlier move into the narrowness of supersessionism.[139] What Jennings sees that Blondel did not is at least two historical "moments" where Christian tradition in some way betrays itself: in its treatment of Jews and Judaism and in its support of and integration into modern colonialism. It is more than possible to add other moments in history where Christianity achieves something like this. Jennings, though, urges us hold in mind not just *any* moment that Christianity is leveraged to execute a historical horror but specifically the ways that Christian theology is distorted according to the economics and geographics and aesthetics of the racial scale.

134. Jennings, 36.

135. Jennings, 83.

136. Willie James Jennings, "New Winds: A Response to the Essays," *Pneuma* 36, no. 3 (2014): 452–53.

137. Jennings borrows for Alasdair MacIntyre to describe what he means by "tradition." See MacIntyre, "Acosta's Laugh," in Jennings, *Christian Imagination*, 65–116.

138. Jennings, *Christian Imagination*, 71.

139. See, for example, Jennings, 211–13.

It is important, however, to recall Lonergan's warning from the last chapter, which is that historical models are helpful, but not infinitely so. And in that sense, Jennings's analyses of colonial patterns and their impact on Christian theology are more heuristic than summative. These heuristics are useful, particularly as forays into common dynamics articulated theologically in colonial, racial systems. They are meant, too, to insist to theology that it must think about its history with race, a gate of inquiry long shut. Still, the heuristics themselves strain to encompass the many, many overlapping gears of colonialism and its historical situations. There are the several noncontiguous phases of colonialism; there is the distinctness of locations, their varying iterations of colonial conquest and racialization; there are the complex relationships within what became "Europe," its various elements that made imagining and accomplishing conquest possible; there are the complexities even of anti-Semitisms in Europe; and so on. It is true, for example, that the complex applications of race in modernity fund a hierarchy, but Jennings's "racial scale" does not always "work" to describe those situations, as in the ways "whiteness" in America often functions distinctly according to class. None of this makes Jennings's schemata useless, but it does limit their use.

And let us remember that there is no *reason* for colonialism. Its every instance borrows intelligibility from its various means and their explanations, including explaining after the fact. This does not, at all, mean that colonization and racialization are not "real" and did not happen. It does not mean that they do not radically transform the Christianity—or leave untouched the Christians—that acts. It does not mean that there are no patterns to discern. Rather the opposite. Colonialism's brute facticity and radical inexplicability, brought into being by human action upon other human beings and their worlds, render what Christians have done and do in colonialism and its lasting structures inescapably true and name it as absolutely wrong. "Modernity," Enrique Dussel reminds us, "is the result, not the cause."[140] And this makes historical facts doubly important to know, in all their complexity and variation, in their patterns and in their lack thereof, since their intelligibility is *the* intelligibility to

---

140. Enrique Dussel, *The Invention of the Americas: Eclipse of "the Other" and the Myth of Modernity* (New York: Continuum, 1995), 11. Or again, "Even the violence inflicted on the Other is said to serve the emancipation, utility, and well-being of the barbarian who is civilized, developed, or modernized. Thus, after the innocent Other's victimization, the myth of modernity declares the Other the culpable cause of that victimization and absolves the modern subject of any guilt for the victimizing act" (64). Notice the odd loop of the "order" of action and its explanation.

be had. Just as a metaphysic of tradition is not a replacement of a tradition or a replacement of knowing about that tradition in its concreteness, so also a heuristic confrontation with Christian tradition's entanglement in sin—both efforts that are made in this book—is not a replacement for knowing this entanglement in its concreteness.

To follow the theory of history that I have established so far, it is necessary to connect the historicity and truth of Christian tradition to Christian action. Underneath the narration of a history is the action of the human beings who together make the event that we try to put into speech. For Jennings, this sort of phenomenon, that of being historical, refers to how Christians "embody" their faith. A Lonerganian, Blondelian framework would emphasize the roles of meaning and of action. But to connect events not only to their ideas but also to human action complicates the ways that Christian tradition is both historical and true.

Blondel articulates his own version of the deformation of Christianity, one that, as in Jennings, wields Christian ideas and Christian action to execute domination. For the monophorists (French integralists), concepts are both stable and immediately grasped. So too, their view of the world endures a rigidity, not only distinguishing the natural and the supernatural, but also separating them and placing one in dominion over the other. Human nature in this model is a passive instrument, designed to receive the exterior, supernatural revelation of God with absolute submission. The monophorists imagine this acquiescence only in its exterior conditions, failing to consider the free assent to grace that grace itself prepares. This failure is more than academic. It makes of Christianity a tool for oppression in the wielding of power. "What made theology a tool of empire?" asks Shawn Copeland. "Perhaps, theologians failed to cultivate the inner drive and desire for understanding and did not allow wonder to move about freely in new cultural, religious, social, and geographic contexts into which they ventured. Put differently: This breakdown of theology was due largely to sin as manifest in bias—dramatic, individual, group, and commonsense."[141] Copeland and Blondel together stress the interiority that is meant to be the instrument of grace; both describe the tragedy of a certain exteriorization that renders sin operable, a failure (as Charles Péguy might say) of "suppleness," a failure with staggeringly grave consequences.[142] Where Copeland describes this

141. Copeland, "Turning Theology," 765.

142. In traditional Catholic theology, sin and guilt are not wholly identical terms, partly as a way to distinguish one's varying responsibility for what one does, whatever its objective nature,

failure on the side of the theologian, Blondel describes it on the side of the world that the theologian, or the Catholic, reflects upon.

I want to emphasize that tradition, in a Blondelian mode, is what Christians do: it is an action in Blondel's sense of the word. It carries some of the valence of Jennings's "performance," but for Blondel, human action must be understood under the integral lights of the natural and the supernatural. Human action, which history *is*, is at the same time more than historical, and in two ways: human action is self-transcending, and human action is, even in its self-transcendence, insufficient for itself. For Blondel, every human action proceeds from out of the "determinism" of the whole "body" of human action, which constantly transcends itself at every point, from embodied consciousness to discrete action to the total solidarity of all human action. But for all this, human action is not self-sufficient. Its origin and its end are supernatural. Human action is doubly "metaphysics in act."

Because human action is "metaphysics in act," it is able to span both history—in its concreteness, its particularness—and more-than-history, which for Blondel is truth or dogma. From out of this dual characteristic, human action can be the subject of human reflection and (because self-transcending) human development. In Lonergan's sense of things, human action is meaningful. It is meaningful, to emphasize Blondel, in its very concreteness. Which brings to human action a further quality not summarized by either facts (history) or truth. Action is a kind of elasticity in motion, always in act and always beyond (an) act, and therefore able to be creative as much as conservative. This elasticity in motion is tradition, which concretely, historically, mediates truth.

Jennings describes not just ideas but also something that Christians *did* and *do*. Indeed, this action is the first fact to remember. Especially in American discourse, the danger is to allow race to "do" the action, when it is human beings who act. Race thus conceals racists.[143] This action, as action, immediately opens out Christian action into Blondel's integral universe: concrete, historical, natural, metaphysical, supernatural. It also exposes Christian *tradition* to its own ambiguity as a mediation, since it, as a mediation of history and truth, is "itself" neither. Or, to put the matter in terms of human action, for Blondel, human

---

a responsibility that is not identical in every case, even in one lifetime. Of these sorts of distinctions and their impact, there are some implications in the next two chapters, but I do not address them directly, nor unfold their every consequence. The constraint of the question of this book leaves such consequences subsequent to the present effort.

143. Fields and Fields, *Racecraft*, 16–19.

action can either change by surrendering to its supernatural origin (God) or remain the same and condemn itself. For Lonergan, this is human action's ability to be for human progress or for human extinction. And so tradition, as an act, suffers the ambiguity of human action, in the ambivalence of its "for."

There is still a further ambiguity, which has to do with human freedom. It is not only the case that human beings can choose to change or not to change; it is not only that we can contribute to progress or extinction; it is also that we have to supply the acting at all. As I have argued, there is a "gap" of sorts between ideas (whether true or false) and human action (whether for human progress or decline). To know the truth is, in this life, not to act according to it—not until it is done. Truth and falsity, progress and extinction, allow for the evaluation of human action's meaningfulness. But human action also escapes this, since for human beings, knowing is not doing.

Into this gap, into this ambiguity, enters tradition's possibility for development and its entanglement in sin. Because Blondel insists on the supernatural, there remains the possibility of judging what is true and good in the totality of Christian reality and what is not. There remains that divine revelation that proceeds to us by way of double *afférence*. The juncture or spring mechanism where truth and history meet is in Christian practice, which for Blondel is the opposite of "subjectivism." "We must realize," he says, "both what the Church does, and her *reason* for doing so."[144] This reason, while always discovered in the concrete, is more than its concrete circumstance, either of exterior situation or of interior subjectivity. And so again, history and truth are not the same, and they are brought together concretely in Christian action, with its reason. But to follow that logic also means that there is no escaping the concrete situation of tradition, no way to enter its purified alternative, where human action is disambiguated from sin and where revelation is cleanly severed from its site in Christ's and the Christian's life. Divinization, in its intimacy and in its glory, is a supernatural action in history—the place of human *grandeur et misère*.

Blondel calls Christian tradition consciousness of Jesus's consciousness, which bridges the distinction between truth and action. I develop this more in chapters 3 and 4. For now, on the one hand, it allows for an evaluative discernment, a judgment, of whether a Christian action is an expression of Christic consciousness or not, and on the other hand, it exposes Christian action to its own ambiguity in its concreteness and in its freedom. Christian tradition therefore acquires two faces simultaneously: it is what all Christians have done

144. Blondel, "History and Dogma," 277.

and do; it is also in particular a Christic doing. It is possible, for example, to (like Jennings) speak of a deformation of Christian action as non-Christic while nevertheless calling that action, concretely, Christian, since it is the action of Christians. Catholics might want to supply here a distinction between "Tradition" and "traditions," or between "sacred tradition" and "tradition," but the point is that both would persist together because both are Christian action, and so there is no getting around having to discern that action's reason. At the level of facts, all we will "see" is Christians acting (whether unto *grandeur* or *misère*). Discerning a difference requires more than the facts and so also is further from the "body" of Christian action.[145]

Which brings us back again to Jennings's problem of traditioned reasoning. At least in a Blondelian frame, there is no other kind of reasoning; there is no "outside" to escape to, not a pure Christianity apart from its history, not even a pure metaphysical horizon, since human action will always remain integral and concrete. Calling an action un-Christian does not, after all, undo it. Nor does condemning the racial scale, or understanding its breathtaking scope, end it. Nor indeed does claiming the equality of human beings result in their concrete treatment as such. There is a real helplessness here, both in its concreteness (with no other situation to be in but the one we are in) and in its freedom (since to be different will require, more than knowing, its doing). The situation is compounded when we realize how history and freedom condition one another, constraining possibility according to the reality of what has been done.

Though both Blondel and Jennings have mechanisms by which to identify an authentic Christianity and an unauthentic one, I want to stress the razor edge of their distinctions regardless. I want to emphasize that distinctions do not separate what is found together in the concrete. In both Jennings and Blondel, the very engine by which Christianity operates becomes the machinery of injustice. Indeed, for Blondel, the monophorists deploy a partial understanding of Christianity that they then absolutize, and for Jennings, Christian salvation becomes racialized and spatialized. Human action is, again, self-transcending or self-condemning—and in either case, the gear turns on human action. It means that there is no guarantee, in the mechanism itself, that action is free of injustice. It was the monophorists who thought that having all the right ideas promised all the right action. A Blondelian frame cannot.

Here a metaphysic of tradition runs up against rich, historied, and extant fields in theology, most centrally that of ecclesiology. If discerning the "reason"

145. Blondel, 279–87.

for Christian action is essential to tradition—and if discerning where Christian action is and is not, complexly speaking, "consciousness of Jesus's consciousness" is also important—then, with or without every necessary metaphysical accoutrement, Christian traditions have already and for a long time developed various "organs" in the "body" of Christian action by which to judge themselves. The Catholic tradition has formalized many of these systems. Blondel himself references the magisterium. There are other important keys too, including the *sensus fidelium*. But here, and not for the last time, a "metaphysic" of tradition encounters its limits—that is, the way that it is a heuristic for understanding human historicity, the truth of God, and the truth of God in history but is not more than this. Theology has many more tools, and so here I want to limit the competency of a metaphysic of tradition to make way for other theological endeavors.

By way of summary, I have noted two things at once. One is Christian action's ambiguity, which Christian tradition also endures because its mechanism is fundamentally that of Christian practice (in Blondel's sense: deeds with reasons for their doing). This general ambiguity takes up a concrete historical shape: Christian tradition is that which Christians have done and do. At the pure level of facts and action, the "exterior" of tradition, it is impossible to parse out a Christian tradition somehow free of its ambiguous involvement in justice and injustice. Such a crisis brings about a second insight, which is that it is possible to evaluate the meaning or truth of Christian practice. Here a Blondelian frame stresses tradition as "consciousness of Jesus's consciousness," which is not only the manner of tradition's meaningfulness but also a way to evaluate Christian practice. Tradition does not so much escape its concrete ambiguity as gain a further horizon, one where God's appropriation of human action in Christ is what Christian tradition is "about" as well as what it is meant to "do" and so is what ultimately measures Christian action and its relationship to "consciousness of Jesus's consciousness."

But these mechanisms do not allow any evasion of what Christians in fact have done, or those attendant meanings. Jennings underlines Christian tradition's enmeshment in colonial existential frames (concrete structures for acting) and their reasons (their logic) such that Christian tradition not only provides essential frames and reasons for the colonial project but also recapitulates both rather helplessly. Christian practice is not always good or reasonable. Yet this is not quite a confrontation with what Jennings is saying, because for Jennings, Christian practice is always caught up in its own determinism. Christian practice is dynamic and it is structured, as all human action is. What Christians have done, and why, is the ground of what Christians do now and why. To call a thing untrue or unjust or even un-Christian is not yet, not at all, to undo it. *Is* there any undoing? If it is not available to us to undo what was then, then what about *now*? Or does history swallow us up in a new, and purely negative, determinism?

Both Blondel and Jennings conceive of a Christianity that is not *only* its sins, even as both work to understand what it means for Christians to sin, to be a part of history in their sinning. For Jennings, the possibility for Christianity takes the shape of a gospel that is reuniversalized because it is pulled away from its suffocating relationship to human bodies and their unreal coloring. It involves treating the long-term wound of supersessionism. For Blondel, it involves a confrontation with integral reality, and with the way that supernatural revelation operates in this reality, such that human freedom is not robbed so much as it is healed and elevated.

The uneasy heart of human being-historical is human freedom, which Blondel says emerges from the "determinism" of human action. Part of what is free in human beings emerges from numerous overlapping and sublating systems of determinism, one of which is the past as it lives on in the present, which is also creative of a situation. Freedom, as free, is that necessary "leap" that makes the present effective, either in repetition or in renewal, either by continuing or by changing. To remain the same is condemnation, and to change is redemption. But the human will, though in one way infinite, is in many more ways finite and so cannot divest itself of history, tradition, situation. It is cold comfort to note, with Blondel, that just because it *did* happen does not mean it *must* have, or must now. That is in some ways worse: the evils of the past were not inevitable, and the noninevitable future is hidden from our sight. It is hidden in part because it is not inevitable. But it is also hidden because all our acting supposes in its action an infinite against which we adjudicate our present action, and in which our action burgeons its status as metaphysics-in-act.

In the face of this challenge, Copeland offers her double heuristic measure for enacting human freedom in its authenticity. The first is her turn to persons, whose most concrete form is that of turning to the oppressed. It pushes against the shattering of human solidarity by effecting a compassion for those crushed under the feet of other human beings.[146] It is also expressive of human being under the revelatory light of God in history. And as a heuristic, it serves

---

146. This is a brief reference to an essay I wrote on Charles Péguy. See Anne M. Carpenter, "Charles Péguy's Difficult Hope," *Church Life Journal*, November 27, 2018, https://churchlifejournal .nd.edu/articles/charles-peguys-difficult-hope/.

as a guiding star for a human action faced with acting in a way that breaks through the facts of history to be more than their pure facticity. Turning to the oppressed is an imperative to be fulfilled in an infinity of ways, as many ways as human intelligence can discover. In this way, it is a guide that activates freedom rather than overdetermining it or playing the game of predicting a future that remains in serious ways indeterminate.

But the facts of our situation contain in themselves the absurd, which is sin and evil—including the surds that Christians themselves have embedded in the situation. Human power is not equal to a situation such as this. We can neither undo the past nor resolve the absurdity of the present. It is a situation disproportionate to us, however much we made it to be. The response that is equal to the situation is a supernatural one, God in Christ, in a divine action that Lonergan terms "supraintelligible." And here is where Copeland's other marker in her double heuristic measure is so important: the mystical body of Christ. As an effect of God's action in history and as a cooperation with it, the mystical body of Christ is more than a restoration of broken human solidarity, since it is also a supernatural solidarity, made possible and made real by the eucharistic presence of Christ.[147] It is also heuristic, since in its concreteness, it takes the myriad forms that this single body has borne and will bear in its supernatural unity as God's sacrament in history.[148]

Conclusion

This chapter has made a study of Maurice Blondel. In many ways, it has been a further specification of what it means for human history to be human action. Blondel's conception of a *réalité intégrale* emphasizes the distinction and the intimacy between the natural and supernatural, a perspective that both clarifies his understanding of the positive sciences and allows him to develop a wide-ranging "science" of human action. It is this latter science that then enables a definition of tradition: it is the mediation of history and truth; in the case of Christian tradition, it is the mediation of history and dogma.

The chapter also expanded and complexified the book's engagement with the puzzle of Christianity, race, and colonialism, this time through Willie

---

147. Esp. Copeland, *Enfleshing Freedom*, 128.

148. This way of speaking can be found most influentially in recent Catholic tradition in Vatican II's *Lumen Gentium*.

Jennings. So Blondel's thought came into contact with what he himself did not originally imagine, and his theory of action and his theory of tradition endured the weight of their ambiguities. Christianity's involvement in race and colonialism became a problem, both at the level of historical facts and at the level of truth. Here I but sketched the nature of that problem, outlining its conditions and possibilities, while also encountering the limits of philosophical analysis to treat of that problem—let alone its solution—in its totality.

With the supraintelligible, a metaphysic of Christian tradition passes over from various theologically inflected philosophical grounds to fully theological ones. To complete that movement is to transition into a theological metaphysic of Christian tradition. This transition will occur in two phases that are aspects of a dynamic whole, one meant to provide a theological explanation of Christian tradition. These two aspects of a single, theological whole are, first, the writings of Charles Péguy and then those of Hans Urs von Balthasar.

3

REVOLUTIONS

Heat of God's wrath in the cupful
of her vault, measure of the faithful
gone white at the bone, end-of-days
brought to the dreadful hour:
dies irae in the crash and bell

This chapter effects its turn to theology on an unusual axis: Charles Péguy. It is unusual not only because Péguy was an early twentieth-century French Catholic essayist, poet, and playwright—not a theologian—but also because the man himself was unusual. Péguy spent much of his adult life acquainted with and yet just outside of the fantastic literary, philosophical, and artistic output of the French Third Republic.[1] A committed socialist and atheist in his youth, he felt abandoned by French socialists and, when he returned to Catholicism, felt uncomfortable with his fellow Catholics. It is in his poetry that Péguy was and is most misunderstood: by the socialists who thought he'd abandoned socialism and by the royalist Catholics who thought he'd joined their cause. But Péguy

1. For some resources on some of the artistic, politically charged output during "La Belle Epoque," see Barbara L. Kelly, ed., *French Music, Culture, and National Identity, 1870–1939* (Rochester, NY: University of Rochester Press, 2008); Mary McAuliffe, *Dawn of the Belle Epoque: The Paris of Monet, Zola, Bernhardt, Eiffel, Debussy, Clemenceau, and Their Friends* (Lanham, MD: Rowman & Littlefield, 2011); Mary McAuliffe, *Twilight of the Belle Epoque: The Paris of Picasso, Stravinsky, Proust, Renault, Marie Curie, Gertrude Stein, and Their Friends through the Great War* (Lanham, MD: Rowman & Littlefield, 2014); and James R. Lehning, "Boulevard Spectacles of the Third Republic," in *The Melodramatic Thread: Spectacle and Political Culture in Modern France* (Bloomington: Indiana University Press, 2007).

is too strange, his convictions too singular and unshakeable, for easy company along settled party lines. Instead, he keeps company with the miserable and lonely, the least. With a heart for this decision, Camille Riquier calls Péguy's philosophy "the memories of a fool (*imbécile*)."[2] But these foolish memories are important.

The great advantage of arts like poetry, literature, plays, dance, and other forms that bear various markers of "story" is that they must deal with time. (This is Paul Ricoeur's great labor in *Time and Narrative*.)[3] And because they are each forms of human phantasmagorical self-presentation and self-reflection, they intensify the shape of human temporality, allowing us to "look" at it. This chapter is an investigation of that temporality, a study achieved by way of Péguy's idiosyncratic writing and art. The turn to theology and tradition is thus accompanied by a turn to what it means to be in time. *Memory* emerges for Péguy as a form of potent human shadow-speak that treacherously reveals and conceals the true nature of temporality. What we remember, after all, is no more. So Péguy runs headlong into a problem that haunts him and thus this chapter: What does it mean to be a member of today when it also and always means the irrevocable loss of yesterday? A trouble of being human is the trouble of time; the present moment makes of itself a perpetual bequest that also forever slips through our fingers. So memory, though usually positive in the genre of tradition, appears at first with an ambiguity, even a venom, that must be treated.

Péguy transfigures the bequest of today in several helpful ways throughout the chapter, with a critique of modern historical method and a sketch of a "temporal, eternal" Christianity and Christology. The theory of *ressourcement* (resourcing) dominates my examination of Péguy, receiving several elaborations throughout the chapter in order fully to describe it as a technique for understanding Christian tradition as a "memory" that is (eternally) true and (temporally) historical. Tradition-memory must endure the crisis of human memory in general, which faces its own passing-away. So also Péguy must endure a crisis, albeit of a different kind—the crisis of a confrontation with colonial and racial memory, through the two wisdoms of a reprised M. Shawn Copeland and

2. Camille Riquier, *Philosophie de Péguy: Ou les mémoires d'un imbécile* (Paris: Presses Universitaires de France, 2017).

3. See Paul Ricoeur, *Time and Narrative*, 3 vols., trans. Kathleen McLaughlin and David Pellauer (Chicago: University of Chicago Press, 1990).

Willie Jennings. Only by passing through this crisis can Péguy the fool-genius be revolutionized.

Because of Péguy's genre-rupturing way of writing, I ask for the reader's patience with and openness toward varied interpretive techniques, and I will employ those varied techniques. I will step through Péguy's work at a few angles, ones that "read" the genre of his writings and that organize the operating concepts in them so that they might explicitly contribute to my developing metaphysic of tradition. At more than one point, I will practice a method of "reading-off" the theological form (*Gestalt*) of a work of literature at length, a reading of form that in some ways resembles literary-analytical strategies but that in a more technical if subterranean way mimics Hans Urs von Balthasar's method of theological reading, which is governed by a theological rather than a literary horizon.[4] Each of these literary-theological moments is followed by a more discursive one, both as a way of clarifying what is discoverable in the poetry-plays and as a way of assembling Péguy's complicated endeavors as an essayist. Together with their final, resourcing "crisis" around colonialism, these interpenetrating moments of Péguy's do not so much conclude the chapter as they point beyond themselves to the next chapter, which is another theological tour d'horizon of Christian tradition.

A Prayer against Pure Memory

Péguy's prose and poetry are held together in a knot of memorial time, memorial place, irretrievable loss, and radical surrender.[5] It is not *only* that he invokes these four together through the action of prayer, specifically in the prayer of hope; in his poetic efforts, it is also often prayer that holds them together. This section treats these topics in their temporal valence. Then, after reflecting on that valence, I treat their geographic quality. Both angles of study, the temporal and the geographical, coalesce around the figure of Jeanne d'Arc.

---

4. For a study of Hans Urs von Balthasar's background in Germanistics, see Jonathan King, "Theology under Another Form: Hans Urs von Balthasar's Formation and Writings as a Germanist" (PhD diss., University of Saint Louis, 2016). A related effort can be found in Anne M. Carpenter, *Theo-Poetics: Hans Urs von Balthasar and the Risk of Art and Being* (Notre Dame, IN: University of Notre Dame Press, 2015).

5. I will be citing extensively from Charles Péguy, *Oeuvres en prose complètes*, 3 vols. (Paris: Gallimard, 1987–1992); and Charles Péguy, *Oeuvres poétiques et dramatiques* (Paris: Gallimard, 2014). Unless otherwise noted, all translations are my own.

Early in his writing career, Péguy wrote a play featuring the major moments in Jeanne d'Arc's public life: *Jeanne d'Arc: A Drama in Three Parts*. It was published in *La Revue socialiste* in 1897.[6] I do not want to review the entire work and its underlying Dreyfusard themes here.[7] What I do want to do is examine the role of Jeanne's prayer in this early play and then carry that reflection forward into 1910's *Mystery of the Charity of Joan of Arc*.

Most of the drama in Péguy's *Drama in Three Parts* is spent in the time between Jeanne's major historical actions. The action itself—especially her remarkable military campaign—is left offstage, while dialogues between characters take up the center. A double motivation drives the play forward: the drama between the characters in their conversations and Jeanne's offstage action between each scene. But at several points, this forward movement is interrupted by Jeanne herself, who breaks into prayers that are also poems. These prayer-poems pause the movement of action to comment on it, a little like soliloquies.

From the beginning, these prayers emphasize Jeanne d'Arc's anxiety about the damnation of souls, a theme she discusses in the opening of the play with Madame Gervaise and Jeanne's friend Hauviette.[8] Here, in the first poem-prayer, that anxiety is played out before God in a gesture that enfolds it in a magnanimity that scandalizes Madame Gervaise. Jeanne says,

> O may my human death come as soon as possible, my God.
> O my God, I have pity on our human life, where those we love are forever
>   absent.
>
> .   .   .   .
>
> O if it is necessary to save the bodies of the damned dead,
> Those panicking with suffering from the eternal flame,
> Surrender my body to the eternal flame,
> My God, give my body to the eternal flame.[9]

The prayer thematically places the beginning of the play alongside its very end, where Jeanne d'Arc leaves the stage toward her final condemnation in fire. But before we have arrived there, Jeanne in her heart and before the presence of the eternal God already lives her final vocation. Péguy opens his play with not a

---

6. Noted in Péguy, *Oeuvres poétiques*, 1547.

7. For a brief analysis, see Péguy, 1552–53.

8. Beginning in Charles Péguy, "Jeanne d'Arc," in *Oeuvres poétiques*, 7.

9. Péguy, 16.

memory but a forward gesture. And in this use of foreshadowing, Péguy unveils the secret compassion—later, the charity—of Jeanne d'Arc. Compassion, that is, for the lost souls of the world, most especially the "damned dead."

This compassion is expressed again through other prayers, where once again the dialogue is punctuated, perforated, by a kind of pause. Later, remembering her home, Jeanne says,

My God,

I loved the bell there, I loved its singing voice
That spreads over the Meuse, filling the valley
Like a slow stream of prayer and valor,
Spreading heavily until you sprawl out:

I liked the bell there: I liked its powerful voice;

I loved the church there: with a single gesture it carries
Its ascending and solid prayer,
Prayer of built and strong valor,
Leaning down here to rise more solid:

I liked the gesture in the sky of the stone church.[10]

Jeanne's first major act of memory in the play is captured in a prayer. But this backward glance is also tragic because she will never again see her home.[11] So Jeanne, in her prayer, faces something irretrievable. Her memory calls up a past that is no longer, that will not return, and so her prayer becomes paradoxical: a memorial and a mourning.

The play ends with a final poem-prayer, one that recalls the drama's opening and that radicalizes it by pressing Jeanne's compassion to its absolute:

Oh my God,

Since Rouen must be my home now, listen carefully to my prayer:

---

10. Péguy, 28.
11. See, for example, Péguy, 72.

> I beg you to accept this prayer as my true prayer for myself, because just now
> I am not quite sure what I will do when I am in the street . . . and in the
> square, and what I will say.
>
> Forgive me, forgive us all the harm that I have done, serving you.
>
> But I know that I did well to serve you.
> We did well to serve you well.
> My voices did not deceive me.
>
> Yet, my God, try to save us all, my God.
> Jesus, save us all and bring us to eternal life.
>
> *She goes out.*
>
> *Curtain.*[12]

The play ends with the darkness of its curtain, carried by Jeanne's last act of compassion for every human being ("us all"). In this act of compassion, in its repetition, the play is *like* its beginning. It is a memory resurfaced. But the ending also is not the beginning, since Jeanne's love has endured an absolute expansion.

Péguy is fond of repetition. I mean this metaphorically but also literally: Péguy repeats himself a great deal, begins-again quite often. His use of repetition gives to the present moment (of reading) a further quality: a relationship to the past in a bringing-forward of the past. Yet this past also is no longer itself. There is something irretrievable in the original, in the first acting, that cannot be done-again even when done again, for now is not then. In the human experience of "today," in other words, there is also yesterday, brought forward in a memorial act and even so forever lost. Jeanne d'Arc from the beginning articulates anxiety for the fate of the permanently lost; in a parallelism, the structure of play around *time* features the permanently lost.[13] It is yesterday that is lost. Every yesterday.

Even Péguy the atheist prays. Prayer operates to signal—by way of its dramatic interruption—the permeability of today to yesterday and also the loss of yesterday. In the logic of the play, prayer is that which can remember today.

12. Péguy, 299.
13. See, for example, Péguy, 279–80.

It spans the distance of time because it remembers. It also participates in the "welling up" of the present because it is uttered today.[14] But prayer *also* transforms what it remembers. Yesterday is, today, *different* than it was. Gone is the original moment, which now is forever altered. So as a creature of the present and of the past, prayer is a form of nonnostalgic remembering: it remembers the past but does not retreat into it. By "nonnostalgic," I mean that something about the memory is not old at all but genuinely new.[15]

As the ultimate act of compassion, prayer also surrenders all things (including, as we will see, the future) to what is higher. This is its further character: in the play, prayer lets go of, surrenders, yesterday and today (and tomorrow) into the hands of God. Péguy makes of prayer a recollection that also relinquishes. At the end of *Jeanne d'Arc*, this surrender is quite literal: Jeanne surrenders herself and everyone to God. This is her last act, carrying her forward to her ultimate fate. So too, there is a verticality in Jeanne's final action, which is directed to God rather than to any other interlocutor. Her last utterance is itself an act of hope that no one be left without redemption.

Though somewhat opaque, the vertical surrender-quality of each prayer in *Drama in Three Parts*, culminating in the last, frames Jeanne's action along the lines of self-transcending hope. Her self-transcendence has something of the character of self-forgetfulness, since she widens her existential reference to that of others, to the lost most of all, and lastly, to anyone at all. But it also has something of Maurice Blondel's "transcendence" in it as that which organizes and renders newly effective those "lower" things that it emerges from. It is this self-transcending hope, rather than memory as such, that is the beating heart of the play. Through it, Péguy poses the possibility (and not the certainty) that human action in history can become liberative, which contextually for him would have been along socialist, Dreyfusard lines. In other words, Jeanne is an example of the daring liberative act offered in hope. And so Péguy's memory of Jeanne serves a higher purpose, which is to—in hope—lend possibility to the present moment.

---

14. Cf. the sentiment in Charles Péguy, "Conjoined Note on Descartes and the Cartesian Philosophy," in *Notes on Bergson and Descartes: Philosophy, Christianity, and Modernity in Contestation* trans. Bruce K. Ward (Eugene, OR: Cascade, 2019), 184–89, esp. 195.

15. The phrase and concept of "non-nostalgic" remembering was first impressed on me in Jennifer Newsome Martin's *Hans Urs von Balthasar and the Critical Appropriation of Russian Religious Thought* (Notre Dame, IN: University of Notre Dame Press, 2015), 2: "These chapters venture to characterize Balthasar's method as constitutively orthodox, but thoroughly probative, phenomenological, literary-critical, aesthetic hermeneutic, and . . . quintessentially non-nostalgic."

What the later poem-play *Mystery of the Charity of Jeanne d'Arc* adds to 1897's *Jeanne d'Arc* is in a sense nothing at all. Jeanne still expresses anxiety for the damned, still offers herself for them, still persists in self-transcendence, though here that real ending in fire is entirely a gesture forward and narratively never arrived at.[16] There is still the sharp taste of memory, especially the memory of Christ's life on earth and the lives of the first saints around him, which have a way of haunting every Christian who enters history "after."[17] Once again, prayer-memory bears in itself the unrecoverable, the unrepeatable, since no other time and no other people can claim to have been first with Christ.[18]

But there is a difference. One that unsettles all the familiar pieces in the poem-play. That difference has to do with "where" Péguy places the narrative's first anxiety for the lost and the first surrendering prayer-action in hope for everyone. In *Charity*, as opposed to the *Drama in Three Parts*, Christ on the cross is the one to first experience awareness of the lost, of the "damned dead." Even as Jeanne is first in the order of narration, Christ is the first in the order of history and, as it were, in the metaphysical order. He literally shouts his agony in response.[19] As Péguy explains,

> For the Son of God knew that the suffering
> Of the son of man is in vain to save the damned,
> And he was maddened more than them by despair [*désespérance*],
> The dying Jesus wept over the abandoned.
>
> [He wept] with the common despair.
>
> He was maddened more than they by *their* despair, by the same despair as
>   them, by their own despair.
> He had the same despair as them. But he was God: what did he not have.[20]

The word that Péguy uses for "despair" is *désespérance*, which is a kind of un-hope (*dé-espérance*). Damnation unhinges the damned from a fundamental, temporal

16. See, for example, young Jeannette's reflection in Péguy, *Le mystère de la charité de Jeanne d'Arc*, in *Oeuvres poétiques*, 430–31.

17. Cf. Péguy, *Charité*, in *Oeuvres poétiques*, 547–53.

18. Cf. Péguy, 464–70.

19. Péguy, 523.

20. Péguy, 519.

experience of being-human, which is the experience of self-transcending hope. So if, in the early *Jeanne d'Arc*, it is Jeanne who throws herself in with the damned, then in this later version, it is Christ who first throws himself in with them, by experiencing their despair.

Désespérance has a response later, in *Portal of the Mystery of Hope*. There again, the first "prayer" and action for the lost (the image is of the lost lamb) emerges not in Jeanne but in the heart of God. God himself takes up anxiety for the lamb and hope for the lamb, in a radical act of condescension: God experiences anxiety that the lamb in the sheepfold will be lost and hope that the lost lamb will be found.[21] God himself, Péguy says, fears for the lost and hopes for the lost:

> Singular reversal, a singular reversal, it is the world upside down,
> The virtue of hope.
> All the feelings we must have for God:
> It was God who started to have them for us.
>
> .   .   .   .
>
> It was she [hope] who made this reversal, the strongest of all reversals[22]

Here it is possible to see the difference in the religious Charles Péguy. It is that God is the origin of hope, the first place of hope, the God who by grace makes hope come to be in the hearts of human beings.[23] The last poem-play in the trilogy recapitulates this: in *Mystery of the Holy Innocents* this hope—the child-hope—takes up permanent residence in heaven.[24] It secures, absolutely, a single place in creation where humanity does not succumb to aging and to despair. So it is not just that Péguy gives to God a real responding voice in the later poems, as compared with the *Drama in Three Parts*; it is also, and more importantly, that this divine speech and action is *first*. God's utterance is the foundation of every human utterance. And so, as "founded," all human speech, all human striving, is also gift. Péguy says as much in the voice of *Clio*.[25]

21. Cf. Charles Péguy, *Le porche du mystère de la deuxième vertu*, in *Oeuvres poétiques*, 709–10.

22. Péguy, 711.

23. Cf. Péguy, 632–34.

24. Charles Péguy, *Le mystère des saints innocents*, in *Oeuvres poétiques*, 926–27.

25. Charles Péguy, "Clio I," in *Temporal and Eternal*, trans. Alexander Dru (Indianapolis: Liberty Fund, 2001), 85–91, 109–10.

This givenness changes, in the concreteness of human life, nothing at all. (As in Blondel, to change is redemption, to remain the same is to be condemned.) One could live a life ignorant of it, and successfully. Again in *Clio*, Péguy accuses the modern world of having found a way to be successfully non-Christian.[26] But givenness also changes everything—if we open ourselves to it through the response of self-transcending surrender. Péguy presents this surrender poetically, at one angle, as a kind of balance, one of God both allowing human freedom its own space and of God holding freedom up.[27] At another angle, this surrender is pure grace, an absolute gift, the grace of letting go: the grace of "night," where at last everyone must fall asleep and for once let go before their supernatural origin.[28]

We do not directly see Jeanne's death in the later trilogy. It does, however, appear. Throughout this trilogy, Péguy alludes to Jeanne's life and fate that, in the logic of the poetry, are all foreshadowings. This is because *all* of the speech takes place between a young Jeannette and Hauviette, or between Jeannette and Madame Gervaise. Lorraine, Orléans, the Meuse, and Domremy all show up.[29] And so does that final surrendering prayer and its curtain: in the figure of "Daughter Night" (who first descends on the cross) and in the white shroud over Jesus's body.[30] But this surrender is more radical because it is less memorial, or rather, memorial (since it is still a memory of Jeanne's life, which is past) in a different way. As structured by the narrative of the trilogy, young Jeannette's life still stretches out before her; she is in fact about halfway through what will be the total length of her short life. But rather than offering several moments of surrender through the course of that life, as previously, Péguy's narrative instead remains focused on her in her present tense as a child, focused on her compassion at a midpoint that is not left behind. In a sense, she is (as Péguy says) doubly Christian, in her very youth, in her present hope that has not faded into a past hope, against a hope aged and disintegrated into memory. As Péguy argues a few years after *Charity*, "She had to be Christian and martyr and saint against the French and against the Christians. She found unfaithfulness installed in the very heart of France, in the heart of Christendom. She had to break that long habitude. She had to climb back up that long memory. That's

---

26. Péguy, 127–31.

27. Péguy, *Saints Innocents*, in *Oeuvres poétiques*, 816, 822–24, 840–41.

28. Péguy, *Porche du mystère*, 764–68.

29. Examples: Péguy, *Charité*, 401, 407, 433; Péguy, *Saints Innocents*, 642.

30. Péguy, *Porche du mystère*, 768.

what I call being a saint and martyr twice."[31] So Péguy's memory of Jeanne is in a real way antimemorial; it is a kind of remembering that fixes her in the present tense, ascribing it to her. It is, to be precise, an antinostalgic remembering, because it is not about her pastness but about remembering her presence in the present. And so here, at last, is the ultimate transfiguration of prayer-action in its divine foundation: in the presence-ing of the past "against" pure memory and "against" pure loss (i.e., against pure pastness).

Loss and *Ressourcement*

In his essay "Loss in the Thought of Charles Péguy," Jean-Louis Chrétien notices Péguy's interest in the permanence of loss, which I previously traced through the prism of prayer, especially of the prayer of Péguy's Jeanne d'Arc.[32] There, in two poem-plays, her prayer acquires its tragedy: she recalls what she will not see again. But for Péguy and for Péguy's thinking, says Chrétien, "this tragic song of the loss of innocence, of the initial, of the first time, of childhood, runs through all of Péguy's work, and arises in connection with the most diverse and disparate themes in their extension, from his own life to educational reforms, from the problems of translation to the permanent erasure of entire civilizations."[33] What is more, Chrétien says, "if we stick to this litany of always irreparable loss, Péguy would be a thinker of despair (*désespoir*)."[34] So for Chrétien, there is the potential in Péguy for a kind of absolute temporal despair, one where we cannot but mourn the permanent loss of every original moment, which fades irrevocably into yesterday.

For Chrétien, Péguy's despair is not overcome by way of the *recovery* of the original. It is to be found instead in a second innocence, a recommencement of innocence, which is rooted in hope's power to begin-again today. This innocence must be given, must be "a grace and a gift."[35] But it is also a perpetual struggle, a struggle in each moment, to begin again.[36] It is a struggle, that is, to

31. Péguy, "Conjoined Note," 154.

32. Jean-Louis Chrétien, "La perte dans la pensée de Charles Péguy," in *Pensée de Péguy*, ed. Benoît Chantre, Camille Riquier, and Frédéric Worms (Paris: Éditions Desclée de Brouwer, 2015). E-book.

33. Chrétien, §7 (translation mine).

34. Chrétien, §11.

35. Chrétien, §15.

36. Chrétien, §17–18.

begin again as the present moment requires, and therefore a struggle to make a unique gesture in the present. "The inexorable," says Chrétien, "mercilessly requires the safety of the unique gesture, and therefore the place of possible loss is also the place of the highest nobility."[37] So for Chrétien, Péguy's response to loss with hope is not a hope that the irrevocably gone persists, somehow, as such but a hope that the present moment allows a recommencement of a life. "Hope," explains Chrétien, "as the essential power of recommencement, has nothing of a power of repetition or of a circular return to an earlier innocence, and true human purity is never anything but a purification, with all that it entails, arduous and painful, against our fatal entropy."[38]

The supernatural givenness of human action makes beginning-again possible. Human action is, at one angle, entirely the supernatural gift of God. Human action is also, as made effective by God, capable of self-transcending: simply, in the very act of entering the world (for example), or complexly, under the light of human progress. The supernatural givenness of human action and its self-transcending movement do not guarantee its recommencement; they make it possible. One need not act; indeed, not every act is free or for human progress. This possibility or capacity for beginning-again remains temporal because yesterday remains gone and, inasmuch as it must take place, in order to take place at all, in the present. Thus, recommencement requires a genuinely new act; it must be original to its present moment. Were human action incapable of self-transcendence, this "genuinely new" act would be impossible; in other words, I would helplessly reiterate the ghost of yesterday, which is neither really yesterday nor really new.

For Péguy's original Jeanne d'Arc, the surrender of her final prayer embraces the absolute transformation of her charity—a surrender that rediscovers her original act of charity in the shape of a charity that exists more radically for all. Together with the later poetic trilogy, this newness of the moment, the purified act, is able to offer a yesterday made more than itself in a humanity offered back to God. "The irreversible *nouveauté*," argues Chrétien, "is kept for [Péguy] only in living memory, and therefore it is elective (not so much because it chooses at will, but because it has been required by what it remembers), a memory which is renewal, and, in a breath of meaning, returns to the past, increased, the force which it received from it."[39]

37. Chrétien, §19.
38. Chrétien, §25.
39. Chrétien, §21.

Chrétien leads me toward a first set of insights into Péguy's concept of *ressourcement* (resourcing), which is bound together with Péguy's understanding of *révolution*. It is really a dual concept, since each is understood through the other. I will begin first with Péguy's notion of revolution, since it frames the action of *ressourcement*. A revolution, for Péguy, must reach more deeply into the resources of humanity and human tradition, into the humanity that acts and the human tradition it sets itself against. "A revolution," says Péguy, "is a call from a less perfect tradition to a more perfect tradition, a call from a less deep tradition to a deeper tradition, a reversal of tradition, a going beyond in depth; research [*recherche*] into deeper sources; in the literal sense of the word, a resource [*ressource*]. It is not only because they are also powerful, it is not only because they are also strong, [but also] because they are magnitudes of the same order that only a fully revolutionary situation can face a fully traditional situation."[40] A revolution, which operates by "resourcing," is not a *reiteration* of humanity or tradition but results in something new, in something more perfect. Péguy argues that "a revolution is not really and fully revolutionary and only succeeds as a revolution if it reaches, as if by a strike of sound, if it causes a humanity to emerge and spring up deeper than the humanity of the tradition which it opposes."[41] Similarly, Riquier argues that for Péguy, even the French Revolution, which concluded in violent bourgeois excess in any case, is not to be repeated or imitated. A revolution must be begun all over again every day.[42] What is more—and this is important to Riquier in particular—Péguy himself takes up the position of the outsider, the one left behind, the person that a revolution must most of all emerge from and also reach.[43] It is a kind of protopreferential option, a positioning of solidarity with the least. And it helps make sense of resourcing and revolutionizing because its center of gravity is where humanity most blooms and most needs to bloom: not in the successful, but in the lost.

Here in *ressourcement* and *révolution*, then, is the dual content of Chrétien's "original gesture"—that is, the very act or gesture of resourcing, which "begins again" and, by beginning again, "increases" the humanity, and the tradition, that it sources. Here too emerges a complexity within the dynamic of tradition: a turning face set in opposition to the past, to reach more deeply into what

40. Charles Péguy, "Avertissement," *Cahiers* 5, no. 11, in *Oeuvres en prose complètes*, vol. 1 (Paris: Gallimard, 1987), 1305–6.
41. Péguy, 1306.
42. Riquier, *Philosophie de Péguy*, 152–57.
43. Riquier, 49–50.

was, beyond the constraints of what was. The original gesture is not the past; it is not a return, but it is the arduously purified.

In the last chapter, Maurice Blondel articulated a philosophy of tradition where tradition is both action and mediation, the action of a mediation; it is the mediation of truth and history, bound together through the medium of human action, human action in the wide sense conceived of by Blondel (meriting connotations of both thought and deed). I also explained how, in the Christian tradition in particular, human action is appropriated to the divine life in Christ. It is from out of this primordial, original incorporation that Christian tradition derives both its meaning (its truth) and its movement (its action). Under the light of *this* sense of action, the mediation of tradition allows Christians to cleave to both the facts of history and the truth of dogma by relating them to each other through the auspices of the primordial incorporation of the incarnation. Therefore, for Blondel, Christian tradition is neither a purely intellectual patrimony nor a mechanistic performance, since it is that meeting place of Christian thought and Christian practice.

Péguy's impact here is complex. For now, I want to introduce a temporal accent to Blondelian action. Through it, we can say that the mediatory action that tradition "is"—the *tradere* of *traditio*—is most properly understood and most properly "itself" in the present, in the *action* of Christian existence (in thought, in practice). Tradition, we might say, is alive in the living. Though it is at times characterized as the memory of the dead, its life is to be found in the thinking and practicing of living Christians, a notion that Blondel also stresses. Tradition's value, and what is to be valued in it, is not to be found in its *pastness*. Its value is what it mediates, is its mediation.

And this mediation of tradition is not unhinged from its past. This is not, in other words, the expression of a tyranny of pure contemporaneity. Today is permeable to yesterday, indeed enlivened by yesterday, through human action (in the poem-plays: the action of prayer). But yesterday only lives on in a specific act of remembering, one where the aliveness of the original is reiterated by being begun again, a beginning-again that infuses the original with new richness. Once again, if human action were only the bare shape of its own concreteness, if it were not self-transcending "metaphysics in act" (Blondel) or capable of progress and ruin (Lonergan), this beginning-again that finds the pulse of the past would be impossible. Yesterday, reduced to its facticity, will never be today. Pure memory remains tragic. But living memory, as creature of yesterday *and* today, as a *péguyste* recommencement, is not tragic. Yesterday—in that which is more than pure fact, in its action, in its truth—can be begun-again and so enriched. Or we might say: the letter kills, but the spirit gives life (2 Cor 3:6).[44]

Péguy's interest in the halfway turn of Jeannette's life, in the interrupted halfway curve of Christ's own life—indeed Péguy's own midsentence, midlife end—evokes a figurative reading where all human action remains open to recommencement and, thus, to self-transcending perfection. No human deed is complete or, shall we say, closed upon itself. As such, human action has a memorial capacity, an openness to being-recollected, but in two directions: in the futility of pure pastness or in the aliveness of beginning-again. The spring mechanism for either is the present moment, where one must make a "unique gesture" that enriches the past or make a "ready-made" gesture that closes up the present through pastness.[45] This unique gesture bears the features of surrender, understood not as fatalism but as charity, a charity that in its breadth embraces, radically, every human being, including most of all the lost. It is a charity accompanied by hope, since it begins again.

Péguy sets himself against the reduction of human action purely to the horizon of scientific history or facticity. Hope, on Péguy's account, is inexplicable to such a history. But hope in the *péguyuste* sense is also something other than an insistence that human action is "more than" the facts. As that which begins again every day and as a theological virtue, hope is the secret that animates all human action. It is at once a practice and a doing, and it is more than all human doing as an absolute gift. And here, at the crossway of human action and pure divine gift, we have the crossway of the natural and the supernatural. To be more precise: we have the elevation of the natural in the supernatural.

A Geography beyond Pure Memory

For Péguy, places or locations have a perdurance that outlasts the events, the memories, that occur in their spaces. Places "have" memories, and they are more than their memories. We might say that geography, for Charles Péguy, is historical. But it is also evocative of much more than history, of origins beyond (older than) history and also of times beyond (farther than) the present (of

44. Glenn Roe makes a similar point with respect to Péguy's relationship to literature. See Roe, *Passion of Charles Péguy*, 214.
45. Cf. Péguy, "Conjoined Note," 100, 109–12.

history). Geographical space is that "place" where human beings meet and are outmatched, by God and nature both.

Paris is the place par excellence. Péguy frequently commits the conceit that Paris and France are the same, that the one is the absolute heart of the other. (This conceit has a dark side that I will discuss later.) For Péguy, Paris is the primary place of French memory, which lives on in the physical monuments that populate the city: the Panthéon, Notre-Dame, the Hôtel de Ville.[46] But the real and living center of Paris, and therefore of France, is its people. Péguy exults in their dual republican and royal identity:

> Singular people of Paris, people of kings, people of the king; the only people who have the power to say that they are the king, without making a shameful literary figure; deeply and truly a people, so deeply, so truly, kingly; in the same sense, in the same attitude and in the same gesture people and king; of the same spirit, people and king; . . . really the only people who without preparation know how to give kings an old and royal reception; really the only people who made revolutions and remained not only traditional, but traditionalist to this point; the only people who is traditionalist in the full consent of its good will; the only one who is comfortable and knows how to stand and present itself in history, having a long habit, having an inveterate habit of this form and level of existence, and who is not insolent and unbecoming, a rude upstart; the only people who do not slip on the waxed floors of glory.[47]

In this gesture, Péguy locates Paris in its people, and they in the city. The two are bound together such that, even were all Paris's physical monuments razed, still the city would live on in the lives of its people.[48] Paris in its people will always be renewed: "We too will begin perpetually every morning."[49]

This gesture toward France through Paris is more daring still: in it, Péguy draws together France's royal and republican histories, knitting them into a whole. It is easy for an anglophone, especially an American, reader to

---

46. Charles Péguy, "Notre patrie," *Cahiers* 3, no. 7, in *Oeuvres en prose complètes*, vol. 2 (Paris: Gallimard, 1988), 21–22.

47. Péguy, 23.

48. Péguy, 29.

49. Péguy, 24.

underestimate Péguy's act of creativity here. But as in the last chapter, royalists and republicans—very often Catholics and atheists, respectively—set themselves bitterly against one another.[50] This animosity would eventually see the end of the Concordat between France and the Vatican in 1905. So in its original context, Péguy's invocation of *people* and *king* together, of a people that is king, treats a terrible historical and cultural wound. In a single phrase, he suggests the survival of a single, of a singular, French people, one who need not choose between heritages.

Péguy the poet frequently envisages places through the figures of their saints. With saints there emerges an ineluctable forward movement to Péguy's geographic thinking, an eschatological tenor, which looks forward to that final night that will descend over all of creation. Genevieve, patroness of Paris, appears in a tapestry, and in it I can note several recurrent themes:

> As she had kept the sheep in Nanterre,
> We place her to guard a very different troop,
> The biggest horde where the wolf and the lamb
> Never confused their common misery.
>
> And as she watched every lonely night
> In the farmyard or on the water's edge,
> From the foot of the same willow and the same birch
> Today she watches over this stone monster.
>
> And when the evening comes that will close the day,
> She is the deciduous and the ancient shepherdess,
> Who picks up Paris and all around
>
> Will lead with a firm step and a light hand
> For the last time in the last yard
> The largest flock to the right of the Father.[51]

Péguy first evokes the particularity of Genevieve's original life, imagining her long watches into the night as a shepherdess. He recollects her birthplace

---

50. See Byrnes, *Catholic and French Forever*, 69–84, esp. 85–94.
51. Charles Péguy, "I [Day One]," "La tapisserie de sainte Geneviève et de Jeanne d'Arc," in *Oeuvres poétiques*, 1081.

(Nanterre) and by it alludes to some of the earliest settlements around what would become Paris. The river Seine, which still scythes Paris, appears in a subtlety ("on the water's edge"), and Péguy depicts Genevieve at the foot of a willow that somehow survives into the life of modern Paris, where Genevieve keeps watch over the people of the city, as she had over her sheep. Her gaze looks forward, too, to the end of time, when the place and the people will be guided by Genevieve (who is person and place: shepherdess, "deciduous" like a tree) to God the Father.[52] The saint and the place touch each other and gesture toward a fate that enfolds and surpasses each.

Péguy's geography—this beating heart of an eternal city, Paris, and its eternal people who perpetually begin again; the beating heart of saints and their places—is a memory, a remembering, but it is not mere memory. It is an act of recollection that is reparative in the sense that it is a remembering directed at historical traumas: Jeanne's harrowing and death, the cataclysm between royalism and republicanism, and so on. It is creative because it makes of such traumas a new place of beginning-again. So also, it is concrete; it takes places and people seriously, together, as the concrete sites of living memory. I want to stress how it is a *people in their places, alive now*, who make memory alive, as they are alive, because it is easy slip into a notion where it is the old monuments that do the remembering. But for Péguy, the monuments are meaningless without a living people knitted to their placed-ness, who do the actual work of remembering by beginning again. And Péguy's geography is also an act of hope, because peoples and places outlast their memories, and in two ways: they live through, beyond, great events, to be marked by them forever (as in the Dreyfus affair),[53] and they reach backward to a beginning, to a humanity, lost to memory itself.[54]

There is nevertheless a tragic dimension in places, not least because memory, though rooted in space, always involves loss (of the original). That tragic dimension as a *geography* takes shape in Péguy's critique of the "modern world" (*le monde moderne*). This is a complex conceptual mechanism for Péguy. Rather than reiterating it in its entirety, I want to emphasize that, for Péguy, the modern world is a world fundamentally consumed by memory in a negative sense. It is a deformed memory, a kind of paper memory, that robs the present of its urgency by robbing it of its presence. "Our modern memories," says Péguy, "are only

---

52. An especially evocative version with Jeanne d'Arc: Charles Péguy, "Châteaux de Loire," in *Oeuvres poétiques*, 1131.

53. Cf. Charles Péguy, "Memories of Youth," in *Temporal and Eternal*, 28, 32, 38–39.

54. Cf. Péguy, "Clio I," 109.

ever miserable memories, crumpled and worn-out memories."[55] In the modern world, there is no surrendering action that embraces memory in a way that renders both its presence and its potential for what is new. There is only memory, and pure memory is always dead. And this dead memory unhinges remembering from a living people, unhinges indeed places from their own placed-ness, by applying schemata (like the kilometer) that are "ready-made" and so not at all permeable to the present in its burgeoning potency, to living memory, or to geography.[56]

Péguy thinks a deeply Catholic geography into being: his is a map of (French) places populated by people and, especially, by saints. And these people and saints, like nature, persist in time with a durability that lifts human striving beyond either pure memory (in its pastness) or pure presence (in its contemporaneity). Most of all, this creative and living endurance is made real in the figure of the saint: saints cleave to the world, marking it and also being appropriated by it, so that in their lives, they orient world-and-people toward the eschaton. They, these lives marked by the absolute grace of surrender (like Jeanne d'Arc), enfold the world and are enfolded by it. They are, in their living generosity, a foreshadowing of an absolute and supernatural generosity that is our present and our future—provided we commit today and every day to beginning again.

This saintly enfolding is eucharistic: through the life of the sacraments, by which Christians are supernaturally alive, and through the radical memorial of the Eucharist in particular, by which the living Christ gives life to Christians. In *Portal*, this first sense is envisioned as the living linchpin by which the Word is handed forward in time—not in the sacraments as divorced from human beings but precisely in the sacramental lives of Christians.[57] In *Charity*, the Eucharist conceptually appears as a living body that draws together the temporal parish church and the eternal church.[58]

I might say more formally: the natural is given, is created, by God. Supernaturally given. I observed this in previous chapters, and in the previous section, in the givenness of prayer and of hope and of surrender. And as given, the world, the natural, is that instrument by which we who are natural greet supernatural grace. There is that double *afférence*, the double movement, where grace condescends to nature and where grace prepares nature for its condescension.

55. Péguy, "Conjoined Note," 79.

56. Péguy, 225–30.

57. Cf. Péguy, *Porche du mystère*, 687–93.

58. Cf. Péguy, *Charité*, 448–49, 458–60.

Péguy not only walks that delicate line of double balance, of double movement, but does so by clinging to *places* in the world. He clings to the world (not as an ideal but as) itself. Concretely. In other words, it is not the world *in general* that the Catholic greets, and where the Catholic greets grace; it is the world *in its particulars*. The Catholic, in Péguy's parlance, is the person of the parish.[59]

The Geography of *Ressourcement*

For a second time, it is possible to turn to Péguy's *ressourcement-révolution*, this time from the point of view of his intellectual "geography." Péguy wants to say, with *ressourcement*, that human beings can reach more "deeply" into the roots of their humanity and the roots of the tradition that they share. This resourcing act, the act of the original gesture, results in something genuinely new, a revolution. It alone allows for living memory. And as such, it manages to be *more* human and *more* traditional because it is an enrichment of the past through its originality. In other words, the turning "face" of a revolution, this threatening moment of opposition and overturning, is a recommencement. A *péguyuste* revolution is not a busy deconstruction of the past but a new act where the past really lives, but more deeply, because of the humanizing character of the original gesture.

As a way of connecting Péguy's dual concept to his sense of geography, I want to note how Péguy's efforts here can be conceived of as a move against the excesses of the historical science of his time. "This is one of the capital errors of modern times in the organization of historical work," explains Péguy. "We attribute to methods and instruments—which have their importance, a certain importance, but an entirely methodical and instrumental importance—a capital importance, and so perfectly total that they must make up for everything."[60] In other words, modern historians expect their methods to supply them with reality, forgetting what Péguy calls "probity" (*probité*). Like Blondel, Péguy notes that historians forget themselves, forget the formation of the person that they are, the activity of that person.[61] *Method* cannot, of itself, guarantee an endeavor's success. Only fidelity to reality can be a guarantee. "The life of the honest man must be," says Péguy, "in this sense, an apostasy and a perpetual renunciation,

59. Péguy, "Conjoined Note," 232–33.
60. Charles Péguy, "De la situation faite à l'histoire et à la sociologie dans les temps modernes," in *Cahiers* 3, no. 8, in *Oeuvres en prose complètes*, 2:486.
61. Cf. Péguy, "De la situation faite à l'histoire," 2:488–89.

the honest man must be a perpetual renegade, the life of the honest man must be in this sense, perpetual infidelity. For the man who wishes to remain faithful to the truth must be incessantly unfaithful to all incessant, successive, indefatigable re-emerging errors. And the man who wants to remain faithful to justice must be incessantly unfaithful to injustices inexhaustibly oppressive."[62] That is, good judgment is not a pure criterion to be written down that can do the work *for* me; rather, it is the effort of a human being who must *make a judgment*. It is a person's devotion to goodness and justice that animates this act of judgment, and it is their actual act of "probity" that makes it real. As Bernard Lonergan says, "It is . . . only by reaching the sustained self-transcendence of the virtuous man that one becomes a good judge, not on this or that human act, but on the whole range of human goodness."[63] So too, for Lonergan, a method is not a set of rules to be followed blindly but a framework for human collaboration that, to be done, must be (after all) done.[64] The modern emphasis on method, in other words, forgets the *place* of judgment, of decision, of attention: the human being. Remember, after all, that living memory requires living people and that it is not remembered by dead stone monuments. Péguy's critique here is in a way more radically anthropological, more thoroughly humanistic than this, since people themselves have their *places*: their places of living memory, which lives on in their aliveness, in their aliveness to where they are as much as when. They are what make monuments alive. And even so, the place that will outlast each person gestures forward to a future that is also a present hope.

Péguy's vision will have to be expanded and deepened, but it provides a foundation for conceiving of the temporal, geographical path of a Christianity that (eucharistically) embeds itself in living places by way of living people, resulting in a conception of a tradition that does not so much conquer spaces as take place in their founding breadth and lift them forward into enrichment. Again, it is not the world in general that Christianity is alive in; it is the world in its particulars, in the "parishes" of its details.

62. Péguy, 2:513.
63. Lonergan, *Method in Theology*, 36.
64. Lonergan, 3–4.

A Christological Revolution of *Ressourcement*

In *Clio*, in the voice of history (Clio is the muse of history), Péguy explains the essential "mechanism" of Christianity. For him, Christianity is eternity "founded" in time. Péguy links this founding to the hope of the original gesture, to continual beginning-again: "For it was always necessary to begin anew. To ensure the multiflowering of a people of saints; if only to make good the losses, stop the leaks, the growing impiety, the incredulity. It was always necessary to begin anew. No degree of eternal foundation alters the fact that the foundation is, in a certain sense, in the world, and eternity, in a sense, in time. Such is my worth, my power and my virtue; I am an indispensable part of the mechanism, in the very organism of eternity."[65] For Péguy, Christianity means the divine redemption of human history.[66] From the start, this divine work orients Christianity "toward" the world and also toward history, even as it orients Christianity toward that which is eternal.[67] The linchpin that holds both orientations together remains history: there, Christians participate in time and eternity both. To *lose* this connecting mechanism is also, then, to lose what it connects.[68]

The axle turns ultimately around Christ himself, the God-man, in whom eternity enters history and founds a new beginning of history. God in Christ, in history, "founds" a participation in his eternity. Péguy describes this as the "incrucification" of all of history through Christ. Christian history, too, is incrucified through the divine beginning-again in the Christian, in a time opened to eternity, in a beginning-again that has a share in God's redemption of history in Christ. "It is the binding," says Péguy, "the eternal, temporal binding, the link, the inlay of the one in the other, that incrucification as it were, which makes Christianity."[69]

Theologians like Lonergan argue that the incarnation is itself a created participation in the eternal life of the Trinity, by way of the hypostatic union. This notion overlaps with Péguy's language of "founding"; in other words, both men attempt to describe how God intervenes in history in the incarnation of the Word and how this intervention has a real, created term—because it is

---

65. Péguy, "Clio I," 91.
66. Cf. Péguy, 155–65.
67. Péguy, 101.
68. Péguy, 115.
69. Péguy, "Conjoined Note," 120.

in creation.[70] For both men, this founding is and remains cruciform, which is how God's action is borne out in Christ's life and in history. Regardless of the theological register, humanity's participation in eternity would also be a created participation in Christ's eternity, and so would be a participation in the cruciformity of his life.

Rendering the incarnation in this more technical, less poetic way allows for a furtherance of *péguyuste* memory and geography. The heart of the theological move here is to describe the incarnation as a "place" of "memory." In one way, I can reiterate Péguy's basic positions: the memory of the past requires the original gesture, which offers to the past, enriched, its essential shape; memory also requires the place of its located-ness, which is "most" alive in the people who occupy a place. This dual reiteration, transposed into theology, would emphasize how the Christian memory of Christ must find, or rediscover, the heart of the Christian mystery, the incarnation, a memory that is to be enriched through the original gesture of Christians in history. And Christian memory must, too, search out the heart of the place and the people of the Christ-memory: Israel. Péguy himself follows these lines of implication in his own work.[71]

But in another way, the precision of a "created participation" in the incarnation (which the incarnation is, and which the incarnation is the instrument of in humanity) allows for still more. For the incarnation is also *God's* unique gesture, one that recollects and enriches the past (of Israel, of humanity), binding all human activity to the "place" (in time, in space) of the Incarnate One. And this divine action elevates human action to what is beyond it, giving to it that absolute "willingness" that Lonergan and Doran described in chapter 1 and making the law of the cross effective in human action.

All of which brings me to the eucharistic heart of Péguy's thought. The Eucharist, the sacrament of Christ's bodily presence, is that ultimate site of ecclesial prayer-memory, a memory that does not look *backward* to the Christ-event so much as it participates in the total Christ in the prayer of "today." It is the exemplary original gesture of both church and God. So too, it is the site of living tradition, conceived of as an act of being-assimilated to God in

---

70. For an explanation of Lonergan on this topic, see Robert Doran, *The Trinity in History: A Theology of the Divine Missions*, vol. 1, *Missions and Processions* (Toronto: University of Toronto Press, 2012), 40–64.

71. This is a quality of Péguy's thinking often present. For example, see Péguy, *Charité*, 431–44; and Péguy, "Conjoined Note," 65–71.

Christ, bringing about (in Péguy's borrowed parlance) a cocitizenship in that eternal city founded in time. The Eucharist is also a participation in Christ's own "doing," and therefore in Christ's intending, by which I mean the Eucharist is, and makes to be, that Christian orientation toward the world that is so important to Péguy's thinking.

Such an expression of theology, of the Eucharist's "place" in Christianity, is in truth but a beginning. The eschatological commitments of the involved Christians and theologians will determine much of the interpretation. One committed to a more realized or realizable eschatology might focus on the church's ethical commitments, while one with a more futurist bent might focus more on mystical communion with the divine and the saints. These must, in any truly Catholic response, be held together rather than opposed. The keystone that "holds together" these ecclesial and practical tensions is Blondel's "consciousness of Jesus's consciousness," which Péguy simply renders as charity. What I am assembling, a metaphysics tradition, is but the background for further competencies that it does not replace.

For a third and final time, the door opens to a consideration of Péguy's *ressourcement-révolution*. At one angle, all of the "natural" mechanisms for Péguy's *ressourcement* remain in place: human activity, which bears the mediation of tradition, is perfectible. By an act of recommencing in the present, what is living in the past can be brought to new fruition, resulting in a "deeper," a revolutionized, humanity and tradition. These *péguyuste* principles can be applied to sacred tradition, most of all in the "original gesture" (today) of the Eucharist, which is primarily God's action. What this means is that a turn to the "sources" or "resources" of tradition also involves itself in the purifying act of commencing today. Péguy's rejection of pure reiteration allows instead for "deepening" or development. There are, however, two further angles of insight, resulting in three dimensions.

The first is that the principle of *ressourcement*, together with revolution, is, in Christian tradition, a part of the larger means by which a supernatural act—the triune God's self-revelation in the incarnation—is preserved, and yet "preserved" only (and precisely) in the manner that human action itself remains effective: by its continuation, which is subject to perfection. Now God's own acting is absolutely perfect (and absolutely supernatural) in the exact sense that it is not perfectible. I will return to this in a moment. However, the human action that is the subject of God's action in the incarnation and redemption *is* perfectible, and it is what-is-being-perfected—indeed in ways not available to human action as such. So there is a doubling: human action's native changeability is the (divine) instrument of its transformation, that which God acts upon; that transformation brings about a radical "willingness" (Lonergan) that involves human action in supernatural perfection, by which I mean human action is made perfect and beyond-perfect (with respect to itself) by God. Here I can repeat Blondel's dictum: to change is salvation, and to remain the same is condemnation. *Ressourcement*, then, becomes an act of further assimilation to divine supra-action. Tradition is *one* quality of assimilation, one aspect of human cooperation, and here I emphasize the human cooperation with "divine things."

We, in our very temporality, participate in the working-out of eternity in time. History, says Péguy, "cannot commit anything temporally which is not inserted, physically as it were, into the body of God himself."[72] Our humble temporality is perfected, not destroyed, in the natural action of a tradition that bears the supernatural. At the same time, the eternal, the supernatural, is also beyond us, requiring our elevation, which is achieved by God. Nature, in order to bear the supernatural, requires the absolutely supernatural gift of grace. So we bear up our temporal measure, and we cooperate with God in history, but also God himself is the primary actor, the supernatural fulcrum of Christian tradition's natural-supernatural operation, of its mediating between eternity and temporality. It is not possible, in other words, to understand Christian tradition without understanding it to be, in its own way, a *réalité intégrale*.

As I have said, the triune God's supernatural action in Christ, the "total" action of incarnation, also acts upon the human action under question. By "supernatural action in Christ," I mean more than that supernatural assistance that is latent in all human action, making it effective (though of course I also mean this). In Christ, divine action does the work of assimilating human action to itself—that is, God is the primary actor, making possible and effective all human participation. This divine action is absolutely supernatural. To participate in it requires God. And there is again a doubling: grace precedes and effects human cooperation in the divine act (of redemption and salvation), since such cooperation is unavailable to human action as such; God acts in all our cooperative acting, providentially and really "securing" the supernatural work of the incarnation in our own work. It is not possible, in other words, to follow Blondel's principle that one must know the "reason why" the church acts in some way, nor is it possible to "deepen" tradition through Péguy's revolutionary resourcing, unless this knowing and deepening is elevated to the level of that which it considers and cooperates with: the supernatural. I mean, in a technical

---

72. Péguy, "Conjoined Note," 119.

way, that the church, for all its human instruments, requires the faith that the Spirit gives. "For the Spirit scrutinizes everything, even the depths of God" (1 Cor 2:10 NABRE).

By way of summary and closing, these are the three dimensions of the integral reality that I have articulated here: (1) our humanity, and so that human reality, tradition, is God's instrument for God's action; (2) our humanity, our being-us, and so tradition, is also a cooperation with divine action; and (3) that cooperation requires divine action to be so. This is—if I turn away from Blondel and back to Péguy—Péguy's unity of the "carnal" and the "spiritual," the "temporal" and the "eternal."[73]

Another Revolution of *Ressourcement*

I turn now to that puzzle of Christian action's entanglement with the problems of colonialism and race. Though I did not yet have a way of saying so until this chapter, each act of turning to this problem in each previous chapter has been an act of recommencement and so, in a very precise way, a *ressourcement* such that the various figures under consideration and their ideas might be made more perfect, might endure revolution. In this section, it will not be possible for me to refigure every thematic aspect of Péguy or every previous theme from every previous chapter. An essential shape, a foundational *Gestalt*, is the goal in what is next such that it can be carried forward into the next chapter.

Charles Péguy's thought is, I think, suggestive of a way into the problem of race and colonialism that is neither pure fatalism nor Christianity triumphant. But in an encounter with people like Copeland and Jennings, especially on the order of space (place) and race, Péguy emerges first with a notable ambiguity. I cannot but mark this ambiguity as a first measure of engagement.

There is, for example, the matter of Péguy's explicit relationship to colonialism, which shifts over time. Though early in his writing career, he appears as a critic of the French colonial situation, this position shifts into outright support of France as a colonial power.[74] Nor is his early critique of colonialism anything like a rejection of French interests in, for example, Africa. "Before his conversion

73. Here I refer to a theme prevalent especially in Péguy's *Porche du mystère* and "Clio I," repeated often throughout both works. For example, Péguy, "Clio I," 111–15.
74. This turn is decisive by the time of his later career. For example, see references in Péguy, "Clio I," 85.

to nationalism," explains Achille Mbembe, "Charles Péguy published exposés on the conditions in the two Congos in his *Cahiers de la Quinzaine*. But he called for reform, not for the abandonment of the civilizing mission."[75] Indeed, after his shift toward nationalism, Péguy tends to take up the French colonial rhetoric common since at least France's First Republic: France has a universal mission to give freedom to the world.[76] Though Matthew Maguire unhooks Péguy from the worst iterations of national paternalism, nevertheless a shadow falls across the historical Péguy, one where he is under the sway of ideas that this present text, my own, seeks to respond to, rendering Péguy's contribution ambivalent.[77] Blondel and Lonergan share in this ambivalent shadow, since they share a Western tradition with Péguy, but Péguy's political turn and wandering topical frame of reference involves him more concretely in the colonial ambitions of France.

There is more. Péguy's reinforcement of colonial themes follows him into his geographic thinking. Other than references to the Roman Empire, a complexity in Péguy for which I have not the space, Péguy has almost no thought for geographies outside of mainland France. His geographic spaces are those of "l'Hexagon," a solipsism common to French colonial and racial evocations.[78] So too, his central exaltation of Paris not only does the work of concealing other parts of the mainland but also, and more relevantly, reiterates colonial exaltations of the French "métropole" (i.e., mainland France) over against Indigenous ways of being.[79] I am saying that Péguy reinscribes the shape of the French

75. Mbembe, *Critique of Black Reason*, 76.

76. For an iteration in Péguy, see Péguy, "Conjoined Note," 118; for historical background, see Laurent Dubois, "Republican Anti-racism and Racism: A Caribbean Genealogy," in *Race in France: Interdisciplinary Perspectives on the Politics of Difference*, ed. Herrick Chapman and Laura L. Frader (New York: Berghahn Books, 2004), 23–35; and Nicolas Bancel and Pascal Blanchard, "The Republican Origins of the Colonial Fracture," in *The Colonial Legacy in France: Fracture, Rupture, and Apartheid*, ed. Nicolas Bancel, Pascal Blanchard, and Dominic Thomas (Bloomington: Indiana University Press, 2017), 43–52.

77. See Matthew Maguire, *Carnal Spirit: The Revolutions of Charles Péguy* (Philadelphia: University of Pennsylvania Press, 2019), esp. 1–24, 164–75.

78. See Trica Danielle Keaton, T. Denean Sharpley-Whiting, and Tyler Stovall, eds., *Black France / France Noire: The History and Politics of Blackness* (Durham, NC: Duke University Press, 2012).

79. Cf. Frantz Fanon, *Black Skin, White Masks*, trans. Charles Lam Markmann (London: Pluto, 1986), esp. 8–27. But more pertinently, there is Achille Mbembe, "Proximity without Reciprocity," in Mbembe, *Out of the Dark Night*, 100: "To a large extent, the phraseology of universalism [in France] has always acted as a screen for the ideology of nationalism and its centralizing cultural model: Parisianism."

colonial empire in his geography, whether consciously or not. A turn to Jennings on theological, colonial, and racial transformations of space cannot but make this a crisis that Péguy's thinking must undergo, not only such that he is made to contribute to the puzzle of colonialism and race in this, my present text, but also so that he himself receives a rethinking in the same horizon. That is to say: there must be a beginning-again with Péguy, here in this chapter, rather than a pure repetition.

Finally, there is the matter of Péguy's use of the word *race*, a theme unexplored in my work thus far but notable in the context of turning to race and racism. *Race* has a broader meaning in French than its version in English and can be translated variously as "type," "culture," "ancestry," "people," "tradition," and "race."[80] Alain Finkielkraut stresses that Péguy does not use the term to mean something like phenotypical characteristics or the broader racialized language of the time: "[There is] no racism, however, in his conception of race. But [it is] on the model which is now familiar to us of a commitment, an inscription, or, better still, a 'rooting' [*racination*] of the spiritual in the temporal, a definition of France as a 'great nation of hospitality.' When Péguy speaks of race, he is not designating a physical category or the hereditary traits of a collective entity, he is affirming the intimate connection of a people of an idea. [An] intimate and fragile bond."[81] But Finkielkraut is not at all the best interpreter of the problem of race in France.[82] And it is too much to expect Péguy's way of speaking here to escape its own context ("no racism") given racism's prevalence and intensity in the late nineteenth and early twentieth centuries, and not least because Péguy engages in a debate over human lineages *against* the explicitly anti-Semitic Charles Maurras.[83] The irony of Péguy's insistence

---

80. Note 24 in Charles Péguy, *Note on Bergson and the Bergsonian Philosophy*, in *Notes on Bergson and Descartes: Philosophy, Christianity, and Modernity in Contestation*, trans Bruce K. Ward (Eugene, OR: Cascade, 2019), 46. The translated text also notes the work of Alain Finkeilkraut (for more, see my subsequent discussion).

81. Alain Finkielkraut, *Le mécontemporain: Péguy, lecteur du monde moderne* (Paris: Gallimard, 1991), 94–95 (translation mine).

82. See the discussion of some of Finkielkraut's remarks in Achille Mbembe, "The Long French Imperial Winter," in Mbembe, *Out of the Dark Night*, 140–41. Mbembe cites an interview with Finkielkraut from 2005, in which he displays profound aversion to racial others, specifically French Arabs, and considers French racism to be a myth. Finkeilkraut has since contributed other troubled readings of the French contemporary situation with respect to a number of matters, including race.

83. As Finkielkraut himself mentions in *Le mécontemporain*, 95.

on the "hospitality" of a France with a colonial empire is, for example, not to be lost. So even if *Péguy* means no such thing as *race* by "race"—itself a difficult claim that requires knowing the mind of a dead man to prove—it is impossible to ignore the valence of France's actual situation and that of Péguy's contemporaries, and so it is impossible to avoid how Péguy must again undergo a crisis regarding this theme too.

One of the present tasks of this present book is, after all, to bring the problem of race and colonialism to its various twentieth-century Catholic interlocutors, an endeavor worked out through the lights of other, fellow interlocutors. And one of the themes of the Catholic encounter with historicity in the nineteenth and twentieth centuries, even before the turn to the realities of colonialism is made, is that the time and place of ideas matter, to their nobility and ignobility. We are, then, also confronted with the facts of a Christian tradition caught up in the colonial project. What I mean is that theological responsibility requires historical understanding, even as such understanding complicates theological responsibility. So something like a *ressourcement* and *révolution* of Péguy himself takes place next, achieved centrally through the thinking of Willie Jennings and Shawn Copeland.

I want to begin by returning to an idea surfaced in the last chapter, which is Willie Jennings's argument that one of the central elements of colonialism, and of Christian theology's involvement in colonialism, is the rearrangement of space. By this, Jennings means something quite literal: Europeans traveled to new places, renamed them, rearranged them, and brought new people to them. But Jennings also means that the relationship between people and land underwent transformation. People were detached from their land, constrained to their bodies as their "identity," as the European body underwent a universalization into that which is intended for all land in the world. In this last movement, the universality and flexibility of the gospel, according to Jennings, is identified with European bodies, a displacement presaged by the church's replacement of Israel. This, then, is the heart of whiteness: not in a personal attitude (though it involves this) but in a radical theological reorientation that is also a practical transformation. "At the foundation of our current racial order," explains Erin Kidd, "is therefore a theological distortion of the relationship between identity and place, founded on a misunderstanding of God's love of creation, the election of Israel, and the incarnation of Jesus of Nazareth."[84] Here is a

84. Erin Kidd, "The Scaffolding of Whiteness: Race and Place in the Christian Imagination," in *You Say You Want a Revolution? 1968–2018 in Theological Perspective*, ed. Susie Paulik Babka, Elena Procario-Foley, and Sandra Yocum (New York: Orbis, 2019), 17.

profound collision between human thought and action such that Christian doctrine, which for Blondel has its heart in Christian practice, funds a new Christian "doctrine" and "practice," a colonial, racial doctrine and practice. Both are entwined so intimately that it is difficult, historically speaking, to surface which emerged first: the Christian practice of racialization or its rationalization.

While relying on Jennings, Kidd emphasizes how human cognitive development and activity participate in a "loop" with the physical spaces that surround a person, informing thought and also being-informed by thought. This makes the organization of persons and space, and the way people think about their spaces, an important and difficult matter.[85] Colonial legacies live on, for example, in de facto segregated spaces.[86] For Kidd, such dynamics underline the complexity and vastness of modern racialized existence. "The well-worn ruts of our colonial history continue to direct us," she argues, "so that awareness of and resistance to racism require not just engaging with our past, or our embodied habits, or our entrenched social structures, but also with the environment's role on our cognition."[87] Thus, the colonial separation of humanity into "white" and "Black" along the racial scale is physical in a double sense, treating bodies and places. This involves *places* in racism not only as relics of past action but also as active interpreting guides for present human thinking and action. Monuments come alive in a living people.

Jennings implicates Christianity and Christian theology in the actions of race and racism. For him, Christian theology and its educational institutions emphasize white, male possession of knowledge as its central arc.[88] This is a reiteration of a familiar theme, one where Christianity and whiteness are rendered identical to each other.[89] Herein is Christianity's sin and responsibility for Jennings, a situation that is not only ideological but also practical.[90] The pinpoint of this crisis, at the end of last chapter, was in whether Christian tradition is implicated in its own history to such a degree that it is capable of nothing else. Tradition's immense power of reiteration, in other words, would here be a kind of permanent condemnation. Jennings himself expresses doubts

85. Cf. Kidd, 18–21.

86. See, for example, Kidd, 20.

87. Kidd, 23.

88. Willie James Jennings, *After Whiteness: An Education in Belonging* (Grand Rapids, MI: Eerdmans, 2020), 29–32.

89. Jennings, 19–20.

90. Jennings, 37.

about tradition's ability to iterate anything but a "white" and "privatized" "property."[91] It is a doubt about tradition that, again, not only references *ideas* but also includes the spaces and places of the world.

I do not want to move to Péguy quite yet. First, I want to consider some of Shawn Copeland's other, as yet unexplored insights. In several works, Copeland performs a complex mode of resourcing while confronting the troubled historical entanglements of Christian tradition. In one such gesture, Copeland emphasizes the discovery of a concealed history: that of Black Catholics in America, a lengthy and layered history forgotten (and never really expressed) under the banners of Spanish Catholicism and Catholic European immigration. She highlights the work of Cyprian Davis in this regard.[92] This is a kind of resurrection of memory, a discovery and cherishing of its lost fragments, however fragmentary.

At the same time, Copeland rearticulates the nature of Christian tradition by examining theology's early structure and noting its transformation over time. "During its first thousand years," she explains, "Christian theology was international and *catholic*, intercultural and pluriform, and included contributions by women. But, increasingly Christian thinkers and clerics isolated, metaphorized, and contemptibly enclosed Christianity's Semitic origins within the Vulgate; pruned its African and Syriac roots; and conjoined (perhaps, better, subordinated) its identity, nearly exhaustively, almost exclusively to Greco-Roman culture and philosophy."[93] This timeline is compound, involving more than one operating shift, and Copeland compounds it further with the advent of colonialism and modernity (together) as a yet more radical reconfiguration of theology and tradition. What is notable from Copeland, for my present purposes, is not so much the exact timeline as the dual action of her argument: she concretely describes what theology has been such that it might be so, and concretely describes what theology has been such that it might avoid being so. Copeland says, "Uncritical acceptance of the paradigm of Christianity as a purely European reality has had grave consequences for theology, for Christian believers, and for peoples pushed either to the periphery or beyond the boundaries."[94]

---

91. See Jennings, "New Winds," 452–53; also cited in the last chapter.

92. See M. Shawn Copeland, "Building Up a Household of Faith: Dom Cyprian Davis, O.S.B, and the Work of History," *U.S. Catholic Historian* 28, no. 1 (2010): 53–63.

93. Copeland, "Turning Theology," 756.

94. Copeland, 762.

There is a further, more theoretical turn in Copeland's methodical retrieving of Christian tradition. She calls for what she names "anamnestic solidarity."[95] Solidarity here invokes that absolute human being-together from the first chapter. Copeland interprets it as a "realization of the very meaning of humanness," one that recognizes the other as other. Solidarity links human beings to one another not only by way of a common humanity but also by way of active regard for the uniqueness of human persons, in a furtherance of human being-together. And the term *anamnesis* specifically has to do with remembering. Copeland's solidaric rendering of the term means that the "memory" in question is a memory of the "victims of history," which is in part a response to history, an explicit move toward justice where there has been injustice. At one level, anamnestic solidarity is a more technical outworking of Copeland's earlier insights relying on Cyprian Davis, as well as an expansion of her work as reviewed in chapter 1: there is, in the ways that we discuss human action, a concealing of the full range of that action—restricting it to victors, to (white) central actors, to various narratives. Copeland asks for a narrative consideration of human action that is closer to its actual reality, one that includes *every* human actor. This is not a *supplement* to "regular" history but an essential pivot toward the real as such. Finally, anamnestic solidarity's valuing of the "other," of the person, also commands a participation in justice, a preference for making-right by making central what colonial whiteness by its nature leaves out. I will repeat that Copeland here has eyes, as in chapter 1, for those who have been historically oppressed.

Copeland's anamnestic solidarity, which she considers a part of the turn to persons, is an articulation of a quality of Christian tradition, not by absolutely mimicking this or that trait in a place or time—though she garners concrete instances—but by making a judgment about the value and meaning of the gospel, as lived by Christians, and then reflecting that judgment. If, for Péguy and Blondel and Lonergan, human action is in some way "more than" its pure facticity, then it has to be engaged as "more than." Its meaning and value as enacted have to be confronted. Here Copeland does so by indicating meanings and values that can serve for judgments about what was or is the case, so that a twofold transformation can take place: concrete Christian existence can be judged (by which I mean affirmed or denied as Christic), and therefore, certain modes of that tradition can be elevated/reclaimed/revisited, so that concrete Christian existence can be expanded and better hewn to the real (of what was,

95. Copeland, 772.

and is, of human action and God's action) by adhering to the concrete goods of greater authenticity.

I want to highlight a theme in Lonergan that is operating underneath here, which in turn recollects one of the themes of Péguy's *ressourcement-révolution*. In the essay "The Origins of Christian Realism (1961)," Lonergan argues that for Christians, the real is the truly affirmed. That is, the real is that which is judged to be the case. The root of Lonergan's claim is the meaning of *homoousios* in the Nicene Creed, which says that the Son is "one and the same substance" with the Father. Lonergan explains, "When you take the real as what is known by a true affirmation, then the Son is God if you affirm the same things about the Son as about the Father."[96] Reality, in other words, is the truly affirmed. And true affirmation hearkens back to Péguy's claim that the "honest man" must be a "perpetual renegade"—perpetually adhering to justice not by way of pure method (as in the historical sciences of his day) but by way of judgment—and for him, judgment must be ever-again achieved, in a person of *probité*. In other words, the justice of one instance does not guarantee the next; justice has to be discovered and adhered to again and again, just as true affirmation must. *Probité* supports the logic of Péguy's "original gesture," the strenuous achievement only of today, which alone can preserve the past by beginning-again, an act that enriches the past. In other words, *ressourcement* in the truest sense is a purification; rather than merely receiving what was, it breaks into the reason-why (Blondel) of human action. *Ressourcement* intends with the same intention of this action, intending a noncontradictory affirmation, an intention that can only be recaptured, as it were, in a fresh affirmation. This freshness brings about a "deeper" tradition and a "deeper" humanity—which is to say, it brings about a revolution.

So Copeland's anamnestic solidarity functions as a mode of *ressourcement* in at least two ways. On the one hand, it is a response to a present situation, one where the real scope of human action is dramatically narrowed and misunderstood to be basically identical to "white" and/or "European" action. It is a move toward justice in response to an unjust error about reality, and it is *also* an affirmation of the reality of nonwhite action. As an affirmation of reality, however, it is a recapitulation of what Christians understand reality to be, which is the truly affirmed. Péguy, for his part, is keen for a Christian charity that embraces the permanently lost, the "damned dead." And Riquier underlines

96. Bernard Lonergan, "The Origins of Christian Realism (1961)," in *Philosophical and Theological Papers*, 91.

how Péguy includes in this group anyone left outside of anything. Copeland lifts the victims of history into this sort of charity. But Copeland also radicalizes and concretizes such a charity, purifying it, by taking into account the reductive and myopic effects of colonization and racialization, which Péguy in his own context only partially grasped in his opposition to anti-Semitism. In Copeland, *ressourcement* undergoes its own revolution.

This model of *ressourcement*, the sort that integrates Péguy's and Copeland's insights, serves as a first and important clarification of the crisis of Christian tradition's entanglement in colonialism. In the last chapters and in this one, I observed Jennings's concerns that such an entanglement prevents Christian tradition from doing anything but repeating its troubled gestures. Tradition's self-repetition here dooms it. And surely it is possible to say, in a play on Péguy himself, that a "modern" tradition, a tradition of worn-out memory, is something like a hollow repetition of yesterday, one that robs today of its potency and dooms it. Or we might say that pure repetition, of whatever sort, dislocates the present by placing it in the past. Regardless of the description, the *fatum* is the same: there is no opening for grace or change, and past actions are reinstated even if in different clothing. But this situation is itself only a partial description of tradition's situation, of the integral reality it partakes of.

The response I might be tempted to offer here is that tradition, non-"modern" tradition, humane or humanizing tradition, is not repetition, not in Péguy's sense. It is beginning-again. So Christian tradition "truly" cannot be the iron playing out of only what it has been. But though I will say this, I have not yet earned its saying. First, there is the matter of a clarification by way of Blondel, Copeland, Lonergan, and Péguy together. And here I want to be clear that I am not so much correcting Jennings, who has his own methods of responding to this problem of a tradition trapped in its sinful repetition, as I am applying a broadly Catholic pattern to the problem. For the fundamental situation of human tradition is not that of container and contained (Péguy might indict the "ready-made" here), nor is it that of historical or material facticity alone. Not if the real is the truly affirmed.

One temptation, when trying to wrest tradition from the perspicacity of Jennings's concerns, is to imagine a pure silver vein hidden in stone: a pure set of ideas, or actions, or writings, that escape accusation (in their meaning, or intention, or status). But this is to imagine a soul without a body. It is to say, if I recall Blondel, that the truth is not related to the facts (of history). Against such a conception of tradition, it is necessary to argue that tradition is not a box that holds the truth, which might be variously extracted or reboxed. And still another temptation, which Jennings himself pushes against, is to turn to despair—a despair where the past is found in the present inevitably, in a renewed application of historical determinism (what happened was all that could happen because it happened).[97] In this model, the facts are all that there is, or all that there will be. Tradition contains nothing distinguishable from itself—it is all and only "boxes," facts, history. This model, too, is a problem.

Péguy is correct: we will not have purity except arduously. And Blondel's *réalité intégrale* urges us not to understand God as other than everywhere in this struggle, as its supernatural principle, as present by a double *afférence*, as the ultimate intelligibility of our reason as it makes its judgments. An undifferentiated notion of human reality threatens always a self-contradictory rupture of the world, one where truth and goodness are assured, not in the mind that must ask and answer questions, but by God's own presence, conceived of "out-there." In this way, the triune God's unwavering commitment to the church supplies the beleaguered justification of any ecclesial action at all, or—in a reversal that admits the same premise—God is present in and to the truly just alone and not present in and to others (e.g., to the conquerors).[98] Thus vanishes the necessary and explanatory complexity of Augustine's phrase "You [Lord] were with me, and I was not with you."[99] Thus too vanishes the sharp-toothed irony of James Baldwin, who says that the Black Christians he grew up with "were no more 'simple' or 'spontaneous' or 'Christian' than anybody else—who were merely more oppressed."[100] Finally, fundamentally, there now vanishes what Baldwin loves in jazz and the blues: "Something tart and ironic, authoritative and double-edged."[101] Baldwin will speak at length in the next chapter.

97. Jennings, *After Whiteness*, 10.

98. Justifications of colonialism run something like the first use of the premise, and every such justification is grotesque. But its inversion is available too: "Rather than pointing to God's presence, [Peter] Claver's sainthood in fact reveals where God was absent," writes Katie Walker Grimes in *Fugitive Saints: Catholicism and the Politics of Slavery* (Minneapolis: Fortress, 2017), 107. Grimes, I think, desires to judge Claver's actions as immoral. Especially in their character as coercive, which Grimes emphasizes, they are. But notice that God's presence and the morality of human actions are, in this sentence, identical. What is grotesque in such a claim is "merely" this: that the God-man who became sin for our sake revokes his solidarity with the sinner, abandoning them to his "absence."

99. Augustine, *Confessions*, trans. Henry Chadwick (New York: Oxford University Press, 1991), 201.

100. James Baldwin, "The Fire Next Time," in *Collected Essays*, ed. Toni Morrison (New York: Literary Classics of the United States, 1998), 310.

101. Baldwin, 311.

My adherence to Augustinian complexity, my reverence for Baldwin's reverence, takes the shape of judgment. To call a deed just or unjust is to make an affirmation or denial about its value, or lack thereof. It is a judgment *about* the facts. So also tradition, as "consciousness of Jesus's consciousness," affirms the truth of Jesus's own self-understanding by way of its own particular, concrete self-understanding. At the level of pure facticity, I have argued, tradition suffers the ambiguities of the human action that it is a part of, and in turn Christian action renders Christian tradition ambiguous, for Christians are and have been both martyrs and fiends—even in the intimate horizon of one individual. But it is necessary also to judge such action, to judge its goodness and truth or their lack. In Christian tradition, the truth of Jesus, by which I mean the truth of Jesus's self-understanding, forms the measure of the facts and their relationship (or nonrelationship) to truth and goodness. This is a truth, ultimately a reality, that is only ever mediated; Christians do not know it as if they *are* Christ. So I am saying that the reality of Jesus is who he affirms himself to be and that it is a reality that Christians affirm as it is mediated to them in the concreteness of their history. Christian tradition, in this more constrained sense, mediates a judgment *about* the facts.

What this means is that Christian truth, and so also Christian tradition, is only ever discoverable in its concreteness (the martyrs and the fiends). But this also means that Christian tradition, because it facilitates a judgment about the facts, is not only its own concreteness. Maintaining both insights at once is the difficulty, at one level. At another level, the principle of *ressourcement* demands a furtherance. What can be begun-again is not the deed that is past but its truth, and not by way of pure repetition but in reapprehension, in *probité*, in a fresh judgment made in today's concreteness. For Copeland, such reapprehension requires the movement toward justice as much as it does affirmation. For Péguy, Christian innocence, like Christian truth, is not a thing returned to; it is the arduously purified. We might say *ecclesia semper reformanda est* (the church must always be reformed).

At the same time, it is important to recall a principle from my earlier reflections in this chapter, which had to do with the multiple angles, the three dimensions, in which Christian tradition can be understood. There is not only the horizon in which human action cooperates with God's action—for example, the act of beginning-again that actively constitutes Christian tradition; there is also that horizon where God is understood to be the primary actor, the one who appropriates human action to divine action in the church. Human beings are not the only, or indeed the primary, guarantors of Christian tradition's fidelity to Christian truth. God is. This divine work is especially attributed to the Holy Spirit. All the same, the *means* of this divine work remain that of human action. As human, this ecclesial action is not rescued from its various ambiguities, especially at the level of individuals. But God also will not abandon the church, in an indefectibility that is corporate.[102] Which is to say, though the church is preserved in its relationship to the Holy Spirit by the Holy Spirit, the church is not preserved from the risks of human endeavor.

The Eucharist, under this horizon, is that absolute act of beginning-again guaranteed and made effective by God and participated in by the church. It is sacramental anamnesis or remembering, a perfect share in the presence of the "total Christ" and, as such, is not at all a reiterative remembering but is each day the original memory itself. The Eucharist is the sacrament of the church, of what God makes the church to be: a living memory for a living tradition, a judgment about who Jesus is that is alive in Christian practice.[103] Again, this is not a guarantee of all Christian action. It is, however, a sign of God's guarantee to be with the church. And God's being-with the church is also a call for Christian being-with, for Christian solidarity. Here Copeland reminds us of a turn that Péguy also effects: the Eucharist asks Christians to commit themselves in solidarity with the oppressed, a group that has concretely, historically included people of color. In this respect, God's eucharistic presence can also be a judgment of the world order and of Christians. For Copeland, all the sacraments "pose an order, a counter-imagination, not only to society but also to any ecclesial instantiation that would substitute itself for the body of Christ."[104] In the Eucharist, in a presence that is *more* than its social or ethical implications, Copeland finds that ultimate meaning and value, that ultimate Someone, that allows a dialectical stance toward tradition (enabling affirmation and denial, that turning face) and that urges tradition's deepening (through *ressourcement-révolution*).[105]

At last, it is possible to arrive at the puzzle of colonial spaces, or racialized geographies, which so often are spaces that Christianity has made and makes to be. There is a type of eucharistic pivot that avoids the question of physical spaces, elevating Christian togetherness "above" them. But Jennings and Copeland in their separate ways demand otherwise. Christians must respond with a

---

102. Special thanks to Jakob Rinderknecht for pointing out this notion to me and helping me fit it together with *ressourcement*.

103. Cf. *Lumen Gentium* §10–11.

104. Copeland, *Enfleshing Freedom*, 125.

105. Copeland, 128.

eucharistic conception of bodies and spaces that is differently ordered. If, similarly, Christianity is animated by the eucharistic call to solidarity, then this must also be a solidarity of spaces. Indeed, Péguy, with his Catholic of the parish, points in this other direction too. The question, in other words, is now this: How is a Christian understanding of tradition to countenance not just the world in general but the world in its particulars; how is it to confront not just bodies but also spaces; how is it to face up to the concreteness of a history that has radically rearranged the world's spaces, and the peoples in them?

Such questions anticipate in themselves the pathway toward non-"modern" geography. And since I am working within a metaphysic of tradition, my answer is more heuristic than descriptive. To begin the heuristic, I want to look toward where the chapter also began, which is with the vertical moment of a prayer that confronts the tragic and the irretrievable: when Jeanne d'Arc recalls the home that she will not see again. Now I can bend this moment to embrace a different but not opposite devastation, the one where peoples were torn from the places and spaces they lived in, taking part (willingly or not) in the radical rearrangement of the world. Here Jennings emphasizes fragments. "It is life formed in fragment," he explains, "in memory of loss and in loss of memory."[106] With the advent of modern colonialism, entire ways of life were shattered into pieces in successive phases, leaving only fragments of what was. Jennings underlines that some things *are* remembered ("precious saving work") and that other things are permanently gone. So here is not only Péguy's pattern of the loss of the original, of the first moment; here is a type of violence, one where resourcing gestures are mangled or prevented entirely. Instead of this, Jennings wants a world where fragments are allowed to "touch" one another, where there is allowed a "play" between pieces. What prevents this kind of play is the totalizing act, either in the performance of white self-sufficiency or in jealous guardianship of fragments.[107]

Jeanne d'Arc's prayer enters into this tragic and potent situation with two parallel movements. There is, first, the *recognition* of loss. The elevation of the tragedy into words, words that can only be garnered from the fragments themselves, in a movement of self-transcendence that is also a movement toward the real, reality. In Péguy's geographical thought, the lives of the saints leave a permanent imprint, a piece of a memory, in a place, in the very topographical shape of a place. So the prayer of recognition, applied to the colonial situation,

---

106. Jennings, *After Whiteness*, 35.
107. Jennings, 39–40.

would have to actively unearth the fragmentary touches of the peoples who have occupied a place. Here Copeland adds a feature: these memories of places need to include the victims of history.

But such recoveries do not eliminate the tragedy; Jeanne still never returns home. History has in it the unrecoverability of yesterday. So there must be a second movement, an act of charity, where loss is elevated into the hands of God. What I mean by this is less *resignation* and more *refiguration*, an act where the "welling up" of the present makes its request, asking not what was but what will be. "Chattel slavery, lynching, and segregation," says Copeland, "are part of American Catholic history, but their continued extension in contemporary racist behavior need not be."[108] In other words, the present is not inevitably the past. But for this to be so requires that radical act of charity that would embrace *all* of humanity, especially the lost ones, thereby restoring the elemental reality of human solidarity by way of a new, supernatural solidarity, the mystical body of Christ, in an absolute willingness that comes from God alone.

The extension of this logic for Christians would involve a turn to the preferential option for the poor and simultaneously to the law of the cross: the oppressed take up the center of attention, and good is exchanged for evil. What I want to do, though, is reconsider that prototypical pivot along the lines of Péguy's creative geography. For there is the task, the precious work, not only of the recovery of past fragments but also of their play. This requires a geographical reconception on the level of Péguy's efforts to treat French historical trauma in such a way that the people of France are not forced to choose between their various heritages. So when he imagines that it is the continual "beginning-again" of the French people, rooted in their spaces, that enables them to embrace the full breadth of their own fragments (monarchy, republicanism), he presents us with the possibility for a similar drawing-together of human fragments elsewhere.

Such drawing-together requires at least three elements. There is, of course, the act of beginning-again: the strenuous original gesture, made not individually but communally. Such communal living requires, however, the actual, physical, spatial act of living in landscapes side by side. Being a people made of peoples, together. In contrast to what Frantz Fanon refers to as the "Manichaeism" of the colony, *péguyuste* geography, reconceived under the lights of Jennings and Copeland, enjoins an alternate living-together that is integral,

108. Copeland, "Household of Faith," 62.

treating one of the fundamental traumas of colonial, racial history.[109] Integral living-together requires, finally, the sharing of space in the fullest sense: sharing resources, sharing livelihoods, sharing values and meanings. It requires a new and renewed (Lonergan: an empirical view of) culture that can bear the weight of cultural plurality. As integral, such sharing is both concrete and made; it is a whole made of "many." As shared, it creates new potencies for the original gesture itself, for a resourcing in the present that offers to the past a new and un-thought-of richness.

It is worth wondering where Péguy's christological gestures might be placed in these reflections. I want to hold off on that line of inquiry, however, because it first encounters its own incompleteness: Péguy never quite confronts the trouble of a Christology that is the inverse of his surrendering vision, one where Christology is the instrument of domination. Though he does intimate this trouble, it is Blondel who in the last chapter spells out a concrete version of the crisis in his encounter with *Action française*, and still more do Jennings and Copeland in their articulations of the persons, actions, and ideas that struggle to explain themselves "as" colonialism and race. Rather than resolving the matter in this chapter, I want to shift directions to a fuller response, one that can elevate and reintegrate the insights that a transformed Péguy has offered here. That will be the goal of the next chapter.

Conclusion

In many ways, this chapter has been an elaborate effort to understand Charles Péguy's oft-referenced *ressourcement* in a richer, more complex manner. This complexity has involved an examination of the tragic dimension of Péguy's thought, and an examination of his response with the hope of the "original gesture" made today. It has also involved a reconsideration of Péguy's poetic expressions of memory and of geography, organized in a particular way around Jeanne d'Arc. Lastly, it has reunderstood Péguy in an encounter with the shadows of colonialism and race through the thought of Willie Jennings and Shawn Copeland. So I argued that Péguy's *ressourcement* is always accompanied by a *révolution*, achieved in the newness of today—a twin action that, when confronted with colonialism, endures its own transformation. Now it is to include not only the

109. Cf. Frantz Fanon, *The Wretched of the Earth*, trans. Constance Farrington (New York: Grove, 1991), 40–42.

tragedy of yesterday's loss but also the tragedy of racial refigurations that are both conceptual and physical, and also always enacted by persons. This tragedy receives a response in the act, in the hope, of an original gesture, one conceived of as a gesture of radical solidarity in Christ, effecting a revolution into a deeper tradition and a more human humanity.

Most retrievals of the *ressourcement* concept emphasize a somewhat triumphal attitude or understanding, where the strength and eloquence of the past find their way into the present. This chapter has not refuted that aspect of *ressourcement*, but it has also contributed a less triumphal, indeed a tragic, aspect to the concept. It is, I must stress, an aspect original to Péguy. He meditates on the loss of original innocence and on the deceptive power of pure reiteration. He proposes instead an act of arduous purification in which alone the past can live. I underlined these features to elaborate two lost original "innocences" in a *péguyuste* mode: the loss of Christian innocence in Christian sin (Péguy might more nearly say: the loss of charity) and the loss of every original cultural, societal past in the wake of colonial action. But since Christianity is a religion not of the naive recovery of an original innocence but of arduous purification in Christ, the door is also opened to the bequest that today makes of us, which is to commit to a different sort of originality: the original, the new, gesture. In this gesture, the past lives on as alive, and so as enriched. Similarly, and no less importantly, this enrichment offers itself in hope to the God who makes all things new.

Thus, naive triumph makes way for the reality of failure, and for Christian tradition's sinful involvement in historical evils. The prototypical return to strength and eloquence is accompanied by the turn to the violently fragmented ("precious saving work")—the turn to, most of all, persons. This is not in order to indulge in tragedyism or self-lacerating histrionics but in order to expand the history under question, dilating the gaze of *ressourcement*, so that the human action in consideration is more readily human by more readily embracing *every* human in the perpetual labor of *probité*. In this, theology participates in the hope of widening itself more nearly to the breadth of the saving God (cf. Eph 3:18).

4

DRAMAS

of her falling tower. Oh saints!
As you stand beneath her burning ribs,
bend your ears to the ground
of her travail, and plead her destiny
with the apology of yours.

This chapter is a formal theological organization of the previous three, sustaining its effort by "placing" many of the prior conceptualities into a theological frame. That theological frame is Hans Urs von Balthasar's theological-dramatic theory, which is a theory of history under the lights of theology. Since history is human action, and since this action is meaningful, Balthasar turns to the theater as a method for understanding what it is for human beings to act and also to mean. Thus, the chapter works to understand the major facets of "drama" according to Balthasar, and how his dramatic theory is transposed into theological theory. The central axis of this transposition is the question "Who am I?" which Balthasar asks again through the "I" of the Incarnate Son. This "I" is the "I" that illuminates and reveals the triune God and that illuminates the "personality" of human beings cooperating in the work of the Trinity in history.

The pivot that makes this double revelation possible and historical is the action of Jesus Christ, characterized as obedience. The category of "mission" offers a way to speak of "roles" that are freely given by God and freely appropriated (in action) by the human subject such that this human "I," like Christ's divine-human "I," illuminates both the self and God. Christic en-missioning provides a way to understand the Balthasarian version of Christian tradition as the free "play" of a loving personality, which is to say, self- and divine-expression. Similarly, Christ and especially the kenotic obedience of the cross provide Balthasar a manner of critiquing Christian action and tradition.

The last section of the chapter encounters again the trouble of a Christian tradition caught up in the mire of historical colonialism and the things its action has produced. James Baldwin and Joseph Drexler-Dreis offer means by which to understand the "undersides" of colonialism from the point of view of the marginalized Black subject who, from out of their situation, provides a key for showing Eurocentric and white acting and being for the unreality that they are. Christian tradition here suffers the concreteness of its entanglements. A theo-dramatic construal of Christian tradition's predicament with respect to race both *expands* the instruments of the theo-drama and provides a manner by which to conceive of a hope for renewal, an expansion and a provision founded together on many of the major themes the book has explored thus far: history as human action, human action as "metaphysics in act," and human action as "original gesture." In a Balthasar who exists in the wake of Baldwin in particular, these principles become an expression of a Black "I" that outstrips its Blackness, revealing the inadequacy of race with respect to human subjectivity, and that in love breaks open the possibility of human "I's" that act anew and in whose acting God acts.

Being's Situation

This first volume of Balthasar's *Theo-Logic* is a philosophical and theological reflection on truth as it is existentially confronted in the world.[1] The accent of the text is on truth as an "unveiling" of being, lending to truth both its objective (or universal, generalizable) and its subjective (or experiential) character.[2] Balthasar underlines the "place" of the thinking subject first of all and yet without surrendering truth's objectivity. "Consciousness," Balthasar explains,

---

1. A general exploration of this achievement is not my focus. A helpful study of it can be found in Aidan Nichols, *Balthasar for Thomists* (San Francisco: Ignatius, 2020).

2. Aidan Nicholas has another study, one that focuses on the *Theo-Logic*. See Aidan Nichols, *Say It Is Pentecost: A Guide through Balthasar's Logic* (Washington, DC: Catholic University of America Press, 2001). A more recent guide is Matthew Levering, *The Achievement of Hans Urs von Balthasar: An Introduction to His Trilogy* (Washington, DC: Catholic University of America Press, 2019).

"implies not only the abstract property of being *conscious* but also, with equal immediacy, the reality of *being* conscious, the being of consciousness."[3] So to know oneself as conscious is at once the revelation of an *experience* of being and of *being* itself. In this notion of truth, subjectivity and objectivity inhere in each other. So Balthasar, in an elaboration of the work of his mentor Erich Przywara, articulates a largely Thomistic account of metaphysics that also makes a turn (like we already saw in Bernard Lonergan) toward human consciousness. This double emphasis on subjectivity and objectivity, with its starting point in subjectivity, follows Balthasar into the rest of his trilogy.[4]

For my purposes here, there is an important elaboration of worldly being that Balthasar offers later in *Theo-Logic I*, one that decisively turns its attention to worldly being as *historical*. As with so many thinkers of his generation, the turn to being-as-historical, while it is (still) a turn to being, is also a turn that underlies a central challenge for Catholic thought: the problem of historicity itself, what Balthasar calls the "situation" of being.

Balthasar begins by noticing that in all existent beings, but evermore so as we rise to conscious beings, there is "an interiority that is not completely reducible to any universal."[5] This presents a problem for metaphysics, since metaphysics is a form of reflection that bases itself in abstraction, in the movement from a particular instance of being into a generalized (or abstracted) understanding thereof. Metaphysics is, in Lonergan's sense, "heuristic." But this heuristic does not totally describe the world as we in fact find it to be. (Lonergan: "Metaphysics is the whole in knowledge but not the whole of knowledge.")[6] There is a *particularness* to individuated being that is not generalizable. Most of all, Balthasar notes, free human actions are irreducible to a pure set of heuristics, refusing the generalities of metaphysics and of predictive natural laws. This is because human action is an instance, an instance in time, that is not repeated.

So Balthasar moves to express the *ratio* or reason of individuated being with a method that can "change along with it." This method is what Balthasar refers to as historical science. Nevertheless, individuated being—beings—remain under the lights of both natural science (here including metaphysics) and historical

---

3. Balthasar, *TL* 1:37.

4. Prototypical in this regard is the first volume of *Glory of the Lord*, which sets the stage for repeating its model: "subjective evidence" takes up the first measure, and it is followed by "objective evidence." He explains some of this in Hans Urs von Balthasar, *The Glory of the Lord: A Theological Aesthetics*, vol. 1, *Seeing the Form*, 2nd ed. (San Francisco: Ignatius, 2009), 419–23 (hereafter *GL*).

5. Balthasar, *TL* 1:181.

6. Lonergan, *Insight*, 416. See also the discussion of metaphysics in chapter one of this book.

science, because each being "is" by nature and by history at the same time.[7] By way of this logic, Balthasar acknowledges the role of metaphysics, the role of the natural sciences (especially in their classical forms), and the role of modern historical science all at once while differentiating what it is about "being" that each seeks to understand. In other words, each "science" asks about what-is under different aspects of *how* it is what it is. Balthasar, for his part, strives to develop an account of being that incorporates being-as-generalizable (metaphysics) and being-as-situation (history), taking up an overall vision that is not so much "between" the two as it is stereoscopic, allowing an understanding of being with depth, of being as subject *both* to abstraction *and* to history.

In this way, Balthasar describes how created being becomes. He sketches the matter classically: being comes into existence (into act) according to its essence, and its essence is evermore brought into being by its existence. Things, in other words, at once have a "supratemporal idea" and a "plastic potency." They become by a kind of pattern or idea, but that pattern also changes, or becomes, as they become.[8] Concomitantly with this reflection, Balthasar considers a different quality of creaturely becoming: it is chronological, developmental, taking place over *time*.[9] Indeed, for Aristotle, time is a measurement of change, and in that sense, it is an aspect of becoming. Balthasar travels in a slightly different direction, though, to elaborate a (theological) philosophy of truth in time according to its "positive" and "negative" aspects.

Because of the knowing subject's experience of time, truth acquires a temporal character, which Balthasar calls "presence." It is a movement, a "coming toward" (positively) and a "passing away" (negatively). Being, the truth of being unveiled as presence, is *always just now coming toward us*, says Balthasar, in a movement by which it bears a sense of futurity. Balthasar, following Augustine, rejects a notion of a future that is laid out before us independently of the present; the future is instead a feature or direction *in* the present.[10] Which is to say, being comes to be in the present—heading forward, as it were, toward more being—and this is its quality of futurity: not as an existent line stretching out in front of our feet but as "laid up" in the "toward" of the present. Balthasar calls this future-form of the present "a beginning, a promise, a *hope*." It is possible to invoke Charles Péguy here: the present perpetually "wells up," and hope is the

7. Balthasar, *TL* 1:182.
8. Balthasar, 1:194.
9. Balthasar, 1:195.
10. Balthasar, 1:196–97.

founding virtue of freely responding to the present welling-up of the real; it is hope that surrenders itself forward by beginning again. Yet for both Balthasar and Péguy, this presence of the present, because it is temporal, also takes the shape of passing away. "What you do not seize now," explains Balthasar, "is a lost opportunity that will never return in this form."[11]

For Balthasar, there is a certain dynamic thread that links together truth with decision or action and that therefore links truth and freedom. In a Blondelian frame, this would be the way that we, by our own dynamism and by way of the dynamism of our integral world, are always caught up in action, whether we like it or not. To be confronted with truth in time is not only to be confronted with a judgment of the intellect; it is also to be confronted with something that must be decided about: "What you do not seize now is a lost opportunity." To explain what this means, Balthasar first highlights a subject's "openness" to being (and thus to truth) itself.[12] This fundamental disposition is not an act of the will as such, but it is volitional inasmuch as human nature's basic orientation to being is accompanied by its full spiritual faculties; this accompaniment is not *subsequent* to a subject's awareness but constitutive of the act of consciousness itself. Balthasar elaborates the structure of this openness by pointing out how the *ratio* of intelligence contains in itself an "abiding will" that partakes of the *act* of the unveiling of being. The notion here is resonant with Lonergan's "willingness." And it is not meant to undercut the role of intelligence in knowledge, but it serves to posit knowing as also loving, which again harkens back to Augustine.[13] Balthasar emphasizes that though this abiding volition is constitutive of the essential pattern of human consciousness, it also can be and must be cultivated. He calls this cultivated willing of truth an "attentiveness" and an "attitude of justice" that defers itself to the full unfolding of being's expression of truth.[14] Balthasar stresses that since knowing is also loving, every form of knowing ought to take up the "open" attitude that is the basic disposition of love.

But human knowing is also an implicit or indirect reference to the divine light by which the human intellect knows (as Thomas Aquinas insists).[15] Balthasar draws this implicit feature to the center to *de*center human knowledge

11. Balthasar, 1:197.
12. Balthasar, 1:110.
13. Balthasar, 1:111.
14. Balthasar, 1:112–13.
15. Cf. Thomas Aquinas, *De veritate* 22.2.

and its power: "One finite man has neither the strength nor the authority to lay an absolute claim on another."[16] To act apart from *this* truth is to render one's knowing "Promethean" and despotic.[17] So there is a kind of "ultimate" loving dispossession necessary to responsible human knowing, one that surrenders itself to God and to divine truth, not as something had, but as that ultimate measure that no human being can lay claim to. This attitude of surrender becomes the form of human responsibility toward one another in an act of deference that encourages the unfolding of every truth of every person, each one in a unique way reflective of divine truth.[18]

Much like Péguy, Balthasar's metrical-chronological "ictus" is on the decisiveness of the present moment—"decisive" in the sense of *urgent* and in the sense of requiring *response*; and much of what Péguy has already established in the previous chapter can carry me the rest of the way into the purifying dignity of the original gesture. Furthermore, Balthasar's reliance on Thomas and Augustine, together, embeds the experience of truth in history with a moral character, ascribing to it a decentered, self-transcending love. This love and its disfiguration (Promethean despotism) is important to Balthasar and will be important to me in what follows.

Theological Dramatics

Balthasar's first volume in his *Theo-Drama* is a prologue. It exists in order to establish dramatic "categories," *instrumentarium*, that organize a dramatic theory that can then be transposed into a *theological*-dramatic theory.[19] He is working in an expressly theoretical mode of reflection, providing a higher viewpoint that is able, by way of its heuristic nature, to measure what human drama is without overdetermining its concrete contents.[20] But Balthasar also effects a transposition of his dramatic theory into theology, a move that integrally "keeps" the categories but that also changes them as the horizon of meaning

---

16. Balthasar, *TL* 1:120.

17. See Balthasar, 1:120; cf. 114, 125–30, 211–12, 272 (this last is its thematic conclusion).

18. Balthasar, 1:203.

19. Hans Urs von Balthasar, *Theo-Drama: Theological Dramatic Theory*, vol. 1, *Prolegomena* (San Francisco: Ignatius, 1988), 130 (hereafter *TD*).

20. Cf. Balthasar, 1:15–16.

itself shifts. Therefore, none of the terms that Balthasar uses in the prologue can be deployed in theology univocally.[21]

There is a danger here even this early in the project of allowing dramatic theory to be overdetermined by the drama of the West. And it is entirely the case that Balthasar's central examples, though they contain references to non-Western theater, are Western. But to understand the original Balthasar better and in order to understand a more helpful Balthasar, I think it is important to hold to the *theoretical* shape of his outlined task, which demands a heuristic rather than a descriptive manner of reflection. Though it is probably the case that Balthasar's heuristic is incomplete, it *is* heuristic. And heuristics of themselves cannot cast an apriority, which means that revision occurs as they are applied to various ongoing concrete situations.[22] (I myself provide elements of a concrete situation requiring supplement and critique, though my work will also remain essentially heuristic.)

"Theatre," Balthasar says, "intends to be an interpretation of the world, in its 'unreality' shining a ray of light into the confusion of reality."[23] For Balthasar, this interpretation (really, as many interpretations as there are plays) is by no means straightforward; every "drama" is simply an attempt, a gesture, even if that attempt unveils merely the ambiguity of being.[24] Theater is, whatever its gesture, a confrontation with human action, transforming "the event into a picture that can be seen," and so also creating an existential-aesthetic bridge by which human beings wonder about human meaning, its places, its possibilities, its ruptures, its failures.[25] This is not the same as saying that theater is, itself, a philosophy. It is instead a form of play, an "interplay of relationships," that is necessary and nascent to reflection.

Whatever human beings are, whatever existence might be—here Balthasar foregrounds concepts with attention to theological possibilities—human beings "gesticulate" (to borrow a term that shows up in *Theo-Drama IV*).[26] This gesticulation's ultimate meaning is not self-evident, but the point is that human

---

21. Balthasar, 1:18.

22. Special thanks again to Jonathan Heaps for explaining this to me by way of Bernard Lonergan.

23. Balthasar, *TD* 1:10.

24. He mentions this a number of times. See, for example, the "extreme ambiguity" in Balthasar, 1:265.

25. Balthasar, 1:17.

26. "Existence gesticulates in the face of death, and death is its innermost certainty." Hans Urs von Balthasar, *Theo-Drama: Theological Dramatic Theory*, vol. 4, *The Action* (San Francisco: Ignatius, 1994), 117.

beings do rather helplessly make meaning. So Balthasar argues that "existence itself contains an accompanying reflection that is immanent in it and which the theatrical process only makes more explicit." And like human gesticulations, human theater "exhibits a confusing ambivalence."[27] This linking thread of a human existence that wonders about itself in play and in reality is what Balthasar means by *Welttheater* (world-theater). It is the simple fact that human beings represent themselves to themselves, making a mirror-world through which to see, however dimly, their world.

Theater offers a "tension" in which human life, which is a question for itself, quests after an answer to itself. The actor is that primary location in the world-theater where the questing problem of representation becomes acute. That is, the actor is the one on the stage who, for the audience's sake, surrenders themselves to a "role"—an incarnate speculation—that provides a reply to the question of meaning, even if (as in some modern theater) it is revolt or negation. It is the actor who *represents* humanity in the facility of *their own* humanity. Aesthetics (image, representation), human action, and human meaning spin together in the actor. "He himself," Balthasar says, "is the relationship established between the 'reality of life' and 'aesthetic reality'; the disguise (*Ver-stellung*) of the role ministers to the presentation (*Vor-stellung*) of that reality that can only enter the realm of reality through disguise. Thus, the actor is seen to be the center of the encounter between two spheres of existence and truth."[28] For Balthasar, the actor playing a role embodies a fundamental dichotomy: that between a person's mysterious inner life and the "role" that they play for themselves and for society.[29] So representation emerges as a kind of Janus-face in the actor: they play a role that they represent (in terms of the play), and they also represent the role-playing of human living. This Janus-face "reveals" meaningfulness, at the very least in the form of the author's meaning as interpreted by the actor.[30] But the actor also is not their role. Balthasar does not associate "role" here with any negative connotation—it is only that human beings, like the actor, *also* escape their roles; it is by embodying this Janus-face that actors perform a making-present.[31] In them, theater posits an idea made incarnate (whatever that idea might be), which is serious for the audience even as it is

27. Balthasar, 1:248.
28. Balthasar, 1:261.
29. Balthasar, 1:264.
30. Balthasar, 1:265.
31. Balthasar, 1:281.

also fictional, nonserious.[32] Theater is serious in its play because of the "horizon" of the stage. The horizon is an "ultimate," even if an illusory one; it is a place against which or "before which" the question of existence is embodied in action. It is a backdrop where we see the shadows thrown by the lights.

Balthasar notes the cultic origins of early Greek theater, which for him illuminate the horizon in the terms of an open question. Human existence hurtles forward, and the question is whether its horizon of action, the outer limit before which human beings act, cares or can care at all. It is in this sense that Balthasar describes the emergence of a dualism in Greek theater between personal providence and impersonal fate, with the theatrical "action" ambivalently incorporating one, then the other, without a resolution that integrates them. "In the ancient world," he argues, "the spectator's gaze toward the horizon of tragedy must remain obscured: the whole realm of mortal man can provide a stage for great events and actions, but it contains no fixed point to which the heart might attach itself."[33] The horizon remains "veiled."

Human beings do not have a premade character that they *then* express; their character is in their action, which means that there is an inbuilt forward directionality to human being, which for Aristotle means bearing an inward goal (*entelechy*). "The actual (the here and now)," explains Balthasar, "makes sense only as the 'now' of something that is moving toward its goal (and hence toward its self)."[34] The temporal forward-movement of human being, because it is not the pure succession of moments but integrated through development, gives to each human moment a "tension" that is "pregnant with the future."[35]

Dramatic action is organized around a "situation," one that undergoes transformation in the action.[36] Because a play is often composed of several characters, "situation" is not only understood as an individual's unique reference point(s) in history or in the play on the stage but also understood to be the interactive positionalities of all the characters with one another, in a situation that is an interpersonal "constellation."[37] But this play-constellation is only comprehensible (to the characters, to the audience) because it has a valence toward or

32. Balthasar, 1:311.
33. Balthasar, 1:317.
34. Balthasar, 1:345.
35. Balthasar, 1:348.
36. Balthasar, 1:353–61.
37. I borrow the "constellation" phrase from Balthasar, 1:353, but it also appears in Balthasar, *TL* I and elsewhere in Balthasar's writing, for example, in Hans Urs von Balthasar, *Convergences: To the Source of Christian Mystery* (San Francisco: Ignatius, 1983).

transparency to the "real" human situation-as-constellation. The shared and real humanity that underlies the fictional action gives to it a weight, however frivolous the action. That weight is, simply, the dilemma of being-human, the question it is to itself, the question that we are to ourselves together, *as* together. From out of this dynamic, Balthasar produces a vertigo: the constellation represented on the stage steps backward into the constellation of being-human, which steps backward into being-at-all, and before each, the individual faces the question of their meaningfulness.[38]

The eyeless face of "destiny," the horizon, appears again here, as human existence gesticulates before the possibility of an ultimate that also judges it. This horizon is not purely external; the "above" is also found in the hero's "ought," or we might say: the horizon is experienced not "out there" but in human *entelechy*. What makes human drama fundamentally or most "itself" is the presence of this horizon, even if it is a pure question to God, or an articulation of revolt or despair (to/against God). Absent of this horizon-dimension, the action ceases being "dramatic."[39] In other words, a humanity that is not puzzled by itself through the "tension" of the question, either in inquiry or in play, abandons drama altogether, since now there can be no illumination of the tension that underlies human being.[40]

Something of this destiny-horizon, however it is understood, emerges as human helplessness toward forces not under human control (individually, collectively) and only becomes "dramatic" when placed in a dialectic with the "possibility of liberation."[41] Human beings find themselves in a situation marked perpetually by their limitations as finite and by the evil they introduce to their own situations, rendering it concomitant with the absurd as well as meaning. To put it another way: drama is not mere struggle but a struggle around *meaningfulness*, and a struggle around human being as *situation*.[42] Pure animal existence, while it is the basis without which human existence would not be, is not yet a full description of human experience, and so also not a full confrontation with

---

38. Balthasar, *TD* 1:354.

39. Balthasar, 1:359.

40. Balthasar, 1:357–58.

41. Balthasar, 1:360–61; "liberation" then becomes an explicit theme in Balthasar, 4:367–83, 477–87.

42. As Balthasar later makes explicit, "Thus, the question of meaning provides the real basis for dialogue between the Church and the world." Balthasar, 4:479; cf. Balthasar, 4:83.

human action, which is embedded in a perplexing (and explicating) world of meaning and its perpetual transmutation as situation.[43]

"Who Am I?"

To transpose his dramatic categories into theology, Balthasar recalls the tension and thus the difference "between what I represent and what I am in reality," which appeared on the stage in the form of role-playing.[44] Maurice Blondel shows up in the midst of Balthasar's text in order to highlight this difference-tension: here again is Blondel's dilemma over how the subject wills itself. Balthasar draws directly from *Action* and summarizes one of its major keys: "What is done or yearned for always contains less than the one who performs this doing or yearning."[45] And in the same gesture, he recalls Blondel's emphasis on a concrete, integral universe as the only serious starting point for thinking about this dilemma, the dilemma of being human. It is a dilemma that emerges in a subject who is possessed of a will that cannot "equal" itself. Thus, the turn to theology is a question of *who* acts in the drama of human existence and not *what*.[46] In other words, Balthasar eschews a retreat into essences (though not essence-talk itself) in favor of the existential emergence of the human question, which has to do with "me" and this difference that I feel between my "I" and my "role" in my world, which is founded on the difference between my willing will and my willed will.[47]

The Blondelian understructure that explicitly supports Balthasar is significant because it provides the essential thrust by which Balthasar moves into theology, following the manner in which Blondel himself gestures toward that movement. By tracing human action's inability to equal itself to its very end, Blondel posits a disproportionate entitative order, the supernatural, that gives human action its fullness. Balthasar's pivot into theology is organized around a natural, supernatural *réalité intégrale*, but considered from a different, which is

---

43. Cf. Balthasar, 1:417–18.

44. Balthasar, 1:481.

45. Balthasar, 1:481.

46. Balthasar, 1:482.

47. This is, as I have mentioned, a dramatic version of a question that appears aesthetically in the first volume of *Glory of the Lord*, with its dialectic between "subjective evidence" and "objective evidence," a dynamic that begins with what is subjective. It is also a dramatic version of the truth of consciousness and being as it appears in *TL* I.

to say a theological, angle.[48] The transposition into theology borrows in such a way that philosophy and drama continue to operate "in" theology, and they do so in a transfigured but analogous fashion. Theology performs its reflection from "within" disproportionate or supernatural (to the human intellect and will) actions and truths, and it does this by using proportionate human means that are "elevated" by faith. Which is to say, human faculties remain themselves but must deal with the world in new but related ways in the struggle to make sense of supernatural revelation. This is the methodological heart of Balthasar's pivot into theology.

Theater allows Balthasar to navigate the difficult dialectic between "meaning" and "action" that emerged in my previous chapters between Lonergan and Blondel. Human history, as human action, as what human beings *do*, receives an elaboration as action that is embedded in meaning, as generative of and impacted by both human and divine meanings. The axis of the "now" (from *Theo-Logic*) is laden with history in a triple way: as a product of human decisions, as emerging from human meanings, as creative of future situations (of/for decision and meaning). Moreover, history is more properly understood as a series of constellations made up of fellow, indeed all, human beings. Theater's common dynamism, which is propelled by the interactions between its multiple characters, gives us a way of seeing humanity as "one" yet materially "many." So *Theo-Drama* presents its readers with an *operating theory of history*. As a *theory*, Balthasar's work offers heuristic points of contact for the theologian to understand history by, and as an *operation*, it reorganizes traditional theological loci according to *Theo-Drama*'s transformed notion of what historicity is and means.

The horizon of the stage is in one sense a gesture toward Blondel's supernatural. At the same time, it is an essential existential argument that posits a confused human posturing toward some ultimate that is ambiguous or ambivalent and so is, existentially speaking, real and unreal, known and unknown.[49] Human beings must inexorably make judgments and decisions, which evinces in some way some kind of absolute, but that absolute does not appear in the world as such, leaving no human being the power of absolute judgment or

---

48. First intimated in Hans Urs von Balthasar, "Part III: The Form and Structure of Catholic Thought," in *The Theology of Karl Barth* (San Francisco: Ignatius, 1992), 251–378 (originally published in 1951, which is to say, decades before the trilogy).

49. Cf. later in the dramatics: Balthasar, *TD* 3:19–20.

decision, especially over another.[50] This decentered dispossession before a "horizon" that is interior yet transcendent is the dramatic version of truth. It is essential, because it carries in its structure the credibility of the human subject as limited and as exalted.

The primary meaning of *action* in *Theo-Drama* is *the action of God*.[51] This action includes the valence of God as Pure Act (in himself as Trinity) and the valence of God's action in proportionate being (the triune act of creation, and that of salvation). Similarly, the turning axis of humanity and human temporality—as one and as individuated—becomes Christic. The world-stage is, in Balthasar's terms, *in God*, and in the "theo-drama," God is "now" (i.e., in theology) the primary actor. Here is the dislocation of philosophy and of theater, because its center of gravity is not the world at all but the Trinity. In a way, this dislocation intensifies when the dramatic horizon itself enters in upon the action of the stage as a "player," as the Incarnate Word. This event transforms everything. At the same time, the world-stage that is "in" God (because where else would it be?) remains the place of action understood as history. Human history in its dialectical, temporal expression of human action and of human meaning is what God redeems by entering into and by becoming a "one" in the many, a one who is also (vicariously) the many. Worldly being is the instrument that the transcendent God uses to "speak" himself to his creature without remainder.[52] So the concrete, integral universe is and remains the means of God's singular self-revelation in Christ. Balthasar's transposition retains its existential elevation of the human subject while also describing a fundamentally theocentric universe.[53]

God's Action in History

Because history is the drama of human action and theo-dramatic action is the action of God in history, anthropo-drama and theo-drama must be linked

---

50. Cf. Balthasar, 1:424.

51. "God has the chief role in the theo-drama." Hans Urs von Balthasar, *Theo-Drama: Theological Dramatic Theory*, vol. 2, *Dramatis Personae: Man in God* (San Francisco: Ignatius, 1990), 17.

52. Cf. For example, Balthasar, *GL* 1:29, 430–36; Hans Urs von Balthasar, *Theo-Drama: Theological Dramatic Theory*, vol. 3, *Dramatis Personae: Persons in Christ* (San Francisco: Ignatius, 1992), 506.

53. Lonergan is similar in this regard, performing the same elevation of human subjectivity in a nevertheless theo-centric universe in both *Insight* and *Method in Theology*.

without collapsing into each other.[54] This link at once organizes the movement between the eternal God and the economy of salvation and provides theological-dramatic theory its propulsion through the rest of the *Theo-Drama*. And this organizing-motivating link is the obedience of Jesus Christ.[55]

At one level, the obedience of the God-man is the free agreement of his human will with the eternal and divine will for salvation.[56] It is a "yes" uttered in freedom, throughout his life, that is reflective of a divine and eternal utterance. In Jesus Christ, says Balthasar, "is the revelation of that hidden freedom that is expressed in his total obedience to the Father, a freedom that is not only divine but also human."[57] As such, his human freedom is expressive of the divine will, the will for salvation. In Balthasar's words, "It all goes back once more to the loving decision made by the Trinity."[58] But this human "yes" to the divine decision is also a created term, a created reality, that ratifies and makes true in creation God's saving will for the world.[59] As Balthasar says elsewhere, "The Passion, as a bearing of the sin of the world and descent into the hell of God-forsakenness, is the divine way of making true in [Jesus] that which he always wanted and sought: that the Father's will be done on earth as it is in heaven."[60] In a unique and supernatural way (i.e., in a hypostatic unity), God acts in this created action of Christ's.

But what "act" of the eternal God's is this "action" that acts in the human action of the Incarnate Word? It is the simple and eternal act by which God is; this act is the act that brings about the incarnation.[61] In other words, the change

---

54. Balthasar, *TD* 2:13: "One last thing: a theodramatic theory is not primarily concerned with spectating and evaluating but with acting and the ability to act." Cf. Balthasar, 2:54–55, 68.

55. "The first thing to be defined is the longitudinal axis, as it were, the vertical beam of the Cross: at its top is the Son's eternal readiness to obey the Father, at its lowest point is his obedience even in forsakenness. And this gives the horizontal beam its definiteness: his obedience is the internal norm of every human life and work." Balthasar, 2:281; cf. Balthasar, 2:68.

56. "The entire theo-drama has its center in the two wills of Christ." Balthasar, 2:201; cf. Balthasar, *GL* 1:507.

57. Balthasar, *TD* 4:364.

58. Balthasar, 4:501; cf. 3:183–84.

59. Note, for example, the intensification of the Son's mission or "hour" in terms of its willing here: "Like no other hour, it is an integral part of the Son's mission; whatever it may contain, he affirms it from the very outset. *He* accepts it: it is not imposed on him from the outside." Balthasar, 4:334; cf. 4:494; 3:519.

60. Balthasar, *Convergences*, 42.

61. Balthasar is relatively explicit in *TD* 2:261 with respect to creation first of all: "The living God does not pour himself forth by nature, all the same, the freedom in which he determines that the

is in creation, not in God, and the created term of Jesus's "yes" is expressive of God as God is. Everything that Jesus is and does in history is also (in the communication of idioms) the being and doing of God.[62] And because this human obedience under question, this "yes," is none other than the obedience of the Incarnate Son—that is, since this is the obedience (through the hypostatic union) of a divine person—it is expressive of this divine person in a special way. The Son reveals himself in this "yes," as he also reveals the triune God in his being-Son, and reveals the unchanging triune "yes" to creation that is his.

Christ's obedience is a human action, and so it is historical in the strictest or most precise sense, even as what it brings about is divine. To put it another way, the hypostatic union is the major hinge of a divine turn effected in human history, and Jesus's complete humanity is essential for this "in history," an *in history* that changes history, as Balthasar says, from "within."[63] Because the two natures of Christ cannot be confused, Christ's obedience maintains the difference between God and the world. His obedience is, in other words, an economic term.[64] This obedience is created; it is action in time. It is an action in time that reveals the divine action that is wholly without time. And Jesus's human nature is also a full expression of the humanity that is his, that we share with him, connecting us together.[65] So the complex divine-human (theo-anthropic) action of the incarnation in this way allows Balthasar a historical action that does not submerge God in history while also serving as an explanatory account of God's effect ("initiative") in history, which we partake in.

The incarnation allows Balthasar a further, a "play-within-a-play," format: the theo-anthropic play of freedoms in Christ forms the stage for our own play of freedoms *in* Christ.[66] This opens the way for the elevation of our freedom

---

world shall exist is, according to its nature, none other than the freedom by which he wills eternally to be what he is." Bernard Lonergan is clearer here, however. See Bernard Lonergan, *The Collected Works of Bernard Lonergan*, vol. 7, *The Ontological and Psychological Constitution of Christ* (Toronto: University of Toronto Press, 2002), 137: "By what is entitatively the same infinite act of being the triune God is able to be, and God the Son is, not only what he necessarily is but also what he has contingently become."

62. Cf. Balthasar, *TD* 3:157–59.

63. Balthasar, 2:161.

64. See "obedience" as it appears in Balthasar, *TD* 4:362. Note carefully, however, that Balthasar here speaks of the economy and how in the resurrection it "returns" in some way to the immanent Trinity—that is, there is an element of eschatological time underlying the analysis.

65. See Balthasar, 3:37–40.

66. Balthasar, 2:63; cf. 2:91.

into the supernatural initiative for salvation in history. "The fact that the drama is grounded in Christ," says Balthasar, "is no hindrance to it: on the contrary, from every angle, it is what makes it possible."[67] This play-within-a-play works in more than one direction: the incarnation *reveals* the original "play" of freedoms in the Trinity, and it *grounds* ours. In other words, it is Jesus's free obedience in history—the action of his whole life, but especially on the cross—that serves as a point of axis, one that Balthasar can "turn" in the direction of the Trinity that it reveals and that acts in history in Christ and one that Balthasar can "turn" again in the direction of humanity, revealing and effecting an "acting area" for our own freedom.

Balthasar typically refers to Jesus's obedience as "kenotic," or self-emptying—a phrase derived from Philippians 2:5–11 and a notion for Balthasar frequently attached to sayings from the Gospel of John—thus alloying it with love: "For the power of the Son's absolute obedience is love."[68] Kenosis is a version of the dispossessive, loving attitude that characterizes, among other things, the open attention of the knowing subject toward truth in *Theo-Logic*. So at one angle, the connotation for kenosis is of a making room, or in Balthasar's parlance, a "letting-be." Since this kenosis is an action of a free nature, in this case the freedom of the humanity of Jesus in his obedience, it is helpful to underline that this letting-be is a *willing* of the other. In other words, it is best to imagine Ignatian *indifferentia* here rather than an exenterated blankness.[69]

Kenosis is also, since it is free and an action, expressive of a subject's interiority, of the "I" that asks "Who am I?" in a mode of that freedom's realization. That Jesus's obedience is kenotic means that his obedience unveils his "I" as the divine Son of the Father, and so this obedience unveils the Father who sent him in an act (really, a lifetime of action) that realizes the Incarnate Son's created freedom evermore really and that reveals the Spirit in the Father and the Son's union of love.[70] That Jesus's obedience is kenotic also means that his "I" makes room in itself for every other human "I" that ever will be—a breadth possible to him as God-man—in an act of compassion that encompasses us at our least and also our worst, at the utmost extremity of the cross but also at the resurrection

67. Balthasar, 3:22.
68. Balthasar, 4:497.
69. As, for example, in Balthasar, 2:167–68.
70. "He does not reveal the Father merely from time to time; he reveals him in every situation of his life." Balthasar, 3:173.

and its universal realization.[71] In the particularness of Jesus's life, in other words, in the freedom of his kenotic obedience, God freely wills the "other" that is all of our freedoms, and so also wills our free action in history, indeed our participation in God's will for a supernatural end to history. "*This particular* history," Balthasar explains of Christ, "incarnates itself in *all* of history."[72]

Jesus's kenotic obedience, which is finite and human, is modeled on infinite, Trinitarian kenotic freedom. Here I want to draw out two points, both of which concentrate around the eternal Son. One is that the Son is the result of or term of a divine procession, a procession "from" the Father. Balthasar characterizes the origin of this procession ("from") as the "Ur-kenosis" of the Father, which Thomas Aquinas would more nearly call "generation" (paternity, begetting).[73] That is to say, the Son is "eternally begotten" of the Father. And Balthasar associates this relation of origin with kenosis. "The Father's self-utterance in the generation of the Son," explains Balthasar, "is the initial 'kenosis' within the Godhead that underpins all subsequent kenosis."[74]

The Son relates to this procession differently than the Father as one who actually proceeds: in the Son's being-begotten, which Balthasar characterizes both as a joyful *reception* of self/divine nature and as a *responding gratitude* (Eucharist) that offers self in return (leading, ultimately, to the spiration of the Holy Spirit).[75] What Balthasar means in one way is that all of the persons of the Trinity are, in distinct fashions, kenotic.[76] This means that the divine nature

71. Balthasar, 3:162.

72. Balthasar, 2:117; emphasis original.

73. "Kenosis" in this type of framework first appears in a major text in *Mysterium Paschale: The Mystery of Easter* (San Francisco: Ignatius, 2005), esp. 23–36; and in Hans Urs von Balthasar, *The Glory of the Lord: A Theological Aesthetics*, vol. 7, *Theology: The New Covenant* (San Francisco: Ignatius, 1989), esp. 211–28; but is laid out "dramatically" in Balthasar, *TD* 4:319–28. These texts were originally published in 1969 (both *Mysterium Pascale* and the finale volume of the aesthetics) and in 1980, allowing Balthasar both an intelligible arc and consistency. For resources around procession/mission in Thomas Aquinas, see *ST* I.43.

74. Balthasar, *TD* 4:323; cf. 2:267–68, 126: "Theological proof must go even farther back, to the eternal generation of the Son."

75. As in, for example, Balthasar, *TD* 2:267.

76. A tricky element of interpreting Balthasar here is forgetting this basic element of the claim. It is tricky because we think of, and Balthasar often uses metaphors of, kenosis as movement from one thing to another (much as "procession" can be similarly perplexed). So "the Father's Ur-kenosis" can lose its connotation as "origin," signified by "Ur." There is no other Ur-kenosis. In Balthasar's usage, at least, it marks out the Father's paternity in a traditional sense, as the "whence" of the other divine Persons, as the one who does not proceed. That *all* Persons are kenotic does

"is" kenotic, but it also means that the persons are not one another while being wholly God.[77] This is, as Balthasar says elsewhere, "the God who, in the three ways of possessing the divine essence *personally*, participates in all the divine attributes."[78] And it means that, embedded in Trinitarian, and by analogy anthropological, kenosis is the notion of a self-giving *willing of the other* that does not eradicate the kenotic person who so wills.[79] Balthasar lays out this logic clearly much later in his trilogy, in *Theo-Logic III*, under the name "self-giving": "Each divine Hypostasis retains its own, irreducible mystery; the Father, in that he is able to be both utter self-giving (*relatio*) and yet One who gives himself; the Son, the answering Word, in that, while giving himself to the Father, he is able to share in the latter's originating power in such a way that, in union with this power, he can not only be love, but produce it; and the Spirit, in that he is both the highest divine, sovereign and perfect selflessness, only existing for Father and Son."[80] In the Trinity, this notion of kenosis is more radically conceived, because the persons are substantive relations undergirded by processions; we must think less of "circumincession" generally and still less of social Trinitarianism so much as we must think of the absolute unity of the intellect and will and nature of the eternal God, a unity that receives the Balthasarian commentary of "self-gift/self-giving" and "kenosis/kenotic."

I have described the Trinitarian life of the Son as one who receives kenosis (the kenosis of the Father) and as one who responds with kenosis (gratitude, Eucharist). By way of kenosis, Balthasar renders a version of the procession of the Son and its term of origin (the Father). And here is the key for my purposes: Balthasar explicitly relates the processions of the Trinity to their saving mission in history, which Thomas Aquinas had done before him.[81] The center of this mission is the Father's "sending" of the Son into history (John 3:16), where ultimately on the cross and in the resurrection the Spirit is breathed over all

---

not abrogate this sense, though the temptation might be to connote otherwise. For evidence of Balthasar's own understanding, see his review of traditional claims around the Trinitarian hypostases in Hans Urs von Balthasar, *Theo-Logic: Theological Logical Theory*, vol. 3, *The Spirit of Truth* (San Francisco: Ignatius, 2005), 117–41 and his own synthesis on 157–64.

77. Balthasar, *TD* 4:331; cf. foundations in 2:256–58, 262–64.

78. Balthasar, *TL* 3:160.

79. Cf. Hans Urs von Balthasar, *Theo-Drama: Theological Dramatic Theory*, vol. 5, *The Last Act* (San Francisco: Ignatius, 1998), 85–87; 4:325; 2:194–95, 258–59.

80. Balthasar, *TL* 3:218.

81. See Aquinas, *ST* I.43; Balthasar, *TD* 3:165–73; *TD* 4:326–27.

flesh (Acts 2:17).[82] As in a created mirror, Balthasar describes the Son in the economy with a double notion: as he-who-is-sent and as he-who-offers-himself in return (which at its completion pours out the Spirit).[83] So the mission of the Son is a mirror of the divine procession. Says Balthasar, "From the very first moment of his entry into the world, sent forth from the Father, he is on his way back to the Father."[84] Or again, "The Son's eternal *processio*, which carries out God's plan for the world, is identical with the Son's *missio*."[85] Since mission and procession are linked, the Son's obedience can be revelatory (of the Trinity) as well as effective (of the Trinity's will for history). Christ's obedience is at one and the same time a *transparency* to the invisible Father, revealing him who sent him, and an action of the Son in the Spirit, ratifying and realizing the one divine will for history.

Christ's obedience is not merely an agreement of his two wills; it is the enactment of loving personality: a personality that "is" in its action and that, because it loves, acts in order to "let-to-be" the object of its love.[86] Jesus's obedience is revelatory of Jesus's *person*. Here Balthasar's axis appears again, able to turn in the direction of the immanent Trinity and, by analogy, in the direction of our own person-ness. Says Balthasar, "In this collapse and rebirth, he maintains his identity; and so, as the matrix of all possible dramas, he embodies the absolute drama in his own person, in his personal mission. Here it becomes clear that this person, in order to preserve his identity, must be trinitarian: in order to be himself, he needs the Father and the Spirit. On the other hand, he makes room within himself, that is, an acting area for dramas of theological moment, involving other, created persons."[87] Even so, I think that ultimately understanding how kenotic obedience is the "enactment of loving personality," as I have called it, requires more than a rehearsal of the Trinity and its processions. It requires stepping backward into the trouble of dramatic representation.

I want to reconceive the problem of representation, which I explored dramatically, theo-dramatically. Jennifer Newsome Martin unveils this problem—which

82. For an example of this type of explanation in the dramatics, see Balthasar, *TD* 3:153, 510; 5:425–88.

83. Balthasar, 4:366–67.

84. Balthasar, 5:83.

85. Balthasar, 5:80.

86. "We render thanks for our selves, therefore, by responding, giving an answering word [Ant-Wort], to the fact that we have been called a 'thou.' We do this by progressively incarnating the word of thanks in our lives." Balthasar, 2:291.

87. Balthasar, 3:162.

I really mean as a complex opportunity—when she explores Balthasar's dramatic concepts in dialogue with his interest in baroque theater, and in dialogue with the "baroque self" as recovered by Julia Kristeva. These dialogues illuminate and inform several of Balthasar's "internal resources" as they operate in his theology.[88] In this vein, Martin highlights how Balthasar adapts the "radical disponsibility" of baroque aesthetics and theater into a theory of representation, one where "the saint" (originally the figure/actor), in a creative act of self-emptying, becomes "transparent" to the divine, revealing both their *own* personhood *and* the incomprehensible light of the triune God through their concrete representation of Christ.[89] This double revelation of concrete self and of (God in) concrete Christ is what Martin calls a "doubling of the self."[90]

When I last spoke of representation, I explained how, for Balthasar, the actor on the stage represents their character and also the human difference between "I" and "role." The actor offers up their own reality to the role that they play, giving it weight, but they also offer that weight to the audience, who share in the realness of being-human. In the transition into the theo-dramatics, this tension and this realness become the burning question "Who am I?" And Martin interprets these dynamics into a fuller range-of-play. Balthasar's consistent interest in a concrete *réalité intégrale* emerges, for Martin, as a complex interplay between "I" and "other" (I/other, actor/character, actor/audience, Christ/humanity, *and* saint/Christ). As we have seen, the conceptual weight of Balthasar's interest in the "other" is available in his emphasis on a deferential "letting-be" that allows the truth/freedom of every "other" to come to be in the creative space, the interplay, between the subject and the other.[91] In the latitude opened up between "I" and "role" in the question "Who am I?" Martin argues that Balthasar introduces otherness into human interiority and so into human "disponsibility."

But it is also a refusal of any absolutized opposition between the existential and the true (evident "already" in *Theo-Logic*, from earlier in this chapter). Balthasar, in Martin's own words, complicates "the identity between 'I' and 'other,' resisting any strong dualism between subjective and objective and challenging readings which would import modern notions of the self as

88. Jennifer Newsome Martin, "Balthasar *avec* Kristeva: On the Recovery of a Baroque Teresa of Avila," *Modern Theology* 37, no. 1 (2020): 28, https://doi.org/10.1111/moth.12595.

89. Martin, 34.

90. Martin, 35.

91. As in Balthasar, *TD* 2:259.

an autonomous ego."[92] Indeed, for Martin, Balthasar *fissures* "the monadic 'I'"
in two simultaneous ways: through "the radical indwelling of God" and, differently, through "a field of other 'I's.'"[93] Whereas I spoke earlier of how the
theater allowed Balthasar's "constellation" to shift in the direction of a *humanity*
that is at once *one* and *many*, rather than referring simply to the constellated
circumstance of the individual subject, Martin shows how Balthasar allows that
shift to carry all the way through to the consciousness of the subject. In fact, the
constellating of the interior subject occurs doubly—in the form of an openness
to and the indwelling of the "other" that is fellow human beings and in the
"Other" that is God.[94] So Martin calls Balthasar's "doubling of the self" in representation also a "porosity" or "liquidation" of self.[95] It is a porosity anchored
in God, and so anchored against absolute dissolution.[96]

Human beings "gesticulate." We create meaning. We at the same time wonder about ourselves and our meaning, representing both to ourselves. And Martin reminds us that, for Balthasar, even the Christian stage bears markers of
ambivalence, just as it also bears up the revelatory illumination of the horizon
by the horizon. As in baroque theater, so also the church: hanging suspended
between glorifying God and self-glorification.[97] This is a function at least in part
of the basic situation of human ambivalence, which is funded by the concrete
experience of an Absolute Good that does not appear in the world as such
(and alas, we must to act always and anyway).[98] That is to say: the world can be
conceived of as a transparency to God, in something like the gestures of Saint
Francis; the world can *also* be conceived of as mute, bare facticity and blind,
pure matter, as in something like Albert Camus or Karl Marx.[99] In *Theo-Logic*,
this is an encounter with the way worldly being and truth point beyond themselves to a center or absolute that cannot be perceived.[100] Human consciousness and indeed the world do not possess an absolute center of their own; they
are both rooted ultimately in the single act by which the triune God knows
himself and is himself. And in *Theo-Drama*, in the drama of God in history,

92. Martin, "Balthasar *avec* Kristeva," 37.

93. Martin, 38.

94. Martin, 38–39.

95. Martin, 37–38.

96. Martin, 42.

97. Martin, 34.

98. Balthasar, *TD* 1:418.

99. Balthasar, 1:424; cf. 1:420–23; 4:144–45.

100. Cf. Balthasar, *TL* 1:35–42, 206–6.

the dispossession at the center of the world becomes the hinge by which the dispossessive Trinity reveals itself without submerging into history. The world and indeed human meaning become the sites of divine speech and action. But this does not erase either how the center of the world and of human meaning is not to be found in themselves or how they can operate negatively to conceal their essential "in-and-beyond."[101] In fact, with the advent of Christ, the crisis is intensified in the decision for or against God, in an act of revealing or concealing—a crisis riven right through the very heart of the Christian.[102]

What Martin has done is show us the ways that Balthasarian representation is a mechanism expressive of what she calls a "fissured/porous" "I." And so, dramatically speaking, underneath the question "Who am I?" is an interplay between "I" and "other," so that the *voice* of the question, so to speak, acquires more than one voice at once, a polyphony: my voice, the voices of other human beings, the voice of God. In the question of my "I," I am fissured, and so I am open to that other who is Christ. "The personal 'idea' of each individual finite freedom," Balthasar explains, "lies in the incarnate Son in such a way that each is given a unique participation in the Son's uniqueness."[103]

But this is not a static stage of persons. It is perpetually transforming, or on the move. All created being, but especially conscious being, comes to be by way of an *eidos* that also comes to be as the subject does, in dynamic mutuality (*Theo-Logic*'s "supratemporal idea" and "plastic potency").[104] So we should add to the polyphonic voice of every "I" the dynamism of a being that is coming into being. This is true, in a complex sense, in the being and becoming of Jesus Christ, since his becoming as man expresses the eternal being of God.[105] And what is more, this "coming into being," for every "I" and for the Incarnate One, is a shared event, for the world is not a series of solitudes. As Balthasar says of the world-theater, so similar can be said of the world: it is a "play of freedoms" whose field of action changes alongside the action.[106]

---

101. This is a reference to Erich Przywara's formula, already mentioned in the first chapter of this text; Przywara has a direct impact on Balthasar. See Przywara, *Analogia Entis*.

102. "Finite freedom, once it has been redeemed and liberated, is now in danger of being able to utter a heightened No." Balthasar, *TD* 4:383; cf. 4:173; *GL* 1:662.

103. Balthasar, *TD* 2:270.

104. Or, in terms of the theo-drama, "it [finite freedom] must come to a decision about itself: it must choose its own 'idea.'" Balthasar, 2:285; *eidos* also appears in *GL* 1:589 and is more generally an aesthetical idea, one that should not as such be removed from the dramatics.

105. Balthasar, *TD* 3:159.

106. Balthasar, 2:189; cf. 2:63, 282, 293.

The question now is whether the *"eidos"* of the Christ-mission can become an *eidos* for any other "I." Balthasar's manner of approaching this problem begins by saying that Christ's "I" and his "mission/role" are uniquely identical.[107] This claim relies on the connection between mission and procession such that the divine Son economically enacts the relation he substantially, eternally is. But it is also an expansion of "mission" in the other direction of the axis, in Jesus's relationship to humanity, because it becomes for Balthasar a way of saying that Jesus is consciously involved in a life given "for" the world, making decisions according to who he is.[108] This is the first connection between Christ's "I" and ours under the aspect of history: everything that he does is an expression of who he is as one *sent forth for the sake of the world*; it is an expression of the divine *"pro nobis."* Jesus's enactment of who-he-is and therefore why-he-was-sent is not "prefabricated." "No," says Balthasar, "he must fashion it out of himself in utter freedom and responsibility; indeed, in a sense, he even has to invent it."[109]

Christ's identity-in-mission is what enables his historicalness, his action, to be the animating pattern of ours without violating ours. It is how the axis is able to turn in our direction without eliminating *our* freedom and responsibility. For Balthasar, Christ's unique identity-action sets him "above" us as the horizon of an effective norm, dramatically speaking our "destiny," but we must understand this "above" as a *space* in which we are left to be and to act according to who we are, and who we are becoming.[110] Balthasar finds this space for us in the idea that we, unlike Christ, are not identical with our roles. Nor are we, to be clear in terms of *theo*-drama, identical with our theological missions ("roles") in Christ. The "gap" is a kind of space of assimilation in freedom, the playing out of our own agreement of wills (and so roles) with God, such that God's *pro nobis* becomes our own. Balthasar speaks in terms of "election" or of God's "name" for each of us, which becomes ours—not *instantly*, but precisely *not* instantly— over time, in our acting and struggle in the world. Balthasar calls it "bringing our innate nonidentity [of 'I' and role/mission] into an ever-closer approximation to perfect identity. . . . In other words, we are to assimilate our own 'I' more and more completely to our God-given mission and to discover in this mission our own identity, which is both personal and social."[111] Our own *difference* from

---

107. See Balthasar, 3:149–201.

108. This opens the way for Jesus's "consciousness of mission" in Balthasar, 3:163–202.

109. Balthasar, 3:198.

110. Cf. Balthasar, 3:15–16; 2:271.

111. Balthasar, 3:270–71.

our "I" and our mission or role is an openness to Christic en-missioning, and that difference is also the potency wherein we bring our mission into act. I mean this in the sense that Martin means it: an infinity of roles is possible in the one Christic mission, each finite role fitted to each "I," and each uniquely transparent to self and to Christ.[112] And I must emphasize that our incorporation into Christ is, fundamentally, God acting in us so that we share God's *pro nobis*. "Discipleship," says Balthasar, "brings with it the gift of participation in the Cross and Resurrection of Christ, and this points to a final element. This participation is bound to extend itself, albeit in a secondary manner, to the *pro nobis* of Christ's Paschal Mystery."[113] The *action* of our participation itself, the thing that makes it historical and human, the thing we *do*, is that of increasingly "able" self-donation to God and to the world ("obedience"), but not as if one were putting on a stone mask that one increasingly and painfully fails to remove. Balthasar instead talks about how God's providence, while itself unchanging, for us appears to change along with us, for we are in history, and history is God's instrument.[114] And this is even true of revelation in history, of Scripture: "This totality [of God's revelation], even in its written form, is continually moving. What is written is continually being reread and reinterpreted."[115]

The center of all this movement is the letting-be or disponibility of the "I" that in freedom is fissured by the "I" of others. And so Martin has allowed us a more complex understanding first of all of kenosis (as disponibility) but also of obedience, which is a mode of representative kenosis. Balthasar, to enable this dynamic coming-to-be and letting-be, emphasizes the *givenness* of our finite freedom and its *movement* (a mirror of the Son's being-begotten and being-Eucharist). Our freedom is, in other words, a power that we always-already "have" and that we must strive toward or realize.[116] We are on the move. From out of this understanding of our freedom, Balthasar argues that human freedom as we find it concretely structured can be described both as inviolate or irreplaceably our own *and* as a coming-to-be, as found most of all in the loving "letting-be" of the other.[117] Remembering Martin is helpful here: we need not understand either the "our own" or the "letting-be" of our freedom as monadic, or as a

112. Balthasar, 3:248–50; 4:384–86; 2:286–87.

113. Balthasar, 4:387.

114. Balthasar, 4:373; 2:273.

115. Balthasar, 2:103; cf. 2:112.

116. Balthasar, 2:207.

117. Here I reference the entire discussion in Balthasar, 2:207–42.

fait accompli between subject and object. And so what I mean to highlight in this regard is that Balthasar structures finite freedom according to an "I" that, *as* on the move, comes to be evermore my own the more articulately, the more responsibly, I am able to love the existence of others. Disponsibility, in other words, is not an act apart from my freedom; nor is it an act subsequent to the act of my consciousness; it is structured by a consciousness-in-act that is also free. And this is important, because it means that losing one or all of the elements results in a violation of freedom, or of consciousness, or of self-disponsiveness. It is no longer dramatic, for it can no longer relate itself freely to its horizon.[118]

So Balthasar's "play-within-a-play" operates by way of divine action in Christ's (human) action, a divine-human action that opens the way for our own action. The basis of this action and its expansion is the kenosis of the fissured "I" before God, which is, as I have said, the enactment of loving personality. "What is given to me," says Balthasar, "is not just any subjectivity, interchangeable with any other, but a subjectivity which, in order that it can communicate itself, is incommunicable. . . . Since I have been chosen to be a unique person, it follows inevitably that I must address infinite freedom as a 'Thou,' however excessive such language may seem." By way of this enactment, I-and-other becomes the frame for incarnation-and-Trinity and also for incarnation-and-human-persons, and similarly, but from the other direction, my "I" can be the fissured expression of myself and of Christ, ultimately of the Trinity. I am in this way incorporated into the redemptive mission of the Trinity and in a way unique to me (a role of my own), one yet "keyed" to the Incarnate Word of the Father.

I have been describing Balthasar's theo-dramatic theory in a way that works to explain, through the phenomenon of action, how God can act in history without vitiating either God's freedom or our own. My description has focused on the generalized mechanisms or instruments of Balthasar's explanation. What I want to do next is orient and describe a Balthasarian theory of tradition in a "metaphysic" of tradition by understanding it theo-dramatically. This is a task that will help relate Christian history to Christ more formally, and it will place cruciformity and resurrection within the frame of a theo-dramatic struggle against iniquity.

118. Cf. Balthasar, 1:358–59.

A Theo-Dramatic Theory of Christian Tradition

The reason for Jesus's mission, while wholly divine and divinizing, is to engage with human history as it is, in the concrete world that is ours, a world containing both sin and evil. Balthasar calls it a "struggle," or "God's struggle" against evil. In it, God enters human history as one among many. Balthasar borrows from biblical imagery to help describe this struggle in terms of a *contest-between* God and every power of darkness.[119] There is, Balthasar says, "first, the overwhelming power of evil in the world, stronger than any human power. God alone is a match for it, but it cannot be defeated by an external act on God's part."[120] Thus, God enters history as a member of it, as one man among human beings, to struggle against evil.

"Struggle" also bears the character of a *contest on behalf of God and human beings both* in the Incarnate One.[121] And it is marked not only by a struggle against "powers" that outstrip human freedom but also and centrally by a struggle *with, before,* and *in* a humanity in revolt against God. Jesus Christ's struggle is *demonstrative* ("before," "in front of" God and human beings)—that is, demonstrative of God's divine love and of the divine judgment of a human situation that sets its teeth against the Absolute Good.[122] But it is not primarily demonstrative, at least in a thin sense. Jesus's struggle is a struggle against a situation, from *within* a situation, such that his acting and his meaning in the situation of history are intended to change this situation. His struggle *heightens* as he acts and means within his situation, evermore revealing himself and evermore resulting in harsher pushback against the truth of who he is and the truth of the humanity that is his.[123] "In the Synoptics," explains Balthasar, "we discern something like a dramatic plot in which the progressive revelation of Jesus' love provokes the resistance of those addressed."[124]

Jesus's struggle from "inside" of history is one spent to overturn the rebellious hearts of human beings without violating their divinely given free sovereignty. This is why he adopts our freedom as his own, and it is why the keystone

119. A theme opened in Balthasar, 2:159–63.
120. Balthasar, 2:160.
121. See Balthasar, "God's Lawsuit," in *TD* 2:152–59.
122. Balthasar, 4:332–38.
123. Cf. Balthasar, 4:11.
124. Balthasar, 4:342.

of his free and finite obedience becomes the compassionate instrument of a divine action that operates within/on human freedom, beginning with the operation of Christ's own freedom. "Here," Balthasar explains, "absolute freedom enters into created freedom, interacts with created freedom and acts *as* created freedom."[125] In this theo-dramatic vein, "struggle" leads up to the cross as that ultimate site where God wrestles against evil, and so with, before, and in a humanity in revolt.

But there is something unusual about the Incarnate Word's struggle against iniquity.[126] Though much of its biblical and patristic descriptive life persists in a contest of strengths, an undercurrent with as much biblical and patristic warrant cuts against such a description and poses instead that the living God has no equal whatsoever, rejecting any notion of evil that would give it any counterface at all, for there is no life but God's, and evil, which cannot be said to be, must borrow its existence from the living.[127] Balthasar cuts against a misunderstanding of *this* imagery in his repeated insistence that the Almighty, who alone bears the face of the Absolute, is all-powerful *by way of powerlessness*. The Almighty God is the kenotic Trinity. As Balthasar argues, "The Father, in uttering and surrendering himself without reserve, does not lose himself. He does not extinguish himself by self-giving, just as he does not keep back anything of himself either. For, in this self-surrender, he *is* the whole divine essence. Here we see both God's infinite power and his powerlessness; he cannot be God in any other way but in this 'kenosis' within the Godhead itself."[128] For Balthasar, one of the things that the cross reveals that human powers could not have anticipated is that the Absolute is absolutely humble.[129] Kenosis appears here to assemble a conceptuality that helps explicate the Trinity as eternal, vulnerable self-surrender and in order to articulate Christ's obedience on the cross as wholly expressive of this eternal reality.[130] And so the peerless God overcomes the power of an evil that bears no face of its own save the borrowed face of a lie; God does so not by strength but by the vulnerability of an infinite love that condemns evil and radically affirms the world. The truth and the crown of this affirmation are the resurrection of

125. Balthasar, 4:318.

126. Cf. the shift in "struggle" as it appears in Balthasar, 2:161–62.

127. See the discussion in Balthasar, 2:118–20.

128. Balthasar, 4:325.

129. "In this being 'made to be sin' and bearing the 'curse,' infinite freedom shows its ultimate, most extreme capability for the first time: it can be itself even in the finitude that 'loses itself.'" Balthasar, 2:245.

130. See Balthasar, 4:326–28.

Christ, which breaks open from the ground of his divinely, humanly unfailing love for the world and breaks forth as the triune God's intention for the world.[131]

Cruciformity derives its nature from its sense as a struggle with evil, one where God out of love for us adopts our fatally injured situation, and in doing that corrects and breaks open human freedom from within. But it also derives its nature from its sense as an unparalleled revelation of the triune God before whom all is as naught, and in whom all is loved with the infinite gaze of self-giving love. Though the meteor-like "impact" of Christ receives the response of a growing brutality and rejection that informs the shape of his cross, its root intelligibility is strictly to be found in God as Trinity.[132] "Of course we can say that the Son dies 'because of sin,'" says Balthasar, "but at a deeper level he dies 'because of God.'"[133] So it is this latter reality, which is wholly supernatural, that in fact governs the theological drama that culminates in cross and resurrection.

And now I have the tools by which to understand *péguyuste* cruciformity. It is, at one angle, a struggle against evil. First God's struggle, then our own. It is also a position, a direction, a "toward" the world to redeem it. "For what we have in Christianity," Balthasar explains, "is an initiative undertaken by God on behalf of the world."[134] Cruciformity and its struggle are guided by a *"pro nobis,"* a "for the world," that must take place in the world to transform it. The cross is Christ's own, an "original" expression of the divine attitude toward sin and evil and toward the world, and the cross becomes each person's in Christ, original to them in their personhood, in all time, in every time. The Balthasarian version of Péguy's "original gesture," of beginning again, is the "doubling of the self."

The original gesture of the Christian in *history*, and so in Christian *tradition*, is doubly revelatory, of God and of self, and this is so because it is also an enactment of a freedom.[135] It bears remembering that I am speaking here not of rigid pictures but of free movement across the stage; I am speaking of human action and its meaningfulness. Christian tradition, Christian history, the Christian community, the "I" in Christ, are on the move. Balthasar describes how Christian tradition, before it is ever an "object," is an act. For Balthasar, Christian tradition is not "any" act but an act of *begetting in time*.[136] The

131. See Balthasar, 4:361–88.

132. Cf. Hans Urs von Balthasar, "The Impact of the Meteor," in *TD* 3:25–32.

133. Balthasar, *TD* 4:496.

134. Balthasar, 2:71.

135. Cf. Balthasar, 2:122–23; cf. 2:201–3.

136. Hans Urs von Balthasar, "Tradition," in *Explorations in Theology*, vol. 5, *Man Is Created*, trans. Adrian Walker (San Francisco: Ignatius, 2014), 358.

Christian, mirrorlike, begets the Son.[137] This is a eucharistic act.[138] And it requires, Balthasar explains, the original gesture that translates the meanings of the past into today: "The complex process of translating and transposing their intended meaning into a new context."[139] Balthasar emphasizes that the Christian has been bequeathed a serious and supernatural responsibility to serve the Trinity's providential gathering of history, and to commit to the task of history's (supernatural) redemption. This, then, is what Christian tradition most "is" and what it "does" and what it is "for": begetting Christ. And lest we misunderstand such action in history, Balthasar insists that it must be patterned after the creative, kenotic attitude of Christ.[140]

Ressourcement, then, would have to be *generative* to be true to Balthasar. It must generate Christ anew, in the Christian who is in history. But to be true to Péguy, Christian tradition could only be so by way of the original gesture, which is made today and in this fashion opens the past to be more than itself. The generative quality in question, the "original gesture," is founded in the reality of the actor on the stage, the one who is acting in a role but who also exists as more-than their role. Which is to say that the original gesture resides in the freedom of being-human *and* in the realization of this freedom. So the newness of Christian tradition is generated by way of the realness of the human person in their self-transcendence. It is the very expression of this "I" in its self-transcendence in history that God acts in and through. Thus, in each Christian is the recapitulation of Christianity in the facts of history, across time. Here I recall Blondel: "The synthesis of dogma and facts is scientifically effected because there is a synthesis of thought and grace in the life of the believer, a union of man and God, reproducing in the individual consciousness the history of Christianity itself."[141]

Ressourcement, as I have articulated it, is understandable as *representation* in Balthasarian terms. To resource is to "represent" Christ, but not in some flat, mechanical way. It has to be achieved by the "I" enacting itself. But it also must be achieved by God's acting in this "I." One aspect of this double effect is the dawn of an "I" that, by enacting triune love, *reveals* the Trinity's supernatural

---

137. This is even so "before" we discuss the incarnation, since humanity is "suspended" in God's freedom and in its own. See Balthasar, *TD* 2:253.

138. Cf. Hans Urs von Balthasar, "Dramatic Dimensions of the Eucharist," in *TD* 4:389–406.

139. Balthasar, "Tradition," 5:367; cf. *TL* 3:327–28; *GL* 1:554.

140. Cf. Balthasar, "Tradition," 5:371–72.

141. Blondel, "History and Dogma," 287.

action. But so also this enacting would involve itself in the *struggle* of God against iniquity. This act of revelation and of struggling-against is, in a dependent fashion, its own recapitulation of the divine economy. The revelation of this "I" in Christ, enacted in history, is an arduously purified "I." In the struggle of every "I," and in God's acting in us, Christianity lives not in its original innocence but in the second innocence of God. Or to be more precise: on this model, Christianity *is* a second innocence, and not a first innocence. But here, at the most glorious page in the illuminated text of salvation history, Christian history and the heart of the Christian split wide open, sundered by evil.

A Theo-Dramatic Critique of Tradition

I want to turn away from tradition in its positive heuristic sense—as "begetting" Christ, as the free revelation of a fissured "I"—and toward its negative playing out in history. Here again, all turns upon the "I" in its freedom, and upon a Christian "I" that gathers power for itself at the price of the other's freedom. What this means, practically speaking, is that the erasure of human *freedom*, conceptually or effectively, is the skeleton key that opens the way to a betrayal of the gospel's content, for fundamentally supernatural revelation is the elevation of the natural by the supernatural *by way of what is natural.*[142] It would be in christological terms the abbreviation of Christ's human nature through the elimination of his free human will; it is in historical terms the concrete act of doing exactly this to any human nature at all, and so to Christ. Balthasar is aware that the very dynamics by which Christianity is, though and even *because* they are embedded in our concrete universe, can and do become gestures of violence, and can and do become gestures of *Christian* violence.[143] It means that the created mechanisms for exchange, change, and gift, which God acts in and through to redeem us, can be mechanisms for suffering or for executing change in a negative sense. "Evil in the world," says Balthasar, "comes from freedom, a freedom that uses whatever power is available—its own power or someone else's."[144]

---

142. This is, to speak technically, how every supernatural elevation works.

143. Notice the dynamic here: "Wherever the self tries to prescind from its rootedness in God and establish its own autonomy, it is attempting to consolidate its freedom; it is attempting to seize power." Balthasar, *TD* 4:147.

144. Balthasar, 4:137.

Balthasar is suspicious of any Christian relationship to power that is not characterized by "Trinitarian" and "christological" powerlessness. This is not the same as having *no* power, since all action requires some kind of *dúname*.[145] But "any success," warns Balthasar, "will always be precarious in earthly terms, however: power, in the hands of essentially covetous men, remains ambivalent."[146] For Balthasar, the powerlessness of Christ-and-Trinity must always connote a kenotic (Martin: "disponsive") affirmation of the other that allows and enables their full unfolding *as* other.[147] This is something like Blondel's double *afférence*, inasmuch as it is concerned with how the supernatural ennobles the natural by enabling grace's own free reception, and it is concerned with a mirror of that dynamic in human relationships and even in human interiority: we ennoble one another. Any violation of these principles is, thus, a type of violence.[148]

Balthasar everywhere repeats that Christian historical action is meant to be "cruciform." And to be cruciform, it must be vulnerable, kenotic love, a love that elevates the object of its love—that is, which elevates the other, the world. In the book *Convergences*, Balthasar discusses the matter at some length in practical terms. I quote in full:

> Christianity is not only to be received in faith, nor only preached, but performed. . . . "Political theology," then, but no longer in the dimensions of the Constantinian era (which extends, inclusively, to the nationalism of modern times), where the sphere of "Church" coincides with the domain of "empire" and expands together with it (and by its methods of expansion); nor corresponding to the concept of the West and its tense political discussion between the "Christian nations," in any event with their expansions into the rest of the world as colonial territory; but where the sphere Church *must* fall together with the sphere World, and in this postulate the center of Christian existence (as mission) is seen: at the intersection, then, of Is and Ought. And this Ought would now be free from over-hasty identification with the earthly "empire" (and its instruments of power and methods of government), and placed instead

145. Cf. Balthasar, 4:155–56.
146. Balthasar, 4:483; cf. 4:137.
147. See, for example, Balthasar, *TL* 3:400; *TD* 4:140–41.
148. Cf. Balthasar, *TD* 5:316.

on the means of the mere gospel, which are less, and at the same time infinitely more, than those methods.[149]

Christianity stands upon the axis of a concrete, integral universe, and by way of the potency of this universe, Christianity brings it evermore into act. Between what "is" and what "ought" to be stands the Christian in hope. But it is a *hope*, not a guarantee, and still less a road map to Parousia.[150] And this hope's *methods* matter: these methods must be a recapitulation of God's own; they must eschew power over against in favor of the kenotic willing of the other. Balthasar's theo-dramatic theory, in other words, not only describes the means of God's action in the world but also provides Christian action with its (divine) standards. And so Balthasar warns, "Anyone who is not focused from the very beginning on this total obedience to the Father's ways with the Son should as a Christian keep his hands off political theology."[151]

Balthasar's interest in Trinitarian, christological powerlessness is something like M. Shawn Copeland's rejection of anything that replaces or confuses the presence of Christ with itself. Here the "powerless" letting-be in question is the letting-be of divine work, because in Balthasar's understanding, the kenosis being asked of the person by God is well and truly supernatural and so cannot be enforced or enabled by anyone but God.[152] This warning explicitly includes the church, which cannot see itself as anything but a "sacrament" or "instrument" of God's grace.[153] Here too stands Balthasar's caution against a theological rationalism that would collect for itself all knowledge and all power, emptied of mystery.[154] The church's experience of itself is meant to be a doubling of "powerlessness," since it means imitating God's willing of the other (and so not holding on to the center of the situation), and since it means not perplexing *itself* with God's willing. Instead, "it is a power to be exercised in

149. Balthasar, *Convergences*, 41.

150. As in, for example, Balthasar, *TL* 3:374: "But this hope, as Paul so insists, does not know what it hopes for; and we, too, the sighing sons of God, cannot describe it, either"; cf. *TD* 2:29–30.

151. Balthasar, *Convergences*, 42.

152. An example that mitigates against the abuse of kenosis while describing it can be found in Hans Urs von Balthasar, "The Claim to Catholicity," in *Explorations in Theology*, vol. 4, *Spirit and Institution* (San Francisco: Ignatius, 1995), 118–19.

153. Even in its tradition, the church cannot hope to "fully contain God's inner self-surrender as act": Balthasar, *TL* 3:322; *GL* 1:541–44; Balthasar, "Claim to Catholicity," 4:66–67.

154. Balthasar, *TD* 4:457–64.

service, and so it uses the criterion of the 'weaker brother.'"[155] And it is exactly here that we run into one of the most important of Balthasar's elaborations on Blondel's critique of authoritarian Catholicism, because we move from the crude violation of human freedom to its exploitation.

It is not just that the church, or anyone, can despotically hold itself over against others—that it can wield power like a cudgel. Nor is it only that the church *has* done so, and here Balthasar notes more than once events like the Crusades and colonialism.[156] It is that the appearance of holiness (or goodness, or truth, or beauty) can secret underneath its lovely face a devastating will to harm. Balthasar frequently and negatively adapts Nietzsche's will-to-power here.[157] What Balthasar is trying to name in this dynamic is the total inversion of letting-be, and in this sense, he calls backward to his concerns about misbegotten attempts at having and holding onto power rather than to powerlessness. But what I am emphasizing here is that it is *also* a kind of lying, a "demonic" lie, because its method is to resemble (while not being) Christ.[158] Thus, Balthasar says, "the power that has been usurped must conceal itself by the lie; the lie cannot abolish itself."[159] It is a radical nonaffirmation of being, being at all or in the first place, but with the "face" of an affirmation. And its method is, further, to enforce the surrender of another's power for its own gain. With a half step, a slight turn of the head, the divine wisdom of a compassionate renewal of human freedom from within becomes a mechanism for evacuating someone else's inviolate freedom or their realization of it, *even should they agree*. If it leaves them an empty husk, it was never the kenosis or compassion it pretended to be.[160] And it performed its task not just by confusing itself with what is God's alone to be and to do but also by feigning otherwise or by executing its new and false status in any case. This false "face" can be worn by the church itself.

A theo-dramatic account of tradition relies on the mechanisms of representation (or mission) and kenotic obedience. What this means is that Christian tradition is "about" kenotically making room for God's saving action in itself,

155. Balthasar, *TL* 3:402.

156. Cf. Balthasar, 3:405.

157. Cf. Balthasar, *TD* 4:157–58.

158. Balthasar, 4:175.

159. Balthasar, 4:165; cf. 4:179–80.

160. I do not have the space here to track the totality of this logic in Balthasar other than its summary. An exploration of it is, however, available in Lyle Enright, "An Art of Divine Protagonism: Questions of Power, Sovereignty, and the Theological Motivations of Contemporary Religious Literature" (PhD diss., Loyola University of Chicago, 2019), esp. 92–139.

an action shaped by the cross. It bears in itself a contemporaneity to Christ's history by making it present, by representing it, in its action, and it also bears in itself that urgent primacy of the present moment. But it also bears an eschatological contemporaneity to the risen Lord of history who now and forever reveals triune love. Balthasar's strong stance on kenotic self-gift also allows a crisis with respect to Christian action in history more generally: it is the crisis of God's own judgment, and whether Christian action is patterned after God or after sin. Both options are not only possible but also real, for Christian action maintains the ambivalence of human action. Here Balthasar's description of the Trinity *in se* and of the Trinity in the economy of salvation is not so much a description of the ontic/historical mechanisms of salvation as it is a hermeneutic for judging Christian action itself. The heuristics of this interpretive key emphasize the freedom of self-gift, the primacy of letting the other be, and nonviolent "power in powerlessness." Christian and non-Christian failure to act in this way—whether or not they explicitly seek to imitate God—results in what Balthasar frequently calls "titanism," which has multiple faces but fundamentally eradicates the potency of a human freedom fissured by others.

Revealing the Beat

At this point, I want to harrow Balthasar's theo-dramatics through the writings of James Baldwin and, in this way, to harrow Balthasar through Baldwin's experience. And essential for Baldwin is how American narrative history and its self-representation conceal a reality that is "more vast" than these, which love is tasked with unveiling. Joseph Drexler-Dreis calls Baldwin's work here "revelatory," a revelation accomplished through a historical praxis (literally: a doing) that is "incarnated" or embodied in action; it is an action that is *placed at* and *revelatory of* the "undersides" of the modern colonial, racial situation.[161] This latter phrase, "underside," is borrowed from Walter Mignolo.[162] What it means is that Baldwin roots himself in the realities that the colonial American mythos conceals, and it means that Baldwin roots himself in the people and places out at the edges of the mythos's central action—shifting the axis away

---

161. Joseph Drexler-Dreis, *Decolonial Love: Salvation in Colonial Modernity* (New York: University of Fordham Press, 2019), 103.

162. See esp. Mignolo, *Local Histories*.

from the apparently powerful and to the apparently excluded. It is a rerooting axis or point of view that Balthasar must undergo.

"In America," explains Baldwin, "the color my skin had stood between myself and me."[163] Baldwin describes the trouble of race, of *all* race, as the trouble of an artificiality that prevents a confrontation with my "I" or "me"—my self hidden underneath the role given me (Balthasar)—a confrontation that we might more formally call self-appropriation (Lonergan). This dilemma of race and self is concretely the case, since it situates people in a cruel relationship (social, economic, etc.) of oppressor and oppressed, of tortured relations of actions. This situation creates a predicament where one is *not* what one thinks: the oppressor is not innocent, and the oppressed is not deserving of oppression.[164] In this way, says Baldwin, "the question of color, especially in this country, operates to hide the graver questions of the self."[165] The untruth of the rôle of race, its demonic "lie," must be broken down to make way for the self. And knowing all the parts of the play as it has happened so far is not, will not be, enough. Recovery, if even possible—and Péguy would remind us that it isn't—is not enough.

We are presented with mutilated selves in history. Says Baldwin, "It is a terrible, an inexorable, law that one cannot deny the humanity of another without diminishing one's own: in the face of one's victim, one sees oneself."[166] In terms of the stage, we might say that the dynamic of representation, this mutual sharing of the weight of one's reality by taking up a role, underlies not only positive mutuality but also its negative mirror, thus sharing in human action's ambivalence. Balthasar breaks down the monadic self such that "I" and "other" are not pure and rigid distinctions. The truth of this remains true even in the terror of its abuse. As Baldwin explains, "What is happening to every Negro in the country at any time is also happening to you."[167]

Breaking out of this tragic situation requires change. For Baldwin, it requires love. Love is therefore the essential motivating lever of action, but because it is *also* breaking apart the (unreal and white) world around it, since it is also concerned with truth that is hidden away by lies, it is also violent. This is violent

163. James Baldwin, introduction to *Collected Essays*, 135.

164. James Baldwin, "On Being White . . . and Other Lies," in *The Cross of Redemption: Uncollected Writings*, ed. Randall Kenan (New York: Pantheon, 2010), 167–69.

165. James Baldwin, "The Discovery of What It Means to be an American," in *Collected Essays*, 136.

166. James Baldwin, "Fifth Avenue, Uptown: a Letter from Harlem," in *Collected Essays*, 179.

167. James Baldwin, "In Search of a Majority," in *Collected Essays*, 221.

for Baldwin, says Dreis, "insofar as it breaks down protective veils."[168] Dreis contrasts this form of violence with that of Frantz Fanon, who focuses on armed struggle. According to Dreis, Baldwin's conception is more reflective or epistemic.[169]

In a letter to his nephew, Baldwin illustrates the grotesque innocence of the white world, the peculiar violence of their unawareness, "still trapped in a history which they do not understand." Untying the strings of this self-delusion is necessary for change to become possible. And, Baldwin explains, in a prototypical inversion, the catalyst for such transformation is not at all that *they* (the white world) must accept *them* (the Black world): "The really terrible thing, old buddy, is that *you* must accept *them*. And I mean that very seriously. You must accept them and accept them with love." It is by way of this love-acceptance on the part of the Black subject that the reality of human solidarity (for Baldwin, "brotherhood") is revealed, and it is by way of this love-solidarity that one brother forces the other ("younger") brother to "see themselves as they are" and so to finally see reality, which only when seen can be changed. In this, Baldwin observes a truth most burdensome: "We cannot be free until they are free."[170] And it is clear that "they" cannot free themselves, for that is the very nature of their quandary of innocence.

There is an unbalancing effect in Baldwin's stance as the "elder" brother who must love his younger brother into seeing himself for what he is. One feature of this unbalancing is to posit, repeatedly, that his place at the underside gives him a window into (a more vast) reality, because he is placed where the tight narrative falls apart. White Americans, by contrast, do not run up against reality; this is their affliction, which they visit on him but most of all on themselves.[171] "In order to face the facts of a life like Billie [Holiday's]," Baldwin argues, "or, for that matter, a life like mine, one has got to—the American white has got to—accept the fact that what he thinks he is, he is not. He has to give up, he has to surrender his image of himself, and apparently this is the last thing white Americans are prepared to do."[172] Whereas white Americans are the center of the world that they have made—in history, in economics, in politics, and so on—Baldwin suggests they are not *really* the center at all, most of all because they are sick with unreality: "In evading my humanity, you have done

168. Dreis, *Decolonial Love*, 115–16.

169. Dreis, 104.

170. James Baldwin, "My Dungeon Shook: Letter to My Nephew," in *Collected Essays*, 293–95.

171. Dreis, *Decolonial Love*, 105.

172. James Baldwin, "The Uses of the Blues," in Kenan, *Cross of Redemption*, 74.

something to your own humanity."[173] So Baldwin unbalances the usual situation by insisting on the privilege of the situation's underside. "The Black subject," explains Dreis, "*already* stands on legitimate ground."[174] But Baldwin also unbalances the colonial universe by suggesting that the modern Western project (in addition to, and especially in, its act of centering whiteness and, therefore, unrealness) needs to be dismantled. This is what revelation from the underside helps do, because it reveals the project's invalidity. "At the very least," argues Dreis, such revelation "[catalyzes] the process of doing one's first works over."[175]

Here I am thrown, from the start, into a question that has more than once occupied me: What is *reality*? So also, What is *history*? And what does it mean, if it is possible, to *speak* either of these? And then, what does it mean to *act* in them? My position has been that history is human action (Lonergan), that human action is "metaphysics in act" (Blondel), that this metaphysics-in-action contains a potency for newness or its abrogation (Péguy) in a struggle over ultimate and relative meaningfulness (Balthasar). This emergent compound theory offers different connotations for the words *praxis* and *historical praxis*, for history *is* the praxis of being human, and its narrational mimetics are secondary to its concrete theorization, which is forced—because the human intellect is not equal to knowing the whole of history—to be heuristic.

And what is more, the major arcs of these theoretical comovements fall together because the *real* is an "integral reality" known not in names but in affirmations—that is, in judgments of what is the case—of decentered truth. Only thus is human action, and so human history, able to be, in its potency, more than what it has been; only thus has it meaningfulness or its vampiric opposite; only thus can it be revelatory, of itself and of its fissured transparency to others and to God.

The European notion of history, in the first place, does not rise to an empirical definition of history at all, since its grasp of "human" in "human action" is not just *truncated* but also *beheaded*: it has no sense. Yes, it describes *some* human action, but this is by literal accident, the bleeding color of a *substantia*, because the European notion of the world aims to describe what cannot be described (the whole of human action) and does so by way of a fabulous understanding of what is human *and* without interest in action aside from what it can be imputed to mean. It would require many contortions of logic to call the

173. Baldwin, 75.
174. Dreis, *Decolonial Love*, 109; emphasis mine.
175. Dreis, 111.

operating concepts that effect this notion a "history" in any theoretical sense, which is the only sense, in fact, by which the "all" of history can be known. Human beings are and have been capable of such contortions. But what I mean is that race is not only phenotypical nothing; it is also—as an attempt to describe *history*—nothing. It describes a no-thing.

This no-thing does *not* mean that race has failed to be real-to-us; it is certainly a violent and convoluted universe of pseudomeanings that inform human action and is also the result of human action, and in this fashion, race is quite devastatingly indeed "historical." For if the supporting structure of a strict theory of history can, to borrow a theo-dramatic theme, reveal the face of a lie, if it can show that this lie is not *history* at all, doing so does not (yet) dis-effect the lie, and it does not do so doubly: lies can provide the reasons for human action despite being untrue, all while, at the same time, we must realize that to unveil this false face is not yet to undo its doing. Reversal, as Balthasar insists, is revelation-in-action.

So what is historical reality now? What would it mean to reveal this realness historically? If the real as the affirmed intervenes here, it means that many names are possible to one reality, each of them affirmable and therefore real.[176] Human speech is not able to utter, *simpliciter*, the whole of reality. But we do have the task of finding as many affirmable notions of it as are possible to us. This would require, too, the task of exposing what is not really so. The real as the affirmed does mean, it must mean, that the price of realness involves the "white man" realizing that "he" is not what he knows himself to be and that he has never been this. It also means the revelation, under the constraints of Blackness, of the truth of human being *beyond* Blackness, beyond a Blackness that never, in reality, expressed the truth of this being. As Balthasar would say, truth is unveiled in its situation, and so the truth of the Black subject reveals the lie of race from within race's historical situation.

At the level of a different horizon, real-as-intelligible (affirmable) "places" its *underside* distinctly. For one thing, it pares away the spatial inferences of "underside," for there is no *where* to be *under*, except that of reality. But I mean this complexly. If "underside" is in at least one sense disclosive of the inadequacies of colonial modernity's measure of the real, it is also disclosive of the ways that these inadequacies create new situations for human beings, new conditions for the challenge of disclosing their being. Undersides are first *made*, and if we are precise, they are made by human action and human meaning, and its nonmeaning.

---

176. Special thanks again Jonathan Heaps for helping me articulate this.

The creative, historical aspect of the "underside" is to break its conditions or to unmake them by reversing them. Or to put it another way: the Black nonpersonal "commodity" of colonial mythos *speaks*.[177] But since there is no "where" that this happens except in the facts of our situation, including their nonintelligibility, there is no pure underside that is not caught up in the ambiguity of its historical situation, that is not in some way determined by its truth and the nontruth imposed on it, that is not entangled, already, with the master narrative that made it to be.[178] This is the tangle of a confrontation with reality as a historical situation.

Something important to Balthasar's theoretical construal of God's action in history is that this action is supernatural, though the fulcrum of this action has created terms. Revelation, the vast more-real in question, is of the absolutely transcendent triune God, discoverable in the heart of the God-man poured out on the cross. But it would be a mistake to *contrast* this with Baldwin's confrontation with historical reality. One reason is Copeland's, and before her James Cone's: the concreteness of Jesus's love in history, and for Copeland his very bodiliness, associates him inextricably with the oppressed. The triune God of the poured-out heart is discoverable in the "least" (Matt 25:40). And this associative measure is both concrete and supernatural. In terms of the theo-drama, human gesticulation, its weltering self-perplexity, and its superhuman predicament in the midst of iniquity are all seized in the work of the Trinity in history in order to doubly articulate this Trinity and this creation. What I am saying is that this Christian association between the triune God and the "least" in the incarnation is not mere word game but a precise expression of what it *means* that God makes human history his own.

And this meaning is also and ultimately divine. So in the theo-drama, what is at work in human history is, in a precise way, supernatural to human beings. Two dangers immediately rise up here. One is a retreat from history to the supernatural, which Péguy describes as a retreat from temporality into eternity and as a reversal of the "toward the world" of the incarnation. It is the banishment of charity. Another danger sinks the proportions of the theo-drama into their purely mundane terms, which for Balthasar is not only erroneous but also monstrous, for now divine authority is exacted upon human flesh by human flesh. It is something like Willie Jennings's description of how the universality of

177. A reference to Fred Moten, *In the Break: The Aesthetics of the Black Radical Tradition* (Minneapolis: University of Minnesota Press, 2003).

178. Dreis, borrowing from Baldwin, emphasizes an act of love that fundamentally means "plunging in" to the ambiguous "city" of colonial modernity. Cf. Dreis, *Decolonial Love*, 102.

the gospel is, in colonialism, applied exclusively to the flesh of Europeans. But I must ask, "Where" is this universal gospel to be found except in the (divine) fulcrum of human flesh? Is the gospel, in a way, trapped in its "toward the world"? This is a way not only to ask whether the crisis of Christian cruelty is inevitable—which, after the fashion of human frailty, it might be—but also to ask if it is *determined* by Christianity's interior form, and so Christianity, in an absolute and not a relative sense, is inevitably cruel.

Here I think Balthasar permits a clarification with his stage-language, since the "what" at work in the divine work in human beings who are "in Christ" is human disponibility and so human freedom, the ability to represent by offering a realness freely. It is an enactment that fissures open to reveal both this finite freedom and its ultimate, infinite source.[179] This offers us a fixed guiding light: the work of the gospel is the breaking-open of human freedom in the intimate space of its interiority such that it can be expressive of infinite freedom (Blondel's double *afférence* might show its face again here) and therefore anything that would violate this opening-up—or prevent it, or impose it—is the gospel leveraged against itself. "The potential with which the Logos has endowed the world he has created," explains Balthasar, "is meant to be recognized and activated by man as his own, in a divinely willed and increasing autonomy."[180] Since the divine meaning and the divine action under question are revealed to be Trinitarian and kenotic, the shape of finite freedom that God makes possible in the theo-drama is of a loving letting-be, which is a willing of the other.

In connection with a loving letting-be, it is worth probing again the burden of the revelatory love that Baldwin articulates from the underside. I think it is worth probing again because it is more than an inversion of the state of things, where the lie of white historical self-centering is exposed by the centered Black subject. It is, in a way, a "more" than underside. A quality of this "more" is the agency effected and expressed in this new center, the reality and authority of the human subject misnamed *Black*. But I want to ask about this agency and the *ought* that it discovers within itself, because I think it is superhuman. By this I do not mean that it is inhumane, though perhaps we might think of the compassion here required of the victims of history in this way, and not wrongly. I mean that Baldwin's love-solidarity is more than human freedom is able to effect, though it *reflects* and *operates through* a fully natural solidarity.

---

179. Cf. Balthasar, *TD* 2:123, which introduces the phenomenon of the "perfect" and free human response, ultimately found in the Virgin Mary.
180. Balthasar, 4:475.

Baldwin senses something of this dilemma when he confronts the fact of death and all our various misshapen efforts at avoiding this fact. Rather than facing death in its facticity, Baldwin describes the mundane ways we erect totems as bulwarks against it: race, nation, flag, even religion.[181] And I think if we take the caesura of our death seriously, then we also run up against the limits—literal, metaphysical, historical—of asking for a love that in truth frees another. It dies, in a way, because we do.[182] But I do not mean that it is impossible. I mean that the nature of its possibility is supernatural.

Exchanging good for evil requires supernatural intervention for its effectiveness, since mere "more good" from us does not dissolve the surd of evil in the facts of our situation. For Lonergan, this is the logic of redemption being a supernatural act at all. And for Blondel, it is wholly possible for religion to fail in its supernatural vocation and to cut itself off at an abrupt and artificial end of human action, which is to say, it is possible for religion to end in "superstition." So again: our acting requires God's acting in it to be effective, to be effectively changed. And in Balthasar's theo-dramatic construal of God's acting in our acting, the turn hinges upon the obedience of Christ, which is achieved from "within" our freedom. It is also God's judgment of evil. "The *krisis* of the world [in Christ]," Balthasar explains, "is not an act or moment that can be distinguished from its perfect affirmation."[183]

A love that in truth frees another is possible in Christ. The incarnation fissures open the uniqueness of a particular human freedom in its unique moment in time, and it fissures open the unique action of God-in-Christ.[184] Here I do not mean that God does things for us, replacing our doing, for God's doing is in our doing. Each of us is faced with the truth of our situation. Each of us is tasked with confronting it. And God makes possible a confrontation that is supernaturally transformative. It is a confrontation founded on the triune God, who is love, and on God's love for the world.

This love would be a *struggle* against the powers of iniquity and a struggle, we might say, for justice, standing between "is" and "ought."[185] So too, this love would suffer *dramatic heightening*, as its increasing revelation provoked further

---

181. James Baldwin, "Down at the Cross," in *Collected Essays*, 339.

182. Cf. Balthasar's discussions of death, as in *TD* 2:37–39; 4:95–136.

183. Balthasar, "Claim to Catholicity," 4:104; cf. 4:102–4.

184. See, for example, Balthasar, 2:38–39; Balthasar, "Claim to Catholicity," 4:108–9.

185. For a more thorough description of such a Balthasarian struggle, see Todd Walatka, *Von Balthasar and the Option for the Poor: Theodramatics in the Light of Liberation Theology* (Washington, DC: Catholic University of America Press, 2017).

resistance. Exposing race for its lie and struggling against it bears the marks of cruciformity, because it will be resisted. But it would also be the expression an absolutely peerless love that has no opposite, not even in evil, revealing not only the radical baselessness of evil but also the more radical founding of all creation in infinite triune love.

And here emerges a difference from Baldwin. Though Balthasar ambivalently permits justified violence in largely Augustinian terms, he does not do so in theo-dramatic terms.[186] For Balthasar, this is the divine love that does not meet violence with violence, thus exposing its greater position not with force but with vulnerability. And the warp and wake of this love, as meaningful action, is properly divine: it is not asked, as such, of the human being by anyone but by the God who makes it possible. So though theo-dramatic reversal has something of Baldwin's loving stripping away of masks, it is also differently ordered around love as "violence," and while I would hesitate to call it the opposite of Baldwin's conception of love, I would equally hesitate to associate the love in *Theo-Drama* with love-as-violence.

To connect these differences, I want to elaborate a dramatic theme. It is that of "Black rage." This rage can be understood as "the expression of freedom under grave threat," says Erin Kidd. It is an "I" that, under the constraints of a role that is violent to it, breaks forth with its "I" with anger. Kidd describes this anger as a provisional "no" to the world as it is. A rejection, we might say, of the "is" in the "is" and "ought" of the world. She explains, "If the objective material of one's freedom is a world hostile to the operation of that same freedom, one's affirmation of God and self can only take the form of a provisional 'no' to the world. What is lost is the chance for one's 'yes' to God, world, and self to coincide, and for one's freedom to be celebrated under any other banner but rage."[187] But this rage is also conceivable as a "yes" to God, and so to the world that God intends, which is not, in this sense, the world as it is.[188]

Inasmuch as, in dramatic theory, the expression of rage in history, a rage responsive of injustice, is the expression of an "I" set against its role, we can also say that the rage of this "I" is expressive of the way it outstrips its role. If,

186. Note, for example, the major discussion of Reinhold Schneider and his pacifism in Hans Urs von Balthasar, *Tragedy under Grace: Reinhold Schneider on the Experience of the West* (San Francisco: Ignatius, 1997).

187. Erin Kidd, "The Violation of God in the Body of the World: A Rahnerian Response to Trauma," *Modern Theology* 35, no. 4 (2019): 672.

188. Kidd, 673.

for Balthasar, the only "name" or "role" that in any ultimate sense could be fitted nonviolently to a finite "I" is the name for the person in the mind of God, then we can also articulate that there are roles in history not only that *do not* aid the appropriation of this divine "name" but that actively conceal and hinder it, indeed violently. The more-than of the "I" that rejects the role assigned to it would be, in the transcendence of its more-than, a referral (a "yes") to the true "name" of the "I" in the mind of God, "against" the names of history. And this would be, finally and with the help of Kidd, a theo-dramatic way to adopt Baldwin's revelatory love that must violently strip away masks, without yet violating Balthasar's concern for love as the expression of personality.

Conclusion

There are those for whom Christianity is in the strictest sense tragic, and menacingly. And the truth underneath this menace and its perpetuation, which makes it tragic, is that the past is not a thing to be escaped, for history is never stepped out of, especially as it lives on in Baldwin's sense: in the throes of an unwitting, false-faced innocence. "Above all," we might say with Péguy, "one must be careful of continuing. Continuing, persevering, in that sense, is all that is most dangerous to justice and to intelligence itself. To take one's ticket on departure in a party, in a faction, and never to bother where the train is rolling to, and above all, what it is rolling on, is to put oneself resolutely in the very best situation for becoming a criminal."[189] And as much as this and the other chapters rattle awake to describe and redescribe the predicament of a Christianity enmeshed in, supported by, and operating to perpetuate colonial structures and most especially the structure called "race," this chapter (and the others) faces an irony, which is that it wakes up as what it is, even if it does not want to be this. The people and ideas that we have met in this book are the truth of their history. It would be understandable, and understandable because true, to accuse any "performance" of theology that brings together the Christianity that suffers its whiteness with its own undersides, of threatening to be, or of being, a reperformance of its own tragedy. There is something that vanishes even in my, the author's, "I," because it is not an "I" of the undersides.

And yet, the facts of our present and their history *need not be*.[190] This "need not be" is an expression in defiance of historical determinism and in favor of

189. Péguy, "Memories of Youth," 29.
190. Copeland, "Household of Faith," 62.

human self-transcendence in the present as it "wells up," and in the future laden in such a precarious present tense. The "need not be" of our present is in its way our only hope for the past too. And it does not, perhaps, seem to be enough. Indeed, I can say with sad certainty that it is not. The situation of human history, and of Christian tradition, is superhuman.

But there is, too, the triune God whose dramatic struggle with evil reinscribes human freedom with its dignity by cleaving it personally to himself. There is the acting of a God who reverses history from within by way of a repudiation of sin and a radical affirmation of being. An affirmation founded in the infinite will of God *and* in a precarious human will like our own. Thus, the glory of divine freedom and its human likeness, beheld in this man (John 19:5), are at last revealed: that freedom wills others to be. And to will another is most of all to love them.[191]

Human power, restored to itself, does not act apart from its vulnerability to the present moment. Such power in vulnerability is where God acts and where Christianity most resides. The effectiveness of power here is not in its "over against," in the iron of a guarantee whose means is the force of its must. No, this power is discovered in freedom's willing of the other—I might also say, in the free willing of another present and its future, one where every "I" can be.

What is not enough for us is enough for God. Thus, we can be only where we are, burdened by the history that is ours. Some might demand more than this, but if there is something to be garnered from these several chapters of mine, it is that there is not more at hand. There is nothing available to us other than the "need not be" of our concrete moment in history, in the arduous task of an original gesture, which God acts within in order to bring about our second innocence. Or, with Baldwin, I could say, we must do our first works over again. This, of course, means that we can *not* do so. But this is not decided. And this not-decided is the vulnerable question that human action and its meaning makes of itself in every moment and that is the fulcrum of God's action.

We are charged with not allowing the moment to slip away. And in this, we entrust ourselves to every hour that faces us with a confident hope in the God who lets nothing that is slip away.

191. Notice, by way of illustration, Péguy's description of the Dreyfusards in "Memories of Youth," 76–79. It is the charity that will not tolerate a single injustice to be visited upon a person by a nation. Indeed, this willing of the other goes further than any earthly love. See, for example, Hans Urs von Balthasar, "Forgetfulness of God and Christians," in *Explorations in Theology*, vol. 3, *Creator Spirit* (San Francisco: Ignatius, 1993), loc. 4600–4604 of 5716, Kindle.

5

ENDS

Oh end of things! When all
is turned to gold, turned too bright
for eyes that presently look on,
wishing for the time and its delay,
mothered urgently by the spectacle

of her, of our, of loss.

Throughout this book, I have brought forward human figures, "saints," through whom we have arrived at an understanding of the being of Christian tradition as true and as historical—and as subject to sin. For Hans Urs von Balthasar, the saints preserve and express, in their living-out of Christianity, a specifically Christian "metaphysics," a strident affirmation of the wealth of created being, achieved through a historical and a personal enactment of a divine love that surpasses both saint and being.[1] And whereas our image of saints might be that of a holiness set so far apart from us that we might even find it discouraging, Balthasar's image is of fools, rogues, failures, "duelists with death."[2] This

1. See Balthasar, *The Glory of the Lord: A Theological Aesthetics*, vol. 5, *The Realm of Metaphysics in the Modern Age* (San Francisco: Ignatius, 1991), 51–52, 646–52.

2. Balthasar discusses these terms with various examples in "Folly and Glory" in *GL* 5:141–204. There is a lively discussion in Balthasar scholarship about the limits of Balthasar's own understanding of saints. It is not my purpose to reiterate and decide the stakes of that question here, even if something like a nascent position is discernible in whom, exactly, I have chosen as my "saints."

book's saints are not, perhaps, fit for a glossy card. But that is the point: they, in their historical being, love in a way that indicates the love that surpasses every concreteness, and so suffuses every concreteness.

Such an all-surpassing love "looks" different in these saints, in each of their faces, but most of all in those faces that we have come to call "Black." These faces, by their very existence, by the (hidden) glory of their self-transcendence, critique the whiteness of these other saints of mine, and of myself. The half step of hesitancy built into Christian historical being, where everything non-white suffers the strangeness of an artificial nonbeing—together with our own traditioned unfamiliarity with associating *their* love and *their* concerns for *their* neighbors with an essentially Christian love and concern for neighbor—is the expression of a staggering dilemma for Christian tradition, the dilemma of how to extricate ourselves from our living-out of colonial existence and its primary actions, most of all in race.

My task in this chapter is to gesture with an eschatological hope—hope in the redemption of human history; in the redemption of the "matter to be redeemed," which is humanity and most of all the pilgrim church;[3] and in the redemption of this church's tradition, which suffers its ambiguity and sin at that axial point by which it is, the axis of human action, in which God acts, and in which the church cleaves to God and to humanity. "The Church," says *Lumen Gentium*, "embracing in its bosom sinners, at the same time holy and always in need of being purified, always follows the way of penance and renewal."[4] If, for Charles Péguy, the worst of deeds is *to continue*, then my task here is to dare an indication of what it means for Christian tradition *to begin again* this day, to seek with God to be the perpetual renegade that is Péguy's "honest man," the dramatic human "I" of a second innocence, a *probité*.

My gesture of hope, made in the rest of this chapter, is one that emerges from four smaller, more fragmentary gestures. The first is a turn to my practical situation as a scholar, to some of the logic that has animated my decisions in making my argument in the previous chapters. This reflection is meant as an example of what it "looks" like to struggle with one's tradition for the sake of its betterment under the light of grace. Then I consider what it means for us to relate to our past in new ways, and after that, I consider the urgency of

---

3. "Matter to be redeemed" is a borrowing from Bernard Lonergan, *Collected Works of Bernard Lonergan*, vol. 9, *The Redemption* (Toronto: University of Toronto Press, 2018), 141.

4. *Lumen Gentium* §8.

our present moment and its eschatological dimensions. Last, I offer a coda that reconceives familiar themes under a new light.

A Return to Practicality

I have written this book as a Catholic with a hope that it will be helpful to more than Catholics. Still, my ecumenical help and hope mean that Catholic history informs me, especially in this: how the Catholic nineteenth century witnessed a major and fraught turn to include history in theology. By "history," I mean not so much a notion that there is a past or a patrimony that we receive, which theology possessed well before the nineteenth century, or even a nascent version of the notion that theology and doctrine develop, which is at least discernible in far older Christian centuries; rather, I mean the notion that historical context fundamentally determines the meaning of texts and theologies and doctrines. *This* turn to history eventually broke open, in the Catholic universe, into the Modernist controversy. Truth itself appeared sundered unto historical relativism, or history appeared vanquished before the objectivity of truth. Yet the historical turn continued apace, in and beyond the controversy, and Catholic theologies flowered into many and various versions of involving history in theology. But this does not mean that the threatened double loss of the Modernist controversy, in its impossible choice between history and truth, has ceased to haunt theology and theologians.

It is my position that we are haunted even still. There is something of the ghost's taste, indeed, almost everywhere, perhaps especially in those theologies that set their teeth against one another. And underneath this new notion of history that haunts us all, underneath its new problems for theology, is a two-edged knife of a question that remains for the most part unasked, or at least, unasked in a way that has managed to soak the fabric of our collective doing: What is *history*, and what does that make *tradition*? We as theologians have yet to provide full-throated theories of these notions. My task has been to break the bonds that separate our many theological inquiries by speculating about human historical being and the mediation of divine truth in it.

Christians will always wrestle painfully and wondrously with and about their tradition. If, as I have argued, Christian tradition is a mediating Christian action, then Maurice Blondel's "literal practice" of a religion and its dogmas remains fraught with questions that haunt us as old ghosts rise to us as new. Weighty interpretive questions about tradition therefore remain, and there remains a need as well for theologians to develop instruments for these problems. I have provided *instrumentarium* by which we might avoid false starts in these hermeneutical (and often deeply ecclesiological) theological questions, by which we might found new questions, and by which we might reconsider old questions without their mere repetition. For the sake of such newness, for the sake of our interpretive problems, I would have us relax, even if only a little, our death grip around the either-or between truth and history, or around their identification, both of which are burdened by questions of truth and sin, in what is an anxiety secreted underneath so many of our theological experiments.

I have applied my speculative theory to the staggering problem of Christian tradition's responsibility for colonialism and race, partly to redescribe that problem using the operating framework that I have assembled. Thus, it has been possible to "see" the work that my theory is able to do, and though it does not resolve what is for Christian tradition a present circumstance, it does effect in its action a potency for new insights about our circumstance such that we are able to take new responsibility for it.

My efforts in this text will have been imperfect. My heuristics will require application, and that application will reveal adequacies and inadequacies that will require a reformulation of the heuristics at work in my theory. After all, the Black subject, as a concrete instance of various oppressed peoples, does not suffice as a figure for all such peoples in every way. Nor is colonialism itself a monolithic historical event. And I have not been able to touch upon the sexual undertow that pulls sharply underneath the process of racialization. What is more, there is a serious struggle to be had in theology around the origins of the church, an origin in the Trinity's intention for history and in a human history marked by sin, and around how that mark impacts our notion of this double origin and its purity or lack of purity. These are but a few of the questions that face the theory, including as they do the much broader hermeneutical methods and ecclesiological questions that a "metaphysic" of tradition simply is not. That I cannot develop all the necessary correlates by myself underlines that the Christian theological task is a collaborative one, or else it does not survive.[5]

This book is a response that strives to be responsible for its concrete circumstance. Accounts of *ressourcement*, as a technique or in its iteration as a historical movement of theologians, tend to be overwhelmingly positive—at least when

---

5. Collaboration became a particular emphasis of Lonergan's. See Jonathan Heaps, "Getting to the Roots of Modern Culture: On Lonergan Part II," *Genealogies of Modernity* (2021), https://genealogiesofmodernity.org/journal/2021/4/21/bernard-lonergan-modern-culture-ii.

not written by a devotee of Réginald Garrigou-Lagrange. But this difference is illusory; even neo-Scholasticism was (and is) a resourcing of Thomas Aquinas.[6] My point is that these wings in the mansion of modern Christian theological reflection tend to view, and to be used to view, Christian tradition through its positive lights. Tradition here is a *resource* overflowing in goodness that can therefore be resourced. That such a treatment narrows Péguy's original meaning is important, but only ancillary to my point: in this book, I am responding to a certain triumphalism about Christian tradition as a resource, a triumphalism discoverable in various forms in contemporary theological conversations. Such triumphalism lives on, indeed, even in radical negations of Christian tradition by Christians. I respond with a *ressourcement* that rediscovers the life of Péguy's intent, and I respond with a view of Christian tradition that is far less triumphal, though it is by no means negative in any absolute sense. Indeed, I have argued that there is an ambiguity of human action in its being, which tradition as action suffers, to its glory and its guilt.

But there is a further illusory division in modern Christian theological reflection that reserves the technique and the history of *ressourcement* as a theological method to the realm of white (European) thinkers, opposing *ressourcement* to liberation theologies and other nonwhite theological movements and their histories at least by implication, if not explicitly.[7] This division is not an accident, and it is not innocent, however unwitting it may or may not be in the minds of theologians. It is a repetition of the colonial separation of white and Black, of its application of these categories to human beings and to places. In other words: Europe does not own the church fathers; that notions of *ressourcement* developed among white Europeans does not constrain its impact to them; and there are resources and methods for students of *ressourcement* in nonwhite theologians and theologies. In this book, then, I am responding to the pressure of this circumstance, which is my own, by bringing together the instruments of white *ressourcement* thinkers and the instruments of Black theologians and thinkers. The division of labor necessary to modern theological thinking through specialization needs for its success a critique of those divisions that recommit us to sin.

Methodologically speaking, I have not been devoted to any purism toward the Ressourcement movement (note the capital R) and its origins in early

---

6. This is a point that Joseph Flipper makes. See Flipper, "The *Ressourcement* of Black Catholicism in Cyprian Davis, OSB," *Modern Theology* 36, no. 4 (2020): 828–29.

7. Cf. Flipper, 829–30.

twentieth-century Francophone contexts, nor have I been a purist in my real focus, which is on the *nouvelle théologiens'* predecessors, Blondel and Péguy. I am devoted, instead, to the life of their thought in a living theology; that is, I am dedicated to giving the past back to itself, renewed—renewed by the present. This involves for me the methodical frames of Bernard Lonergan and Balthasar as forms of supporting and invigorating such a renewal, and in seeing Lonergan and Balthasar together, I continue the legacy of Robert Doran. The thing to understand in what I do here is that the élan of each of these thinkers is not yet complete; it is capable of and requires furtherance. This is the essential claim of Péguy's *ressourcement-révolution*, which enables the giving-back of the past to itself through its enrichment. Because my theologizing is rooted in Lonergan's underlying, organizing cognitional theory and its method, I have been able to press it in the direction of eclecticism, bending it (notably with Balthasar) against pure scholarly lineages for the sake of an enrichment. Thomism, transformed, has supported the efforts I lay out here. Balthasar, transformed, has supported the efforts I lay out here. And so on. It is a type of theologizing that Balthasar calls "constellating," or that I might call *poikilia*, which in ancient Greek usage referred to the variety of color in embroidery and music.[8] From out of such a perspective, mine is a theorizing that has turned repeatedly and deliberately to bringing *all* of these men into contact with the *aliveness*, with the enriching principle of life, with the refracting variety discoverable in the Black thinkers that I have studied here: Copeland, Jennings, Baldwin.

Fundamental to the problem of colonialism and race is the artificial division of human being, and underneath it, the organization of the good of order around only the few. Europe and Christianity are collapsed into one and the same, a thing, a monolith—a will to power. Reiterations of this collapse have taken various forms over the course of modern history, and what renders them consistent is the vanishing of nonwhite historical agency, concretely through various economic and judicial measures and ideologically through various failures to acknowledge the authority of God's testimony in nonwhite (often Christian!) lives. Christian tradition, executed at cross-purposes with itself, suffered and suffers a narrowing of its character. I have turned to Black voices in order to

---

8. On "constellating," see Hans Urs von Balthasar, "The Plurality of Theology," in Walker, *Explorations in Theology*, 5:386. As for *poikilia*, Sappho's "Fragment 1," for example, uses a form of the root in a compound word: ποικιλόθρον. See Page DuBois, *Sappho* (New York: I. B. Tauris, 2015), 23; cf. David A. Campbell, ed. and trans, "Fragment 1," in *Greek Lyric*, vol. 1, *Sappho and Alcaeus* (Cambridge, MA: Harvard University Press, 1982), 52–53.

struggle into being a Christian tradition that more completely enacts its catholic (its universal) character.

Such a struggle has involved a turn to the roots of that which is living in each of the (white) thinkers that I have discussed in this book to break open and renew that life, as if from within. I did so to commit these thinkers to what they themselves did not do, or could not complete, or could not experience—to what they could not do at the very least because they are dead but more often because they, in their ways, share in that guilty narrowing of the Christian life that colonialism and race visits upon Christian tradition. I have sought to bring what is living in these dead men, and in them to bring myself, before the mystery of these Black lives and their reflections on what it means to be a Christian and a modern person. The widening of these old and narrowed lives thus confronts the creative friction of lives that they (and I) struggled to imagine at all. In these lives, we are all, together, further widened but also critiqued for our narrowness and failure. And lastly, I have worked to speak-together all of these lives, white and Black, including their friction, in order to dare that Christian tradition might be renewed in them, through a beginning-again.

On a New Relationship to the Past

As Blondel says of human action, so we must say of our Christian tradition: it either changes or remains the same—and for this is condemned. By this I do not mean that Christian tradition fails in its essential surety as a mediation, together with Scripture, of the "wellspring" of Jesus Christ.[9] I do mean that this fidelity to Christ in history, by way of the Trinity and also by way of history, is an active fidelity, always in act and therefore always requiring action, in the mode of its own precarity. Though Blondel writes 1893's *Action* before his encounter with John Henry Newman, still Newman's words on doctrine apply: "It changes with them [new controversies, new relations to principles] to remain the same."[10] I might say: it changes to remain itself. But this paradox of change and of fidelity, of these together, is a question more than it is an answer, because it is not clear, in the case of colonialism, what changes fidelity to Christ will require. It is not clear in part because what we deal with here is a set of facts that includes surds. It is also not clear in part because Christian tradition, in its everyday

9. *Dei Verbum* §9.
10. Newman, *Development of Christian Doctrine*, 40.

living, is a collaboration with common sense. But common sense cannot supply an answer of practical intelligence for the sake of this problem because race's operative continuation *is* common sense, and common sense once again does not know its own insufficiency.

Tradition's self-coherence and interior continuity, even if for the most part achieved through the instrument of common sense, are nevertheless not a function thereof. For example, though many of our practical, daily dealings with heat and fire bear a certain, implicit verification of thermodynamics, they are not identical with the theory, which in its knowing has informed and transformed everything from keeping warm to preventing fires. And what is more, the theory often moves against common sense: it is possible, indeed, to fight fire with fire. Or, in another example, the transition in medicine from the commonsensical theory of humors to modern scientific methods "still" means that fevers must be lowered, but it also means that sometimes this fever is an immune response that must receive support. Similarly, it is common sense that says that coherence and continuity in tradition are functions of an unchanging relationship to the past, and while such a claim appears to affirm its thesis, it is a theory of tradition that affirms this coherence and continuity through a changed relationship to the past.

In many discussions of Christian tradition, a certain aestheticism reigns—even an aestheticism of the expression of ideas. By "aestheticism," I mean a reliance on appearance, on material instantiation (whether visual, physical, auditory) as the measure of identity between instances. So often this serves us well. But just as often, it mistakes intelligible form for its appearance, and we wait to love the lepers of the New Testament without realizing that they will be different in our day, and thus we fail to realize that keeping this love will require searching out its intelligible shape. Sometimes indeed Catholics would like our Latin to be our fidelity for us, when our fidelity always must be our own, dear, precarious work, divinely graced in the history that we proclaim to be God's. Sometimes, in Balthasar's way of speaking, an aesthetic theology betrays us with its beauty when what we need is a theological aesthetic.[11] Appearance, then, is not the measure of fidelity; form, or intelligibility, is. (Blondel's "reason" for Christian action.) In a temporal existence that is itself change, it is change that retains the original, even while not being the original. Catholics are accustomed to speaking of this dynamism as development, which more clearly secures the link between the original and its intelligent repetition. In this

11. Balthasar, *GL* 1:33–41.

intelligent repetition, even pure repetition receives its purpose and intelligibility. We pray the words of the Creed because we believe them.

If we must change because our repetition of colonial forms is evil, if that moral imperative presses upon us its weighty evidence, then let it be clear that this "must" is not a betrayal of the Christians of our past, by whom we receive our present circumstance in its wonder and horror. This circumstance, even if we did not make it come to be, is our present responsibility. The ictus of fidelity as first of all intelligible rather than material becomes fundamental, not because ideas are free of question and critique—far from it—but because it is intelligence that questions and that critiques. The question (of intelligence) opens the way, heuristically wedges into being, the being of an action that no longer merely repeats the past. The question allows the problem of colonialism and tradition to become the problem of an original gesture made today. A dialectic of thought and action lays hold of the "need not be" of the present moment, and strikes out in a new direction, making of the past a new thing but also making new things in its present.

But the problem of decolonizing a colonial world has at best barely begun, touching as it does a whole world far outside the interior cataclysms of Western Christendom. Perhaps indeed there was not an "outside" from which to retreat; perhaps Christendom was always fissured by the other, and in our colonial modernity, perhaps the "far" colony is "here" after all.[12] Universities across the globe were *founded* to support the colonial task, and they bear up that task in their every field, their institutional organization, their very stones.[13] Older disciplines (like theology, philosophy, even medicine) endured transfiguration according to the racist, economic task, a change that ran across every nerve of each discipline. Every discipline and their every fragment of knowledge receive the touch of a distorting task. And so, if the Renaissance could pretend it was possible to get around medieval Christendom to find the Greeks and Romans, we today know otherwise. Nothing is got around. Nothing that reaches us today reaches us untouched by the time that intervenes between it and us.

In theological circles, this truth means that even the way we teach the church fathers, or Thomas Aquinas, or John Henry Newman, must be transformed. It

12. Cf. Mbembe, "Proximity without Reciprocity," 90–111.
13. A vivid example that comes to mind is Georgetown's relationship to slavery. See Rachel L. Swarns, "272 Slaves Were Sold to Save Georgetown. What Does It Owe Their Descendants?," *New York Times*, April 16, 2016. See also Joseph Flipper, "Pedagogy toward Refusal," *Horizons* 48, no. 1 (2021): 155–71.

means that we must come to recognize that the way we treat any figure itself has a history, a provenance, a traditioned body of action, that must be discovered and dealt with. It means that these figures themselves require a kind of being-perfected by a more perfect intention than their own, and by an origination more originary than their original, since even when saintly, the intention and its originating work is always an intention and a work of its time and place. We are similarly limited, of course. But we are also alive, and we partake of the providential accident of arriving later. Thus, we must offer to the past its present revolution in our day, and we ourselves must hope to be resourced in still another day. Here, historical inquiry is a first measure that roots such figures, including ourselves; but historical inquiry gives way to, or must be transposed into, an inquiry about present problems. This can be positive: Blondel's critique of integralism acquires a new purpose and force. It can also be negative: Péguy's mental geography, since colonial, must be transcended with another one.

There is much in such an unwieldy task that does not recommend itself. A tyranny of a present-ism or future-ism looms its way into fears that I, at least, know well. Similarly, there is a sincere surrender of comfort that takes place in any surrender of the familiar. It is not that I myself do not get annoyed at our wide ignorance of our Christian past or feel no doubt about what is so often thin guesswork about what the young want or need from a reeling church or that I never frown at the suffocating effect of some ecclesiological or theological gestures. I do. But it is also true that "our Christian past" is much more, *and* much more monstrous, than we are often accustomed to thinking; it is also true that knowing *this* past is explanatory of a great deal in our actual present, that this expanded past gives to us an urgent present task—the task, that is, of dealing with the past in its present presence. I suggest not a reduction of Christianity but an expansion, an expansion that rises to meet Christianity in its concreteness through a confrontation with present injustices and their origins. Christian fidelity is rarely comfortable.

Each day seems to witness the rise of programs and institutions designed around restoring attitudes and systems of really a rather recent Christian past. I see the articulation, in words but also in organizations, of devotion to the "true" liberal arts, to "real" Catholic theology, to the glories of the Western tradition, all perceived as under threat. And what is under threat most often are norms and apparatuses no older than the nineteenth century, even if the vintage number on the bottle reads "medieval Christendom." It is so often the bluster of a false history. For the liberal arts, Catholic theology, and Western tradition have never been self-enclosed, monolithic, or stable. The "threat" of loss and change here is the threat of allowing these to be what they have always been—the "always" of their own temporality—that is, to be what the logics of more recent histories conceal. Yes, it is true that many Christian institutions are now this and now that desperate effort to appeal and to survive, in a succession of so many fads, but this failure of intelligence hardly warrants another. And intelligence says that keeping our past requires no less than changing our relationship to it.

The temptation, for reformists and revolutionaries and recalcitrants alike, will be to imagine a history of discrete conceptualities and human actions arriving all at once and whole such that they can be modified, overthrown, or preserved: like a body mottled by tumors that can be removed, or whose only existence is cancerous, or that is in any case a *body* and so always, at least to the mind's eye, clearly bounded. What I have argued for in this text, with respect to Christian tradition, is more difficult, since each of these options is in a sense true and in another sense false. Christianity's entanglement in colonialism will not be a question of simply dropping what is colonial in it, since Christianity does not exist outside its own, its present, colonial shape. Yet this shape was not and is not inevitable, however likely its repetition also is; it is not inevitable even if this "not inevitable" rests only on the thin hope that is the human freedom to do otherwise.

Christian tradition is a body of action. Like all bodies, the "action" of tradition is really many operations operating simultaneously in a system of transcending movement. Like all bodies, its "inside" and "outside" are self-evident only for realisms and idealisms.[14] Something like this insight, where clean lines vanish, sustains the despair that despairs whether Christian tradition can be reformed at all, or ever. For Christian tradition is traditioned ironically, by its own sin. There is no escaping to somewhere other than where it presently is. But a theory of tradition bounded by critical realism affirms one operation of tradition to be the community's judgment of its own thought and action. Here tradition rises, not away from human history and into the hovering realm of ideas, but into human action as an action whose truth and goodness can be judged—that is, into human action in its ambiguity, with a mind for that action's clarification through affirmation. And the being of action can sustain many affirmations at once. Thus can, and thus *must*, a community judge its saints to be saintly and also sinful, and it can do so without making of their historical bodies a menagerie of dislocated parts, and it can judge what those sins might

---

14. The accounts of a self-evident border between "tradition" and "not-tradition" are something like Lonergan's notion of the "body" (i.e., the term in quotations). See Lonergan, *Insight*, 275–79.

be. Rising to the task of decolonization is something of a similar order. Like all judgment, it gives to human freedom a new deliberation. The gift, as it were, but also the command, of a new task with new decisions.

What I speak of here is not easy. It requires, as its primary movement, queries into the Christian past that will unveil that past as less than familiar and whose intelligible goal is to iterate a new, nonhabituated relationship to that past. On several levels, I mean a search that is quite practical: an examination of our history with and in colonialism, of the varying mechanisms by which we and all that we are—our communities, our theologies, our institutions, our councils, our very imaginations—have been and continue to be the active instruments of the violent racialization of humanity and, more profoundly, the violent inequalization of human beings, the rupture of our solidarity. If sin is surd, then its facticity is its only quality capable of genuine confrontation. But the facts of history, even without their surds, are tongueless by themselves; history requires interpretation. So we must interpret and pass judgment over the shadows that persist underneath the gold of our memories, underneath our present actions, because to love the truth is to face the entwinement of each with the other. A past and present perhaps lovely become also monstrous.

It is the death, in a way, of the belief that Christianity is a religion of a first innocence. That this innocence is discoverable, or rediscoverable. In Catholic terms, I might ask, Is it not true that the purity of the "yes" wrought by the Virgin at the annunciation is—as pure and also as "yes"—itself wrought by the work of the cross? And who would we be to be any different, to be better than being also wrought by the cross? Perhaps, then, a certain naivete dies at the foot of the cross. But let us let the dead bury the dead; let ours be the religion of a second innocence, arduously placed; quick now, here, now, and always, in the passion of a charity that responds to evil with a supernatural good: we have the Trinity's work still to do, and to be done in us.[15]

The Pressure of Eternity in the Present Hour

This new exploration of our own past is not only, not even primarily, the uncovering of our many sins; underneath those sins are whole peoples, countless human persons, whose lives we remove from our collective memory, in whom we who so amputate our memory are also found. So in this turning backward,

15. "Quick now . . ." is a reference to the end of "Burnt Norton" in T. S. Eliot's *Four Quartets*.

there is not only a kind of negation—of our own glory, at least—but also a kind of discovery: of persons who were and are also Christians, of persons impacted by Christianity, of persons erased by Christianity, of Christianity as it in fact is, expanded by its own facticity, and expanded in a forward direction, moved by the ground these facts provide for further questions. For these persons are not only in our past; they stand before our eyes in our present. This is a Christianity that is present. And this presence orients our own action and its eschatological realism.

The forward tilt of eschatology tends to disintegrate into a kind of deferral, either of God's hour or of our responsibility in the present hour (which is also, after all, God's). But even a realized eschatology tends toward an oscillation between two reductions, often conceived in terms of whether a theology is "too" political or political "enough." This section instead stands on the notion of the supernatural that I have argued for in these pages; it provides, then, a heuristic glance or indication of matters more explicitly wrestled over in many other theologies. Part of that heuristic will be the Black subject of colonial modernity, as has been my general focus in this book, as a way of indicating the undertow of an "underside" populated by many persons of many kinds.

If a tradition as a present historical situation is to be a transformed situation, then it must be a transformation of the meaning and the action that "make" the situation, and its hinge for transformation is the human person. Balthasar underlines the following about our theo-dramatic historical situation: the *person* who transfigures our situation is the Word sent by the Father in the Spirit, and the *meaning* that transfigures the situation is the divine Word (Logos) of the Father, whose kenotic obedience is the (historical) *action* by which the Trinity transfigures our situation. Now I want to fill out this Balthasarian heuristic in a new direction, one that takes our own situation as its dramatic situation, and so acquires a point of view that considers those meanings, actions, and persons by which the triune God in Christ makes our present situation *theo*-dramatic. Those *persons* are Black subjects in history, the *meaning* is the truth of their dramatic being in history, the *action* is the kenotic self-expression of their personality (their flourishing) in history. So in what follows, we will need a Blondelian stereoscopic eye: for the supernatural action of God, for the natural action that God acts in, for the double *afférence* that animates the integral world that is ours.

The Black subject is already constitutive of our modern situation, the one on whose back we have built our world; but the Black subject *in their self-transcendence* is also relatively supernatural to the world that we have built. After all, no one called "Black" is supposed to bear up their subjectivity with creativity and passion. They exist in spaces and places designed to wreck their subjectivity and their communal solidarity. Indeed, that so many do suffer immensely under the burden of a good of order that tries to explain its injustices as if race and not persons accomplish them, that so many lives are indeed wrecked, testifies to the power of our racialized situation.

I want to be careful here: that so many die in the ignominy of our packed prisons, that so many endure until they can no longer endure, indeed that they *can no longer*, is its own testimony to self-transcendence, to the self-transcendence that cracks apart along the high shores of a world that denies the very being of this self and its transcendence. This is true, while it is also true that Black subjects struggle into being greatly varied personalities of immense communal responsibility, while Black art witnesses to memory and loss and love and joy while demanding justice again and again before an indifferent white universe. So Black subjects embody our situation and also the potency of its demise; in them is a "new situation" that is a revelation of the real, for they are quite real, for they are *already* real, and at the same time, they introduce new possibilities to the real, for in the logic of race, they are not supposed to be "real" to us at all.

What I mean is complicated. It is complicated because I mean to point out a situation of injustice bent around persons of African descent. But I also mean to point out that "African descent" does not contain the situation as container and contained, does not explicate situations constituted by actions, meanings, and persons. For they are not the only persons who act. They are not the only meaning in play. And they themselves are not summarized or explained *by* racism. Not because racism is unreal, psychotic hyperbole but because it is real and unreal; its psychosis is the very real refusal to ask further, relevant questions. I am stressing the reality; I am stressing the refusal. I am concerned that theological discourse about and around race and racism, about and around colonialism, simplifies the situation and therefore impoverishes our understanding. Our temptation, in a situation evinced of sense broken into pieces by nonsense, is to grab hold of one fragment of sense and to totalize it. To solve the situation by solving a part.[16] Thus, Baldwin's claim, "race stood between myself and me,"

---

16. Cf. Lonergan, *Insight*, 8: "We correct old evils with a passion that mars the new good. We are not pure. We compromise. We hope to muddle through. . . . We have to learn to distinguish sharply between progress and decline, learn to encourage progress without putting a premium upon decline, learn to remove the tumor of the flight from understanding without destroying the organs of intelligence."

provides me with many indications rather than only one and suggests a present price that is also a present opportunity, an underside.

Bringing into being a new situation, the situation that God intends for our own, requires a new constitutive meaning. That meaning is Christ, the Logos in the flesh; that meaning is *also* the truth of the human subject called "Black." More heuristically speaking, I mean the truth of the oppressed. This latter, this created truth expresses the truth of Christ, the Logos in the flesh.

These *logoi*, logos and Logos together, are legible without their confusion if we consider that the Black subject's creative self-expression in history is an act of kenotic obedience: obedience to God's intending of their self before the world, obedience to their own will-to-life, obedience to the goodness that God intends for the world through their living self-expression. This self-expression is also a kenosis that makes their expression of themselves an expression of much more: of their communities, of God.

Copeland, Jennings, and Baldwin—representative of a complex thought tradition of many features—posit a Black "I" that is, already, an agent of history and that in this "already" fractures the lie of race at its foundation, since they are not supposed to *have* agency or authority, or must "earn" it. In their anamnesis of this "I" and its expressive history, however composed of fragments it is, these thinkers source the destruction of race in and through the ecstasy of human being (*ens humanitatis*). It is an intelligibility coming into act, into existence, against and despite and beyond the unintelligible. And though expressive of human nature as intelligible or in its intelligibility, the coming into being of this "I" is *also* the instrument of the supernatural and of supraintelligibility.

Every Black "I," expressive of its own mysterious existence as personality, is an efficacious sign of God's work in history. And this "I" is fissured not only by its tragedy, not only by its luminous being in the world, but also by the "I" of Christ. So the Black "I" in its agency is radically fissured by the other: by God, by human being in its being, by *humanity in act* in its radical solidarity. And this fissuring, in Christ, in the supernatural goodness that God brings into being, becomes the present instrument for, as well as the presence of, a future resplendence. "What the enslaved and their descendants mean by Christianity," says Achille Mbembe, "is a space of truth that opens up within an odd scission in a terrain of a truth that itself is always opening itself up—it is a *be-coming*, a futurity."[17]

---

17. Mbembe, *Critique of Black Reason*, 174.

So our hope for Christian tradition's future finds its tomorrow by beginning-again, today, by beginning-again in the (kenotic) beginning-again of Black subjects, today, in their perpetual becoming. And I do not mean that we must leave it to Black subjects to make themselves christological; they already are. Christian tradition begins-again in this "already," which is their own and is also, supernaturally, God's. Our eschaton is near, is near already. It is discoverable in the struggle of the poor of history, which is also God's struggle. In this Black "I," the one already within Christianity but also the one without its visible borders, Christianity—even despite itself—rises to an arduous second innocence that is divinely intended and effected in cooperating action. In these persons, our eschaton stares us in the face. They demand of white Christians a more human humanity, a more traditional tradition. Their present existence calls to us with what we must become, so that our becoming is one enriched by the richness of their own.

Similarly, Christian hope is not for a future far away but for one that is present (cf. Mark 1:15), one that makes its bequest of us in each moment, else the moment pass away (cf. Gal 6:9–10; Eph 5:16). That bequest has a face. It is concrete, just as every goodness is concrete. It is the face of Christ, present in the oppressed, present to us in history. They *already are*. They *already struggle themselves into being*. To recognize them is to recognize the real; it is a return to responsibility, to the fullness of Christ's *pro nobis*, but not one that we effect without the gift, the grace, *that* each of these persons *is*. The triune God is with us already in our yearning for God, yes, *and* the triune God is already on the other side of our unseeing, in the Black subject that we do not (presently) will to see.

Balthasar is explicit about the church's surrender of worldly power before the world, indeed in service of the world. Henceforth must the Christian relationship to the world be one of "mere" gospel and of an absolute commitment, a "yes," with God the Father, to the world. Balthasar did not understand, however, that the surrender of such power is embedded in racial terms and their structures, indeed within and by Christian tradition. So his heuristic, which is that of a church whose historical kenosis includes surrendering its desire for effectiveness-through-power, requires an expansion.

The basic intention of Christian tradition's kenotic obedience, in the case of colonialism, is to perform a self-emptying that results in the dismantling of whiteness. There are many ways to conceive of such a dismantling, and it is hard indeed to intend an absence, a loss, an ending. But the operation of kenosis is not to will a lack. So the destruction of whiteness occurs in, and is ordered by, willing the nonwhite other, by recognizing that they are, by willing them to be themselves, and by following through with concrete action that enables the flourishing and self-transcendence of the nonwhite subject. Theirs is the immanent historical meaning that recollects for us the transcendent meaning of Christ, and so theirs is the immanent meaning that transfigures our situation for the sake of its transcendence. In one sense, what I am describing here is the act of seeking justice for and in their lives, but it is also the act of ordering Christian theological meaning around their lives, not with a merely secular justice, but with a theological justice (as in, for example, liberation theologies). But such seeking of justice and theological ordering cannot be, or at least remain, the domain of theologies specialized around those kinds of concerns, since one of the problems is, very precisely, that the matter is left to them.

For God in Christ is and will be our "all in all" (1 Cor 15:28), and the Christian task in history is to join with the triune God in willing that this surpassing "all" come to be. Much more difficult is, and will be, this task in the wake of a racism, of a colonial world, that narrows our supracosmic willing with God to the space of a strained gasp. In this way, racism ends our Christian action, in Blondel's sense, in mere superstition. But the desire itself remains unrestricted, and our action by its very determinism requires what is supernatural to it. In these realities, we might hope that our struggles as Christians to will the cosmos with the love of God, to will with the passion of a universe that is in love with God, will be made *more* willing and *more* loving, *more* human and *more-than-human*, by God.[18]

We would benefit here by recalling Balthasar's refusal of any strict separation between the objective and the subjective, the "I" and the "other." My language of "we" and "they" suffers, of course, its context, where I indict the "we" that constrains itself to whiteness, including me. This threatens to forever slide the "we" of Christian tradition as I express it into that constraint all over again, partly because that constraint really is the part of our present context that I address. What I say here, however imperfectly, is that this "we" really is not white, never was white, must cease to consider itself white, must in this sense "welcome" no one so much as expand to regard the being that is its own.[19]

Balthasarian kenosis is creative self-expression. This self-expression wills and, in willing, loves another: their freedom, their difference, their own, their

---

18. Cf. Lonergan, *Insight*, 721; and of course Péguy's *révolution* in "Avertissement."

19. I am thinking of the ways Joseph Flipper (correctly, I must stress) critiques ecclesial language in "White Ecclesiology: The Identity of the Church in the Statements on Racism by United States Catholic Bishops," *Theological Studies* 82, no. 3 (2021): 418–39.

expressive personality. This "self" in its willing and loving is fissured, already and evermore, by what it wills and loves. This means, for a racialized Christian tradition, that our kenotic "willing" of the nonwhite other is, at its root, the willing of another's creative and free being-personality in history. We desire that their freedom be their own, that they experience a world where this freedom can be theirs. To desire such a world is to commit oneself absolutely to bringing it into being. To desire it is to be fissured by it. As Balthasar does not conceive of the kenotic Trinity apart from a willing and being of persons, and of each person for the others, so *we* cannot conceive of willing another human person without allowing them and desiring for them their own (since also human) autonomy.

But willing the real autonomy of another is anything but a turning-away or a descent into negative indifference. It means wanting and working for a world that allows this autonomy to be autonomous; it means attending to the creative personalities that thus unfold before the world and in God; it means effecting a kenosis that allows such meaning to affect one's own creative being of a historical personality. There is, in other words, so very much that we who are white must do in order to be freed of our whiteness. It is not a question of not-acting. It is not a question of everyone acting in the same way. And it is not a question to be held off for tomorrow. It is a question of acting now in a way that engenders irreplaceable, personal human action, that recognizes God in the upward *afférence* of this human freedom that is not mine to own, instead of following the model of production that at present so cages us within the empty and impersonal bounds of race.

It is true that here I speak centrally of proximate ends of present acts of justice. But it is also true that this immanence nevertheless points beyond itself to a supernatural justice, the justice that the Christian tradition wills in cooperation with God. Such justice has to mean much more, for example, than grudging cash payouts to our victims. More than apologies. And more than cooperating with the world in bringing about its immanent "ought." For this "ought" also desires, however inchoately, a justice disproportionate to itself—disproportionate indeed even to the church that proclaims the arrival of divine justice and divine mercy in Christ.

With Balthasar, I do not think that the church's relationship to the world will ever be free of irony and self-contradiction.[20] Nevertheless we are dedicated,

---

20. This is a central thesis in Balthasar's book on Reinhold Schneider. See Balthasar, *Tragedy under Grace.*

in Christ, to this world; the Trinity's economic *pro nobis* is implacably our own. And whereas we might have thought that such en-missioning would mean grabbing hold of the ship of state to ensure its arrival to harbor, or that the yoke of discipleship meant the acquisition of a power by which to enforce itself, we know that the concrete action of God in history, of the Incarnate One, does not avail itself of such methods. It is not a power over against, but a "powerless" power that does not seek its own accretion; it is not a controlled outcome but a kenotic willing of the other. We ourselves, therefore, are bound to such methods.

In terms of a proximate action funded by a radical disproportion, I think mainly this means holding out, however imperfectly, the tremulous flame of hope, hope that change is possible at all, or ever. For we are a religion of a divinely wrought change. If we must testify to this divine work by unmaking the world that we have made—by making that world and its people newly unfamiliar to us, by loving a creativity not under our control, by guaranteeing nothing for ourselves—so much more do we, with great risk, recapitulate the essential operation of the redeeming God in history and the operation of a tradition that mediates this truth in its action. To put it a final way: we can make nothing new, and we must make all things new.

Coda

"An eternal precariousness," says Péguy. "Nothing is gained eternally. This is the human condition itself. And the most profound condition of the Christian."[21] He calls this human and Christian precarity a "poor uncertainty" (*pauvre incertitude*) and an "uncertain poverty" (*incertaine pauvreté*).[22] By it, he refers to our very temporality, which consists in the presence of a present that is perpetually coming into being and perpetually passing away. It is poor and human because it is the only thing that in the end any of us, all of us, really do have—and we do not even really ever have it, as it rises into being, as it vanishes as the past. We are forever (or eternally) at a point of departure. And this same precariousness is Christian because its *pauvreté* is that single, exposed extremity of the world,

21. Charles Péguy, *Note conjointe sur M. Descartes et la philosophie cartésienne*, in *Oeuvres en prose complètes*, vol. 3 (Paris: Gallimard, 1992), 1450. My translation mostly resembles Ward's translation in Péguy, "Conjoined Note," 209.

22. Péguy, *Note conjointe*, in *Oeuvres en prose complètes*, 3:1435.

that only chink for a lance, that solitary place of puncture for the "wound" of divine grace.[23]

A theory of the being of Christian tradition, a "metaphysic" of tradition, has for its central work the task of describing the divine wounding of Christianity in its historical existence, the task of clarifying the operations by which such a historical existence might also be the life of a tradition, and the task of illuminating the operations by which the life of that tradition might also be divinely true. If such a task is worthy for its own sake, it is urgent for us today, as underneath our various defenses of the life of our tradition are anxieties about its death. These anxieties are aware, at least implicitly, that the historical guilt of Christian tradition is overwhelming, indeed superhuman.

My theory is designed not to resolve our anxiety, or to consume it in despair, or to swallow it up in false hope but to offer it the sharp edges of a new precision that enables new questions and new answers to questions so that we might rise to greater responsibility through greater understanding. If Christian theology, after all, has figured out how to describe tradition as *tradere*, as a verbal infinitive, as action, still, the operation of such action, its exact nature as action, has remained only partially queried. There remains in our theological inquiries a tendency to waver uncertainly between thought (in a Catholic context especially: dogma) and practice in arguments about which is primary or a tendency to collapse them. The waver and collapse occur not only because of various theological or philosophical disagreements but also because of underlying uncertainties that haunt all our positions. I mean that it is not clear to us what it means that we are a historical religion, that we hand on truth, and that our tradition is somehow involved in these. And it is difficult to argue effectively, to struggle together—a struggle that is in a sense our essential communal task—while standing upon sand. I would have us struggle better, and differently.

Even if the problems of race and colonialism, intimately entwined, appear remote from our struggle about tradition, in fact, they are not. They in their concreteness contribute to the superhuman situation, the situation of surd and of reality, in which we as historical and true find ourselves cohabiting with lies by our very action. But I think the more worrying, the deeply threatening trouble is that staring the facts in the face leaves us uncertain whether we can survive them. Many indeed doubt whether we can or could, or even should, and they do not misperceive the danger at all, even if they have not considered the possibility

23. Péguy, "Conjoined Note," 64–65.

of a supraintelligible solution. That such a solution is required says perhaps everything about how serious a situation we are in as a Christian tradition.

Something that an untheorized Christian tradition and the racialization of human beings share with each other is an inability to understand people, their histories, their cultures, indeed their own traditions, as living. Christian tradition became an object-thing to impose on others. The uneven phases of colonialism and their schizophrenic logics and actions all reduce the human situation (its meaning, its action, its persons) to things, with Christian tradition offered as the best of things. Péguy calls this type of phenomenon a *monetizing*.[24] It makes presence into paper.

Our perplexity about tradition secrets within itself a refusal of that *pauvre incertitude* by which Christianity gains and loses its life. If we hold onto our own solidity, perhaps we can survive the weight of our sin. But this is a refusal of the operation of Christian tradition in the very sense that it is an *operation* at all, that it is mediating action, that it is *péguyuste* "incrucification" and Blondelian "synthesis of thought and grace in the life of the believer." Thus, our tradition becomes something to preserve and something to give to others (whether they want it or not)—in either case, a thing. And it is very easy to lose things or to give them away, which made and makes for glorious Christian objects that are also very threatened or threatenable. We are perhaps instead, perhaps in reality, far poorer and far more vulnerable and thus also more woundable, before and by the grace of the triune God that we proclaim. If only we were willing. If only God makes us so.

"The cult of progress," says Lonergan, "has suffered an eclipse." What appeared so sure with the rise of colonial endeavors, what reached a basically religious status even in the apparently post-Christian West in the twentieth century met with bitterness and ruin.[25] The twenty-first century, our own, struggles over a version of this ruin even still, though in the form of new orderings and dilemmas. Can we, after all, escape our history with more history? Or do we not prove again and again that we do not, and never can?

---

24. This is more the concern of *L'Argent* but is discernible, for example, in Péguy, 214–15.

25. Lonergan, *Insight*, 710. In *Insight*, Lonergan does not draw a line from Christianity to the "cult of progress," by which he means primarily the Enlightenment belief in automatic (white) progress, but Copeland has filled out such a connection in Lonergan, and Balthasar in fact does draw such a line. Regardless of my textual priors, here I do associate Christian colonial ambitions and secular Enlightenment progress.

Lonergan argues that one of the tasks of Christians today is to affirm that human beings do and can develop in history. But this affirmation must endure a recalibration and a correction by way of its actual reality: "development [implies] that perfection belongs not to the present but to the future."[26] This means that our present, our actual reality, is in fact a progress still underway, is a progress wounded by sin, is a progress that is not at all automatic—that threatens regression and collapse. So not only is tomorrow *never* guaranteed to be better than today or yesterday, but also—and more centrally for Lonergan—we will always be in the midst of figuring out what we must do next. (A return of Péguy's *pauvre incertitude*.) Says Lonergan, "[Progress] must be taken to imply, not only a contrast with the past, but also a contrast with its goal."[27]

Since one of my topics has been colonialism and race, it might seem a cruel irony to reaffirm progress at this point, since "progress" became such a rallying cry (especially in the eighteenth and nineteenth centuries) for the "civilizing" colonial, imperial conquests the West executed. But this cruel irony depends on the reservation of progress to certain peoples, according to certain specifying models that do much the same, and it depends very much on the notion that human development must "look" identical everywhere. These are not my claim, or Lonergan's.[28] The point is that human being, *ens humanitatis*, bears a temporal dynamism and that this dynamism is an essential instrument of that interior dynamism, which is the desire to know, the drive of the "pure question."[29] The point is that human communities build on and dismantle their past achievements, and those of others. The point is that in greatly variable ways, human beings are the variable by which their variability is explained.[30]

If it is thanks to Christianity that human beings now doubt whether the postcolony is even possible, if it is thanks to us that whole peoples find themselves trapped by a systematic oppression that thwarts their striving for self-transcendence and thus thwarts all progress, then all the more must we testify with the hope that there *is* a tomorrow buried beneath today, one truly different from today. But this testimony cannot be that of the very certitude and

---

26. Lonergan, *Insight*, 710.

27. Lonergan, 711.

28. Neither in the context of my citations so far (from *Insight*, chap. 20), which is not really about civilizations or who gains the term, nor as Lonergan later develops his notion of progress, a development I detail in the first chapter.

29. Lonergan, *Insight*, 34.

30. The "variable" language is something Jonathan Heaps says a great deal, and I borrow it from him.

exactness that wrought the deaths of entire ways of life by our hands. For we do not know our tomorrow except as it is laid up in our today. "As the thesis of progress never places man on the pinnacle of perfection," explains Lonergan, "it ever asserts that his knowledge is incomplete, that his willingness is imperfect, that his sensitivity and intersubjectivity still need to be adapted."[31] Our testimony, then, cannot be confidence about the outcome, or an assurance about what exactly will come to be, not even for ourselves—for we do not *know*. We only hope. So ours must be a testimony to our own precarious dynamism as human beings, a precarious dynamism that we share with that dynamic intelligibility that we call "human being" and that therefore has to be a testimony not only to that *dynamism* but also to its *precarity*. Lonergan cautions, "Our course is in the night; our control is only rough and approximate; we have to believe and trust, to risk and dare."[32]

If we are to testify to the thesis of progress, it must be a concrete testimony. Essential to such a testifying hope must be, then, the real kenosis of our own, embedded power and the real kenosis that wills the other. In a way, I am saying that we must visit uncertainty upon ourselves, and that we must do so today: we can no longer know with confidence how to relate to our past, for that relationship must be adapted; we can no longer guarantee our sway with the world through a will to power; we can no longer guess the future of our theologies, for those too must endure adaptation. And this uncertainty, our very willingness to be uncertain, our making it real, is itself a votive of the dynamism of human being, a candle lit in its favor, and it is a votive of trust in the triune God who redeems us and who redeems our history by way of our dynamism. Whence this uncertainty will be a chance, a precarious chance always vanishing through our fingers, a chance relying on the flickering flame of our free *need-not-be*: a chance for a creativity that indeed recovers the past, but to new purpose, a chance for a creativity that indeed recovers us to ourselves.

It will not be easy, or simple. It is, and it will be, a kind of death—the death of everything familiar in its familiarity to us. "Present perceptiveness," says Lonergan, "is to be enlarged, and the enlargement is not perceptible to present perceptiveness. Present desires and fears have to be transmuted, and the transmutation is not desirable to present desire but fearful to present fear."[33] Thus, we must ply our fear with meaning so that it can be endured. And that

31. Lonergan, *Insight*, 711.
32. Lonergan, "*Existenz* and *Aggiornamento*," 224.
33. Lonergan, *Insight*, 496.

meaning is the Logos in the flesh, who takes flesh in the logos of our hour. To love this Word, in its immanence and its transcendence, is to be willing to be afraid. How much more perfect will be this fear before the world when it is not a terror visited on others but a fear that supposes what it hopes for in the intimate mechanism of its vulnerability?

We must again be vulnerable to the truth of who we have been, the truth of who we are; we must be vulnerable to the suffering that this truth will cause us, vulnerable most of all to those who suffer because of us. As Baldwin says of America, so it is possible to say of the white Christian gaze:

> There is a sense of the grotesque about a person who has spent his or her life in a kind of cotton batting. There is something monstrous about never having been hurt, never having been made to bleed, never having lost anything, never having gained anything because life is beautiful, and in order to keep it beautiful you're going to stay just the way you are and you're not going to test your theory against all the possibilities outside. America is something like that. The failure on our part to accept the reality of pain, of anguish, of ambiguity, of death has turned us into a very peculiar and sometimes monstrous people. It means, for one thing, and it's very serious, that people who have had no experience have no compassion.[34]

The recognition of a Christian tradition that is capable of immense ugliness—the recovery of our life's pain, of the pain we have inflicted on others—is, then, requisite for the rediscovery of Christian compassion, which Péguy simply calls "charity." And in such charity, God renders these our tears, these tears that we must hope for, that we must yearn to make real, no longer bitter, but a divine gift of a compunction that makes possible for us a divine being in history.

Underneath tears there is joy. Goodwill, says Lonergan, "is joyful. For it is love of God above all and in all, and love is joy. Its repentance and sorrow regard the past. Its present sacrifices look to the future."[35] If, for Baldwin, love must carry in itself a violence that is at one with the refusal to tolerate lies, still this love that is also violence passionately affirms a kind of beauty, the beauty of a consciousness that cooperates with the "more" of reality, the "more" otherwise

34. Baldwin, "Uses of the Blues," 79.
35. Lonergan, *Insight*, 722.

so cruelly denied.[36] In Balthasar, Christian love rises to a (divine) willingness to renounce comfort and happiness, a willingness to choose "alienations that must be endured for the sake of coming together in unity," such that suffering has its key as a quality, in this world, of what is involved in the Christian's struggling exit from alienation. But love's content is not this suffering. It is an assent to the glory that God intends for the world, and so Christian love is joy.[37]

It is not, in the end, for the sake of the past that we relate to the past in new ways. It is for the sake of our present, that urgent present forever welling up. And in committing ourselves today to offering something new to today, new even indeed in our very regard *for* our past, we act with hope for the future that is laid up in our present as its interior direction. "The living is ever now," says Lonergan, "but the knowledge to guide living, the willingness to follow knowledge, the sensitive adaptation that vigorously and joyously executes the will's decisions, these belong to the future, and when the future is present, there will be beyond it a further future with steeper demands."[38] So we cannot rescue our tradition, our Christian tradition, without that God-given grace that grants us the goodwill that is willing to do whatever divine goodness requires of us. It is a will that bears a courage brave enough to surrender what is familiar and safe for the sake of that greater good of our tomorrow, and it bears a fortitude that is strong enough to rise upward along our ever-steepening hill. For we do not really know our tomorrow except through this flickering flame-gesture of our today.[39] We must, then, pray for the zeal that makes us willing to act today. "We are required," says Balthasar, "only not to let go of love, the love that believes and hopes and through both is suspended in the air so that its Christian wings may grow."[40]

Such vulnerability is a decentered vulnerability, a collective openness to divine transfiguration that is itself a sign of the truly vulnerable. We acquire a vulnerability that points beyond ourselves to Christ, and to Christ in our midst, Christ in every oppressed person of history, which in our recent history has been many persons, and profoundly those persons we consider Black. So our vulnerability is doubly decentered, a double request to look beyond itself,

36. Cf. "What will happen to all that beauty?" and its contrast with vengeance in Baldwin, "Fire Next Time," 346–47.

37. Balthasar, *GL* 7:534–36; cf. 7:536–40.

38. Lonergan, *Insight*, 711.

39. Péguy, *Porche du mystère*, 633.

40. Hans Urs von Balthasar, *Love Alone Is Credible* (San Francisco: Ignatius, 2004), 96.

centered as it is upon the "least of these" and upon Christ in these, his cherished ones. Our convincing power can no longer be ourselves, nor can it be achieved through power; it requires instead the creative act of our kenosis, our willing of others and God-in-others. In other words, the purpose of our vulnerability is not for our own sakes; this would simply reconceive our domination. Our vulnerability is for the sake of the *vulnerable*, our poverty (*pauvreté*) is for the sake of the *miséraux*.[41] And our only chance to make it so is in the presence of the present as it wells up.

But we must not imagine the oppressed, we must not imagine subjects like the Black subject, as only passively Christ to us. They are Christ to us in their struggle for self-transcendence. And here is where I have in mind Balthasar's "duelists with death," his saints for when sainthood is no longer legible as it once might have been in Christendom.[42] Balthasar notices, by way of example, two works of fiction that confront death in a way that recognizes Christ's death in it while allowing for postures of defiance, of bitterness, cynicism, even blasphemy.[43] One literary example is François Villon, "Bachelor and Master of Arts, felon, recidivist, and jailbird."[44] The other is Johannes von Tepl, who, though less the sinner and criminal than Villon, writes "not a book of 'consolation,' but of bitter struggle and disputation" in the face of death.[45]

But Villon and Tepl are not the only examples available. It is, after all, the nonwhite "I"—in our history but also in our fiction—whom colonial modernity associates with death. This death is the end of their being-alive, but it is also the "death" of their freedom and subjectivity, and the "death" of their human, sacramental representation of symbols other than death. These deaths constitute the life of colonial modernity. It is they who die as criminals in our prisons, they who die at the hands of our law enforcers, they who die beleaguered of an education that would help waken their freedom, and so on. Indeed, Africa and Blackness, Mbembe explains, came to represent nonbeing and negation: "The Remainder—the ultimate sign of the dissimilar, of difference and the pure power of the negative—constituted the manifestation of existence as an

41. Péguy makes a distinction between poverty and *misère*, which he takes to be an essential (and modern) problem demanding modern economic response. Cf. Maguire, *Carnal Spirit*, 192.

42. Balthasar, *GL* 5:142.

43. See Balthasar, 5:147.

44. Balthasar, 5:148.

45. Balthasar, 5:150.

object. Africa in general and Blackness in particular were presented as accomplished symbols of a vegetative, limited state."[46]

And so the Black struggle in our age has so often been a defiance, a blasphemy, a bitterness, a face-off with this, the modern death. They are our saints who are dueling with death, even if we are quite unwilling to see them as such, and even if we are placing them toe-to-toe with death in the first place. These saints deploy savvy and irony and creativity, at one angle, in order to accost death with their more-than-death, with the glory of their complex existence. At another angle, they work to acknowledge and remember the death and loss that they so intimately endure and face. "Well," Baldwin writes to his nephew, "you were born, here you came, something like fifteen years ago; and though your father and mother and grandmother, looking about the streets through which they were carrying you, staring at the walls into which they brought you, had every reason to be heavyhearted, yet they were not. For here you were, Big James, named for me—you were a big baby, I was not—here you were: to be loved. To be loved, baby, hard, at once, and forever, to strengthen you against the loveless world."[47] If Balthasar is correct, then it is this very human love in the face of a world of death that, in the most precise Christian sense, reminds us of Christ's own death out of love, and it is this very human love that reminds us of the divine intention for the world, which is to overcome our death.[48]

Much of my work in this book has been a struggle to place a tradition familiar to me before the unfamiliar images of these saints, them and their lives. Like all saints, they transcend us as images of what we, the church on earth, must become in Christ; like all saints living in history, they themselves await an eschatological perfection; and, like all saints, they point to the world that we are commanded to serve. In these saints is a divine demand that we, that we and our tradition, that our tradition in us, be remade, once again, in the image of our God. In these saints, we rediscover that very image. So also in these saints, in these Black subjects in the modern world, in every nonwhite "I," is a revelation of our guilt before them and before the world and before the triune God. I would that we were not so guilty, together, in our history. But since we are, we must begin again.

---

46. Mbembe, *Critique of Black Reason*, 11.
47. Baldwin, "My Dungeon Shook," 292–93.
48. Cf. Balthasar, *GL* 5:152. Balthasar compares Tepl to Dante and Beatrice; here, however, the love in question is the Black will to community rather than the marital image that Balthasar cites.

CONCLUSION

Discussions of Christian tradition tend to be backward-looking: toward the tradition-that-has-been, toward the patrimony that one represents or betrays, that one loathes or defends, that one rediscovers or forgets. And in a sense, this book has also turned backward, has also bent the ear of its heart to the voices of the dead.[1] But it would be a mistake to consider my work here a turn backward; it is certainly not a work intended to *teach* a turning backward or to reinforce and reengrain the glance behind one's back, which is so often mistaken to "be" the being of tradition. For, together with these many figures of my study, I have argued that such is not the being of tradition in fact. Tradition is alive; it is a life; it is a mediation that binds together thought and act. It is a human mediation within which God supernaturally acts, bringing about in human lives a divine life. So if tradition is a memory, it is a memory whose presence is present to our present. It is a present that looks to a future that is also present, present in this very gaze that looks forward. Thus, Maurice Blondel can say, "Tradition is less concerned to conserve than to discover."[2]

I have spent the past five chapters building what I have been describing as a "metaphysic" of tradition. It is a theory about "what" Christian tradition is that answers the question by asking, not so much about that tradition's content,

---

1. "Inclina aurem cordis tui" (incline the ear of your heart) reads the prologue to the *Rule of Benedict*, in a semblance of Psalm 44(45):11 and Proverbs 1:8. See *The Rule of Saint Benedict in Latin and English with Notes* (Collegeville, MN: Liturgical, 1981), Prol. 1. Here I echo its language and evoke monastic traditions deliberately, for one's "master" who speaks wisdom is not ultimately the abbot but God.

2. Blondel, "History and Dogma," 276.

as its operation, and not so much about which operative "actions" count as "traditional" or as "tradition" (which is a reversion to the question of content), but about those heuristic activities by which tradition *is*—at all or in the first place, in its development, in its sinful self-contradiction, in God's supernatural action in it. This theoretical stance is what I have been calling a "metaphysic" because it asks about the being of history, the being of tradition as historical, the renewal of a tradition that is historical, and the redemption of history in a tradition that shares with human history its quality of being.

But this book has also been a confrontation with something else. Or, I should not say *else*; I should say that this book has been a confrontation with *reality*, to the heuristic limit that is possible to human beings and possible to my work as a theologian today. And such a heuristic limit is merely so: the categories sit empty, waiting to be filled. This is their power, and their constraint. And I have built this heuristic theory to contend not only with the fact *that* tradition is historical, *that* it is the mediation between truth and history, but also with the equally as historical fact that *this* tradition, our Christian tradition, is mired in and has perpetuated sin. That sin is structurally widest in its impact on us today in the form of colonialism and its central creation, which is race.

The being of Christian tradition and its existence as the central engine of ever-transmuting racial deeds and logics, and as also (and more essentially) the engine of profound inequities underneath racializing categories, need to be thought together—since they are so entangled in the concrete—in order that they might be separated, however painfully. But to make such a study means discovering that the cracked vein of self-contradiction and irony runs its way through Christianity's whole structure. There are ways that certain endeavors attempt to rescue this structure by marking out a boundary between when Christianity was whole or pure and when it was corrupted. No ideology is immune to this fantasy, and so Christians of many kinds dream it. Still, others render the fantasy such that they never have to ask the question of our goodness and our sin at all. Against this dreaming, but also against despair, my book has marked out the ironies that it also performs, performs in the being, at the very least, of its own author and my own place in the world and in history as a scholar. I am what my context has made of me, for good and ill, and not just passively so. I am the drama of my own living. But the book is also a kind of action-beyond-context, a reaching or an intending, embedded in the rôle of the inquiring Christian. This book hopes for more, and in hope, it attempts a beginning-again, however imperfect. A purely horizontal temporality and a fully immanentized metaphysic struggle to lay hold of an action that can or could be both ironic and transcendent, and the same goes for a monphorist vision of kingly and theological domination. Only a *réalité intégrale* can name such a thing as more than contrary—as something real, as M. Shawn Copeland's "need not be" breaking into being, as a struggle for authenticity. This is the reality that I have argued for.

A *krisis* emerges, in the New Testament sense of a judgment and decision, which Hans Urs von Balthasar transposes into drama. On the stage of history, self-contradiction exists in that distinction that persists between the "I" in history and its various mediating historical roles. But this "I" is also self-transcending, because it is permeated to its marrow with the Absolute Other that is the triune God. And so, I am all that history makes of me, and I am one who can, in God, choose God. I can transfigure a historical situation by first transfiguring its meaning and then acting. In other words, I can enact Blondel's dramatic reversal, where I allow an act that I cannot command to change me, to become the primary principle of my own action. Balthasar inscribes this dramatic reversal into the very heart of Christ on the cross, which is fissured by the lance of sin: the heart that freely fixes itself on the saving will of God—even when darkness swallows the hour. This fragile hinge-point in human history, a fragile human will that is the will of a divine Person, becomes the divine instrument of a resurrection intended for the world, of a Spirit of infinite love poured out. And if we thought that this meant that we ourselves need not endure such crisis, Charles Péguy reminds us of the perpetual grief-wound of the Christian, the wound of juncture for grace, in a person who must always be attempting an original gesture.

So I myself do not escape the sinful ironies of a present history that lances me through. But this history *is* the history that is God's, and we do not await another one in order to act. It is possible to recapitulate Christianity through an ever-again begun decision for the triune God: the God who alone can bring good from out of evil. In this act, my act and ours, the act that awaits its own perfection, Christian tradition neither consigns itself to the despair of remaining the same nor unhands its own heart from out of its cracked ribcage. Or, if it does surrender its heart to the world, this itself is a recollection of Christian tradition's intelligibility and purpose. In this sense, my book *resolves* nothing. It is meant for use, for expansion, for correction. It is a heuristic for understanding a theological drama that demands our participation. And after these many pages, we no longer assume that theory has no interest in justice, or that theological justice has no earthly concreteness, or instrument, or urgency—all while remaining supernatural. Thus are we tasked with remembering in our action and its reason, always, the intending action of the divine *pro nobis*, which invites, and which makes, our cooperation with its Eucharist.

Notre-Dame on Fire

She's the end of the world.
She's dipped in flames
the color of the sun.
She's wreathed in the hot sparks
of an ecstasy, of dying wood.

Memory of millions under
the shadows of her archways,
those watchers at her fiery gate,
the dyed at her glass, long
their light gathered at sunset.

Heat of God's wrath in the cupful
of her vault, measure of the faithful
gone white at the bone, end-of-days
brought to the dreadful hour:
dies irae in the crash and bell

of her falling tower. Oh saints!
As you stand beneath her burning ribs,
bend your ears to the ground
of her travail, and plead her destiny
with the apology of yours.

Oh end of things! When all
is turned to gold, turned too bright
for eyes that presently look on,
wishing for the time and its delay,
mothered urgently by the spectacle

of her, of our, of loss.

—Anne M. Carpenter

Selected Bibliography

Works by Major Interlocutors

Baldwin, James

———. *Collected Essays*. Edited by Toni Morrison. New York: Literary Classics of the United States, 1998.

———. "The Discovery of What It Means to Be an American." In Morrison, *Collected Essays*, 137–142.

———. "Down at the Cross." In Morrison, *Collected Essays*, 296–347.

———. "Fifth Avenue, Uptown: A Letter from Harlem." In Morrison, *Collected Essays*, 170–179.

———. "In Search of a Majority." In Morrison, *Collected Essays*, 215–221.

———. Introduction to Morrison, *Collected Essays*, 135–136.

———. "My Dungeon Shook: Letter to My Nephew." In Morrison, *Collected Essays*, 291–295.

———. *The Cross of Redemption: Uncollected Writings*. Edited by Randall Kenan. New York: Pantheon, 2010.

———. "On Being White . . . and Other Lies." In Kenan, *Cross of Redemption*, 166–170.

———. "The Uses of the Blues." In Kenan, *Cross of Redemption*, 70–81.

Balthasar, Hans Urs von

———. *Convergences: To the Source of Christian Mystery*. San Francisco: Ignatius, 1983.

———. *Explorations in Theology*. Vol. 1, *The Word Made Flesh*. San Francisco: Ignatius, 1989.

———. *Explorations in Theology*. Vol. 3, *Creator Spirit*. San Francisco: Ignatius, 1993. Kindle.

————. "Forgetfulness of God and Christians." In Balthasar, *Creator Spirit*, Kindle loc. 4353–4612. Vol. 3 of *Explorations in Theology*.

————. *Explorations in Theology*. Vol. 4, *Spirit and Institution*. San Francisco: Ignatius, 1995.

————. "The Claim to Catholicity." In Balthasar, *Spirit and Institution*, 65–121. Vol. 4 of *Explorations in Theology*.

————. *Explorations in Theology*. Vol. 5, *Man Is Created*. San Francisco: Ignatius, 2014.

————. "Tradition." In Balthasar, *Man Is Created*, 356–373. Vol. 5 of *Explorations in Theology*.

————. *The Glory of the Lord: A Theological Aesthetics*. Vols. 1–7. San Francisco: Ignatius, 1984–2009.

————. *Love Alone Is Credible*. San Francisco: Ignatius, 2004.

————. *Mysterium Paschale: The Mystery of Easter*. San Francisco: Ignatius, 1990.

————. *A Theological Anthropology*. Eugene, OR: Wipf & Stock, 2010.

————. *A Theology of History*. San Francisco: Ignatius, 1994.

————. *The Theology of Karl Barth*. San Francisco: Ignatius, 1992.

————. *Theo-Drama: Theological Dramatic Theory*. Vols. 1–5. San Francisco: Ignatius, 1988–1990.

————. *Theo-Logic: Theological Logical Theory*. Vols. 1–3. San Francisco: Ignatius, 2000–2005.

————. *Tragedy under Grace: Reinhold Schneider on the Experience of the West*. San Francisco: Ignatius, 1997.

Blondel, Maurice

————. *Action (1893): Essay on a Critique of Life and a Science of Practice*. Translated by Oliva Blanchette. Notre Dame, IN: University of Notre Dame Press, 2003. [There is now a 2021 edition with a new introduction.]

————. *L'Action*. 2 vols. Paris: Librairie Félix Alcan, 1936.

————. *L'Être et les êtres*. Paris: Librairie Félix Alcan, 1935.

————. *The Letter on Apologetics and History and Dogma*. Translated by Alexander Dru and Illtyd Trethowan. Grand Rapids, MI: Eerdmans, 1964.

————. *La Pensée*. 2 vols. Paris: Librairie Félix Alcan, 1934.

————. *Philosophical Exigencies of Christian Religion*. Translated by Oliva Blanchette. Notre Dame, IN: University of Notre Dame Press, 2021.

————. *Un alliance contre nature: Catholicisme et intégrisme; La Semaine sociale de Bordeaux 1910*. Brussels: Éditions Lessius, 2000.

Copeland, M. Shawn

———. *Enfleshing Freedom: Body, Race, and Being.* Minneapolis: Fortress, 2010.

———. "Anti-Blackness and White Supremacy in the Making of American Catholicism." *American Catholic Studies* 127, no. 3 (2016): 6–8.

———. "Building Up a Household of Faith: Dom Cyprian Davis, OSB, and the Work of History." *U.S. Catholic Historian* 28, no. 1 (2010): 53–63.

———. "Doing Black Catholic Theology: Rhythm, Structure, Aesthetics." *Chicago Studies* 42, no. 2 (2003): 127–141.

———. "Theology at the Crossroads: A Meditation on the Blues." In *Uncommon Faithfulness: The Black Catholic Experience*, edited by M. Shawn Copeland with LaReine-Marie Mosley and Albert J. Raboteau, 97–107. Maryknoll, NY: Orbis Books, 2009.

———. "Turning Theology: A Proposal." *Theological Studies* 80, no. 4 (2019): 753–773.

———. "Tradition and the Traditions of African American Catholicism." *Theological Studies* 61, no. 4 (2000): 632–655.

Jennings, Willie James

———. *After Whiteness: An Education in Belonging.* Grand Rapids, MI: Eerdmans, 2020.

———. *The Christian Imagination: Theology and the Origins of Race.* New Haven, CT: Yale University Press, 2011.

———. "'He Became Truly Human': Incarnation, Emancipation, and Authentic Humanity." *Modern Theology* 12, no. 2 (1996): 239–255.

———. "New Winds: A Response to the Essays." *Pneuma* 36, no. 3 (2014): 447–455.

———. "Whiteness Isn't Progress: How the Missionary Project Went Horrifically Wrong." *Christian Century* 135, no. 23 (2018): 28–31.

———. "Wrestling with a Wounding Word: Reading the Disjointed Lines of African American Spirituality." *Modern Theology* 13, no. 1 (1997): 139–170.

Lonergan, Bernard

———. *Collected Works of Bernard Lonergan.* Vols. 1–25. Toronto: University of Toronto Press, 1988–2019. Hereafter cited *CWL.*

———. *Archival Material: Early Papers on History.* Vol. 25, *CWL.* Toronto: University of Toronto Press, 2019.

————. *Collection*. Vol. 4, *CWL*. Toronto: University of Toronto Press, 1988.

————. "Dimensions of Meaning." In *Collection*, 232–245. Vol. 4 of *CWL*.

————. "*Existenz* and *Aggiornamento*." In *Collection*, 222–231. Vol. 4 of *CWL*.

————. *Insight*. Vol. 3, *CWL*. Toronto: University of Toronto Press, 1992.

————. *Method in Theology*. Vol. 14, *CWL*. Toronto: University of Toronto Press, 2017.

————. *Philosophical and Theological Papers, 1958–1964*. Vol. 6, *CWL*. Toronto: University of Toronto Press, 1996.

————. "The Origins of Christian Realism (1961)." In *Philosophical and Theological Papers*, 80–93. Vol. 6 of *CWL*.

————. *A Second Collection*. Vol. 13, *CWL*. Toronto: University of Toronto Press, 2016.

————. "Philosophy and Theology." In *Second Collection*, 193–208. Vol. 13 of *CWL*.

————. *Topics in Education*. Vol. 10, *CWL*. Toronto: University of Toronto Press, 1988.

————. *A Third Collection*. Vol. 16, *CWL*. Toronto: University of Toronto Press, 2017.

————. "Dialectic of Authority." In *Third Collection*, 3–9. Vol. 16 of *CWL*.

Péguy, Charles

————. *Notes on Bergson and Descartes: Philosophy, Christianity, and Modernity in Contestation*. Translated by Bruce K. Ward. Eugene, OR: Cascade, 2019.

————. *Oeuvres en prose complètes*. Vols. 1–3. Paris: Gallimard, 1987–1992.

————. "Avertissement." *Cahiers* 5, no. 11. In *Oeuvres en prose completes*, vol. 1, 1283–1316.

————. "De la situation faite à l'histoire et à la sociologie dans les temps modernes." *Cahiers* 8, no. 3. In *Oeuvres en prose complètes*, vol. 2, 481–519.

————. *Note conjointe sur M. Descartes et la philosophie cartésienne*. In *Oeuvres en prose complètes*, vol. 3.

————. "Notre patrie." *Cahiers* 3, no. 7. In *Oeuvres en prose complètes*, vol. 2, 10–61.

————. *Oeuvres poétiques et dramatiques*. Paris: Gallimard, 2014.

————. "Châteaux de loire." In *Oeuvres poétiques et dramatiques*, 1129–1131.

————. "Jeanne d'Arc: Drama en trois pieces." In *Oeuvres poétiques et dramatiques*, 6–299.

———. "Le mystère de la charité de Jeanne d'Arc." In *Oeuvres poétiques et dramatiques*, 399–559.

———. "Le mystère des saints innocents." In *Oeuvres poétiques et dramatiques*, 777–927.

———. "Le porche du mystère de la deuxième vertu." In *Oeuvres poétiques et dramatiques*, 627–768.

———. "La tapisserie de sainte Geneviève et de Jeanne d'Arc." In *Oeuvres poétiques et dramatiques*, 1079–1117.

———. *Temporal and Eternal*. Translated by Alexander Dru. Indianapolis, IN: Liberty Fund, 2001.

———. "Clio I." In *Temporal and Eternal*, 85–165.

———. "Memories of Youth." In *Temporal and Eternal*, 3–82.

Though not cited, Péguy's major poetic trilogy is in translation:

———. *The Mystery of the Charity of Joan of Arc*. Providence, RI: Cluny Media, 2019.

———. *The Mystery of the Holy Innocents and Other Poems*. Eugene, OR: Wipf & Stock, 2017.

———. *The Portal of the Mystery of Hope*. Grand Rapids, MI: Eerdmans, 1996.

Works by Others

Bajzek, Brian. "Cruciform Encounter in a Time of Crisis: Enfleshing an Ethics of Alterity." *Theological Studies* 80, no. 1 (2019): 79–101.

Bancel, Nicolas, Pascal Blanchard, and Dominic Thomas, eds. *The Colonial Legacy in France: Fracture, Rupture, and Apartheid*. Bloomington: Indiana University Press, 2017.

Blackwood, Jeremy. "The Heart of the Mystical Body of Christ: Subjectivity and Solidarity with Poor Women of Color." *Theological Studies* 77, no. 3 (2016): 652–677.

Blanchette, Oliva. *Maurice Blondel: A Philosophical Life*. Grand Rapids, MI: Eerdmans, 2010.

Bouillard, Henri. *Blondel et le christianisme*. Paris: Éditions du seuil, 1961. [Available in translation: *Blondel and Christianity*. Translated by James Somerville. Cleveland, OH: Corpus, 1969.]

————. "The Thought of Maurice Blondel: A Synoptic Vision." *International Philosophical Quarterly* 3 (1963): 392–402.

Byrnes, Joseph. *Catholic and French Forever: Religious and National Identity in Modern France*. University Park: Pennsylvania State University Press, 2005.

Carpenter, Anne M. "Balthasar beyond European Modernity: Re-thinking *Herrlichkeit* through Its Precursors." *Modern Theology* 37, no. 3 (2021): 616–636.

————. *Theo-Poetics: Hans Urs von Balthasar and the Risk of Art and Being*. Notre Dame, IN: University of Notre Dame Press, 2015.

Chantre, Benoît, Camille Riquier, and Frédéric Worms, eds. *Pensée de Péguy*. Paris: Éditions Desclée de Brouwer, 2015. E-book.

Chapman, Herrick, and Laura L. Frader, eds. *Race in France: Interdisciplinary Perspectives on the Politics of Difference*. New York: Berghahn Books, 2004.

Congar, Yves. *Tradition and Traditions: An Historical and a Theological Essay*. New York: Macmillan, 1967.

Conway, Michael. "From Neo-Thomism to St. Thomas: Maurice Blondel's Early Encounter with Scholastic Thought." *Ephemerides Theologicae Lovanienses* 83, no. 1 (2007): 1–22.

————. "A Thomistic Turn? Maurice Blondel's Reading of St. Thomas." *Ephemerides Theologicae Lovanienses* 84, no. 1 (2008): 87–122.

Doran, Robert. *Theology and the Dialectics of History*. Toronto: University of Toronto Press, 1990.

————. *The Trinity in History: A Theology of the Divine Missions*. Vol. 1, *Missions and Processions*. Toronto: University of Toronto Press, 2012.

Drexler-Dreis, Joseph. *Decolonial Love: Salvation in Colonial Modernity*. New York: Fordham University Press, 2018.

Durand, Jean-Dominique, ed. *Les Semaines Sociales de France: 1904–2004*. Paris: Éditions Parole et Silence, 2006.

Dussel, Enrique. *The Invention of the Americas: Eclipse of "the Other" and the Myth of Modernity*. New York: Continuum, 1995.

Enright, Lyle. "An Art of Divine Protagonism: Questions of Power, Sovereignty, and the Theological Motivations of Contemporary Religious Literature." PhD diss., Loyola University Chicago, 2019.

Fanon, Frantz. *Black Skin, White Masks*. Translated by Charles Lam Markmann. London: Pluto, 1986.

————. *The Wretched of the Earth*. Translated by Constance Farrington. New York: Grove, 1991.

Fields, Karen E., and Barbara J. Fields. *Racecraft: The Soul of Inequality in American Life*. New York: Verso, 2012.

Finkielkraut, Alain. *Le mécontemporain: Péguy, lecteur du monde modern*. Paris: Gallimard, 1991.

Flipper, Joseph. "The Ressourcement of Black Catholicism in Cyprian Davis, OSB." *Modern Theology* 36, no. 4 (2020): 826–842.

———. "White Ecclesiology: The Identity of the Church in the Statements on Racism by United States Catholic Bishops." *Theological Studies* 82, no. 3 (2021): 418–439.

Flynn, Gabriel, and Paul Murray, eds. *Ressourcement: A Movement for Renewal in Twentieth-Century Catholic Theology*. New York: Oxford University Press, 2015.

Gillespie, Charles A. "Drama Alone Is Credible: Hans Urs von Balthasar and the Interpretive Work of Theatre and Performance in Twentieth-Century Christian Thought." PhD diss., University of Virginia, 2019.

Heaps, Jonathan. "The Ambiguity of Being: Medieval and Modern Cooperation on the Problem of the Supernatural." PhD diss., Marquette University, 2019.

Heaps, Jonathan, and Neil Ormerod. "Statistically Ordered: Gender, Sexual Identity, and the Metaphysics of 'Normal.'" *Theological Studies* 80, no. 2 (2019): 346–369.

Hemmer, Ryan. "Cathedrals of the Mind: Theological Method and Speculative Renewal in Trinitarian Theology." PhD diss., Marquette University, 2020.

Keaton, Trica Danielle, T. Denean Sharpley-Whiting, and Tyler Stovall, eds. *Black France / France Noire: The History and Politics of Blackness*. Durham, NC: Duke University Press, 2012.

Kidd, Erin. "The Scaffolding of Whiteness: Race and Place in the Christian Imagination." In *You Say You Want a Revolution? 1968–2018 in Theological Perspective*, edited by Susie Paulik Babka, Elena Procario-Foley, and Sandra Yocum, 16–26. New York: Orbis Books, 2019.

———. "The Violation of God in the Body of the World: A Rahnerian Response to Trauma." *Modern Theology* 35, no. 4 (2019): 663–682.

King, Jonathan. "Theology under Another Form: Hans Urs von Balthasar's Formation and Writings as a Germanist." PhD diss., Saint Louis University, 2016.

Kirwan, Jon. *An Avante-Garde Theological Generation: The "Nouvelle Théologie" and the French Crisis of Modernity*. London: Oxford University Press, 2019.

Lawrence, Frederick. *The Fragility of Consciousness: Faith, Reason, and the Human Good*. Edited by Randall Rosenberg and Kevin Vander Schel. Toronto: University of Toronto Press, 2017.

Long, Charles H. *Significations: Signs, Symbols, and Images in the Interpretation of Religion*. Aurora, CO: Davies Group, 1999.

Maguire, Matthew. *Carnal Spirit: The Revolutions of Charles Péguy*. Philadelphia: University of Pennsylvania Press, 2019.

Martin, Jennifer Newsome. "Balthasar *avec* Kristeva: On the Recovery of a Baroque Teresa of Avila." *Modern Theology* 37, no. 1 (2021): 23–43.

———. *Hans Urs von Balthasar and the Critical Appropriation of Russian Religious Thought*. Notre Dame, IN: University of Notre Dame Press, 2015.

———. "Memory Matters: Ressourcement Theology's Debt to Henri Bergson." *International Journal of Systematic Theology* 23, no. 2 (2021): 177–197.

———. "'Only What Is Rooted Is Living': A Roman Catholic Theology of Ressourcement." In *Theologies of Retrieval: An Exploration and Appraisal*, edited by Darren Sarisky, 81–102. New York: Bloomsbury, 2017.

Mbembe, Achille. *Critique of Black Reason*. Translated by Laurent Dubois. Durham, NC: Duke University Press, 2013.

———. *Out of the Dark Night: Essays on Decolonization*. New York: Columbia University Press, 2021.

Mignolo, Walter. *Local Histories/Global Designs: Coloniality, Subaltern Knowledges, and Border Thinking*. Princeton, NJ: Princeton University Press, 2000.

Misner, Paul. *Social Catholicism in Europe: From the Onset of Industrialization to the First World War*. New York: Crossroad, 1991.

Mills, Charles W. *The Racial Contract*. Ithaca, NY: Cornell University Press, 2014.

Moten, Fred. *In the Break: The Aesthetics of the Black Radical Tradition*. Minneapolis: University of Minnesota Press, 2003.

Newman, John Henry. *An Essay on the Development of Christian Doctrine*. South Bend, IN: University of Notre Dame Press, 1989.

O'Malley, John W. *What Happened at Vatican II*. Cambridge, MA: Harvard University Press, 2010.

Prevot, Andrew. "Divine Opacity: Mystical Theology, Black Theology, and the Problem of Light-Dark Aesthetics." *Spiritus: A Journal of Christian Spirituality* 16, no. 2 (2016): 166–188.

———. *Thinking Prayer: Theology and Spirituality amid the Crises of Modernity*. Notre Dame, IN: University of Notre Dame Press, 2015.

Przywara, Erich. *Analogia Entis: Metaphysics: Original Structure and Universal Rhythm*. Translated by John Betz and David Bentley Hart. Grand Rapids, MI: Eerdmans, 2014.

Ricoeur, Paul. *Memory, History, Forgetting*. Translated by Kathleen Blamey and David Pellauer. Chicago: University of Chicago Press, 2004.

———. *Time and Narrative*. Translated by Kathleen McLaughlin and David Pellauer. 3 vols. Chicago: University of Chicago Press, 1990.

Riquier, Camille. *Philosophie de Péguy: Ou les mémoires d'un imbécile*. Paris: Presses Universitaires de France, 2017.

Roe, Glenn. *The Passion of Charles Péguy: Literature, Modernity, and the Crisis of Historicism*. Oxford: Oxford University Press, 2014.

Second Vatican Council. *Dei Verbum*. November 18, 1965. Available at https://www.vatican.va/archive/hist_councils/ii_vatican_council/documents/vat-ii_const_19651118_dei-verbum_en.html.

———. *Lumen Gentium*. November 21, 1964. Available at https://www.vatican.va/archive/hist_councils/ii_vatican_council/documents/vat-ii_const_19641121_lumen-gentium_en.html.

Thiel, John E. "*Dei Verbum*: Scripture, Tradition, and Historical Criticism." *Horizons* 47, no. 2 (2020): 207–231.

Walatka, Todd. *Von Balthasar and the Option for the Poor: Theodramatics in the Light of Liberation Theology*. Washington, DC: Catholic University of America Press, 2017.

Weheliye, Alexander. *Habeas Viscus: Racializing Assemblages, Biopolitics, and Black Feminist Theories of the Human*. Durham, NC: Duke University Press, 2014.

Index

abstraction: and Blondel, 39, 48; definition, 7–8; and history, 2, 24–25 (*see also* facts); and metaphysics, 7–8, 123–24; and modern science, 47; and monophorism, 62–63. *See also* concreteness

action. *See* agency; divine action; élan; human action; obedience; willing

Action française, xviii, 62–63, 65, 118. *See also* monophorism

afférence: from above, 43, 63–64; from below, 43–44, 64. *See also* double *afférence*

affirmation, 111–15, 162–64, 175–76, 186; and Christian tradition, 111, 175–76; divine, 147–48, 151, 161; and lies, 153; and the saint, 165–66. *See also* judgment; truth

Africa, 68, 104–5, 190–91

agency: divine, 41; divine *ad extra*, 40–41, 44; human, 41, 51; nonwhite historical, 29, 160, 170, 179. *See also* divine action; human action

ambiguity: of being, 127–31; of Christian tradition, xvii–xix, 72–76, 80, 166, 169, 175–76; of human action, 127–31, 159, 188

anamnestic solidarity, 110–11

anti-Semitism, 68–69, 112

anxiety, xiv, xvi, 82–87, 164–65, 168, 184–87; divine anxiety (Péguy), 87. *See also* hope

Aquinas, Thomas, 31n, 42n, 125–26, 137–39, 168–69, 173–74

Augustine, 113–14, 124–26, 162

authenticity, 12, 194–95; definition, 15–16; major, 30–33, 110–11, 194–95; minor, 30, 32, 76–77, 194–95. *See also* transcendental precepts

authoritarianism: and Catholicism, xviii, 62–67, 153–54; and human freedom, 65–67, 153. See also *Action française*; monophorism

beginning-again, xix, 89–90, 96, 161, 191. *See also* hope; *ressourcement-révolution*; second innocence

being, 5–7; experience of, 5–6, 122–23; individuated, 11, 123–24; as the intelligible, 6, 28n, 54, 122–23, 158–59, 172–73, 179 (*see also* affirmation; judgment; truth); knowledge of, 6–7; luminous, 47–48, 179; notion of, 6; passionateness of, 31; as situation (Balthasar), 122–26